LAW & DIVERSITY PROGRAM

Moral vision and professional decisions

Moral vision and professional decisions
The changing values of women and men lawyers

RAND JACK and DANA CROWLEY JACK
Fairhaven College / Western Washington University

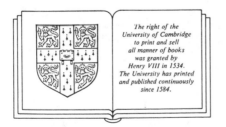

The right of the
University of Cambridge
to print and sell
all manner of books
was granted by
Henry VIII in 1534.
The University has printed
and published continuously
since 1584.

CAMBRIDGE UNIVERSITY PRESS

Cambridge
New York   Port Chester   Melbourne   Sydney

Published by the Press Syndicate of the University of Cambridge
The Pitt Building, Trumpington Street, Cambridge CB2 1RP
40 West 20th Street, New York, NY 10011, USA
10 Stamford Road, Oakleigh, Melbourne 3166, Australia

First published 1989
Reprinted 1989

Printed in the United States of America

Library of Congress Cataloging-in-Publication Data
Jack, Rand.
Moral vision and professional decisions: the changing values of women and men
lawyers / Rand Jack and Dana Crowley Jack.
   p. cm.
Bibliography: p.
ISBN 0-521-37161-9 hard covers
1. Legal ethics – Washington (State) 2. Practice of law – Washington (State)
3. Women lawyers – Washington (State) I. Jack, Dana Crowley. II. Title.
KFW76.5.A2J33   1989
174′.3 – dc19   88–32974
                                                                       CIP

British Library Cataloguing in Publication Data
Jack, Rand
Moral vision and professional decisions: the changing values of women and men
lawyers
1. United States. Lawyers. Professional conduct. Ethical aspects
I. Title II. Jack, Dana Crowley
174′.3

ISBN 0-521-37161-9 hard covers

To Darby and Kelsey

Contents

6 Toward a more morally responsive advocate   156

Preface

When we told people that we were writing a book on lawyers and morality, the common reply was "It must be a short book." This response betrays a misunderstanding of the often obscure, sometimes conflicting moral maze in which lawyers work. What is perceived as a lack of morality may in fact be the result of a double dose of morality in which the training of church and childhood is canceled by the ethics of courts and clients. To understand the attorney's dilemma requires insight into lawyers as both persons and professionals.

This book, like all others, has a special history. It grew out of a marriage between psychology and law, literally and figuratively. One of us is a developmental psychologist; the other, a lawyer who practices and teaches. The main ideas for our work arose from a coincidence of two phenomena that concern women and their place in law: first, the rapidly rising number of women entering the legal profession in the United States and, second, a growing body of psychological research regarding gender differences.

From our conversations came the idea of applying the psychologist's interest in morality, social roles, and personal identity to the world of practicing attorneys. In that world lawyers are supposed to think and feel in a prescribed way — neutral, detached, objective, rational. We wondered how spending life in the legal system affected lawyers' moral values and psychological development. How do attorneys reconcile personal values with the conflicting demands and obligations of their trade? How do lawyers think about their work? Do women bring a different point of view to the practice of law? What is happening to the growing number of women lawyers who are entering a system designed by and for men?

To explore these questions we talked to thirty-six attorneys about who they were, what they did, and what they thought about practicing law in a county of 120,000 people in the state of Washington. The interviews explored moral conflicts and posed hypothetical moral dilemmas. Before the interviews, attorneys were told only that we were conducting "research on how lawyers understand their responsibilities to each other and to the legal system. Of particular interest is how individual attorneys think about themselves as attorneys, about the practice of law and about moral choices lawyers have to make in the course of their work." The letter further stated that they would "be asked open ended questions for which there are no preconceived right or wrong answers."

In 1984 we interviewed every woman practicing law in the county, and matched each with a male counterpart who had a similar type and length of practice. This excluded older attorneys and those with sophisticated corporate or commercial practices, and it gave domestic relations and criminal work a disproportionate presence.

In spite of its obvious limitations, our sample has strengths. The eighteen male and eighteen female attorneys we first approached all agreed to be interviewed. They averaged just over six years of practice, and thus the women represent the recent surge of females entering the profession. All of the lawyers were intelligent, reflective, and articulate. They responded to our questions openly and honestly, allowing us to enter the inner world of practicing attorneys, a world as yet unexplored by developmental psychologists. Conclusions from our small sample cannot be generalized to an entire profession. Our findings do, however, point to critical questions for a profession undergoing significant change. From our work emerges a new model for thinking about patterns of moral thought among lawyers.

Attorneys who appear in this book grew up, went to school, and have practiced law across the United States. They work in civil and criminal law and with public agencies. Like most lawyers in the United States, these attorneys are in small firms; they are regularly active in the courtroom and see clients daily. American lawyers have much in common. Whether in large cities or in small towns, all share a similar law school experience and adhere to a common code of professional ethics. All play the same game by approximately the same rules. Although the careers of our attorneys differ in a variety of ways from those of corporate lawyers in metropolitan areas, we cannot guess whether a different sample would produce significantly divergent results.

The attorneys we interviewed were not always consistent, were sometimes caught in paradoxes, and, like the rest of us, did not neatly separate emotions from reason. We try to convey their uniqueness. While the results of our research invariably oversimplify, we acknowledge the complexity of each person's adjustment to the legal system. We also recognize a major concern for attorneys with which we do not deal. In concentrating on moral issues, we ignore conflicts that lawyers increasingly experience between self-interest, usually financial self-interest, and expectations dictated by professional role. As law shifts from a profession to a business, these conflicts are growing in social importance and demand their own study.

Chapters 1 and 2 explore the presuppositions of our work. In Chapter 1 we examine gender-related moral perspectives in the work of developmental psychologists, and similar themes in political philosophy and law. Defining characteristics of lawyers in the legal system are the subject of Chapter 2. Chapters 3 and 4 integrate material from our empirical study with concepts from earlier chapters. Some alternative ways of relating to the legal system that female attorneys have pursued are described in Chapter 5. Chapter 6 concludes with a look at future possibilities for more morally reflective advocates.

In pursuing this project we make assumptions about oral interviews and about the relationship between qualitative and quantitative data. With reluctance, we assume that we can translate paradoxical, contradictory narratives into objective data by assigning numbers and performing statistical tests. How does the computer digest rambling, often hesitant, subjective searches for honest answers to perplexing questions? We found no way to factor in long pauses, tone of voice, nervous laughter, or the subtle nuances which are the tools of the trade for legal wordsmiths in our society. To complicate matters further, it is risky to assume a direct relationship between how people consciously think and how they will act in tense situations.

Because our work describes gender differences, certain dangers accompany its conclusions. In the past, when psychologists have found such differences, men have been taken as the norm with women considered deviant or lesser. In law, gender differences can channel women and restrict them to certain types of practice. Recognizing that women's current reality has arisen in particular cultural and historical conditions, how do we describe gender differences without their being used to rationalize and justify women's assignment to fixed roles? What does society do with the differences? Can we use gender differences to suggest productive changes in the legal system?

Difference does not have to connote inequality; it is simply another way of marking diversity. As biology shows us, diversity provides strength, creative innovation, and the improved likelihood of survival. Rather than see differences as a basis for subjugating one group or another, one should see differences as a source of enrichment and of an increase of human possibilities.

Acknowledgments

First and foremost we thank the lawyers who took time to share candidly with us their thoughts and feelings about practicing law. We deeply appreciate their willingness to describe their personal conflicts and uncertainties about their profession. Their names have been changed in the text. We gratefully acknowledge the encouragement offered by Carol Gilligan in helpful discussions regarding the ideas in this book. First as Dana's doctoral adviser and later as a friend and colleague, Carol has provided inspiration to see things in new ways.

The study for this book was supported by a grant from the Russell Sage Foundation, which allowed us to transcribe more than two thousand pages of interviews. We also would like to thank Fairhaven College and Western Washington University for their institutional support, as well as Gail Fox, Dabney Bankert, and Gail Weir of the Bureau for Faculty Research for their manuscript preparation. The law firm of Brett and Daugert and Mary Claire Hopper gave us indispensable logistical support. Carl Simpson, Robert M. Thorndike, and Michael Kosten provided diligent, creative assistance with statistical analysis. We appreciate the work of our four coders — Laurie Rathbun, Connie McCollum, Leslie Rogers, and Mary Manix — and the helpful advice of Jane Attanucci, Kay Johnston, and Carol Gilligan regarding the Coding Manual and the training of coders. Robert Keller gave useful comments on substantial parts of the manuscript, and other friends read portions of the work in progress.

Several persons doing editorial work for Cambridge University Press were indispensable to the completion of this book: Susan Milmoe, Laura Dobbins, Martin Dinitz, George Andreou, and Brian MacDonald.

Finally to our children, Kelsey and Darby, our love and gratitude for their patience and forbearance while this book consumed us.

1   Care and rights: two ways of perceiving the world

In this book we weave together three themes dealing with problems of morality and social order. First, we consider contrasting ways of understanding what it means to act morally. One approach relies on rights, duties, individual autonomy, and generally applicable rules; the other, on care, responsiveness, avoidance of harm, and interdependent relationships. One has dominated political and social moral discourse in our society. The other has been limited to the private sphere but is now an emerging force in public life as part of a dialogue of moral perspectives.[1] Traditionally, men in our culture have followed one path and women the other.

A second theme involves the potential tension between personal morality and institutionalized professional morality. Personal morality develops over time in each of us as a product of complex personal and social forces. Professional morality – the established ethical obligations that come with a profession – we meet fully fashioned and ready to be slipped into like a new suit of clothes. Codes governing professional behavior may fit well with an individual's personal morality, or they may not, depending on whether personal ethics coincide with the values and goals that shape the institutional role. A conflict of personal and professional morality creates dilemmas for individuals and pressures on institutions.

Our third theme concerns the conjunction of personal and professional morality in lawyers and how that meeting affects the legal system under which we live. People structure the form and content of the legal system to provide social order, and, not surprisingly, the legal system reflects the values of those who construct and nurture it. These are primarily lawyers, who work under an elaborate and detailed codified morality. What happens to lawyers and the legal system if the personal morality of many new lawyers, mostly female, no

1

longer fits the mold of professional morality? How do the attorneys fare, and what changes might occur in our system of social ordering?

We begin considering these issues of morality and social order by reviewing an ancient tale.

Antigone and Creon: a conflict of world views

In *Antigone* Sophocles tells a story about conflicting ways of comprehending rules and relationships. After quarreling over heirship to the throne of Thebes, Eteocles took royal power and drove his brother Polyneices from the kingdom. When Polyneices returned to seize the throne, the two brothers killed each other in battle, and Creon, as next of kin, became king. Viewing the dead Polyneices as a traitor and as a potential model for insurrection, Creon decrees that his body be left where he fell in battle outside the walls: "No man is to touch him or say the least prayer for him; he shall lie on the plain, unburied; and the birds and the scavenging dogs can do with him whatever they like."[2]

Antigone perceives this decree as a challenge to her most fundamental obligation to her brother Polyneices, to her commitments of love and relationship. Faced with the penalty of death by stoning, Antigone resolves to attend to her brother's body. Seeking the company of her sister Ismene in this deed, Antigone implores:

> And now you can prove what you are:
> A true sister, or a traitor to your family.[3]

Ismene responds with an appeal to the authority of law; Antigone counters with the power of familial attachment:

Ismene: The law is strong, we must give in to the law. . . .
Antigone: You may do as you like,
             Since apparently the laws of the gods mean nothing to you.
Ismene: They mean a great deal to me; but I have no strength
             To break laws that were made for the public good.
Antigone: That must be your excuse, I suppose. But as for me,
             I will bury the brother I love. . . .
Ismene: Go then, if you feel that you must.
             You are unwise,
             But a loyal friend indeed to those who love you.[4]

This dialogue establishes an essential dialectic of the play — strength of law and duty of compliance versus allegiance to human relationships and to the bonds of personal commitment. In conversation with Antigone, the Chorus lends support to Ismene:

> Reverence is a virtue, but strength
> Lives in established law: that must prevail.[5]

As the giver of law, Creon embodies both its strength and the security of the state. Recognizing the threat to the safety of the state posed by personal loyalties, he sets them in proper relation: "No one values friendship more highly than I; but we must remember that friends made at the risk of wrecking our Ship are not real friends at all."[6] To allow the personal loyalty of Antigone to subvert the rule of law is to court "Anarchy, anarchy! Show me a greater evil!"[7]

After Antigone is arrested for ministering to the body of her brother, her fiancé, Creon's son, pleads with his father for her life. Once again confronted with the imperative of human commitment and invective against further hurt, Creon responds:

> I'll have no dealings
> With law-breakers, critics of the government:
> Whoever is chosen to govern should be obeyed —
> Must be obeyed, in all things, great and small,
> Just and unjust![8]

The seductive strength of a woman contests the power of lawmakers. Here, however, it is not sexual seductiveness that is at issue but the seductive power of allegiance to familial relationship. Her strength lies not in the law but in opposition to the law. Having proclaimed the requirements of law for absolute obedience, Creon returns to the theme of the authority of law, now identifying it with his own masculinity:

> We keep the laws then, and the lawmakers,
> And no woman shall seduce us. If we must lose,
> Let's lose to a man, at least! Is a woman stronger than we?[9]

Sophocles grounds this opposition of law and relationships in gender. The masculinity of the lawgiver is again emphasized when Creon confronts Antigone with her crime:

> This girl is guilty of a double insolence,
> Breaking the given laws and boasting of it.
> Who is the man here,
> She or I, if this crime goes unpunished?[10]

Antigone reverses Creon's hierarchy, which places obedience to law as the pinnacle value. A higher natural law surpasses kingly laws in strength and justifies defiance of them.

> *Creon:*   And yet you dared defy the law.
> *Antigone:*   I dared.
> It was not God's proclamation. That final Justice
> That rules the world below makes no such laws.
> Your edict, King, was strong.
> But all your strength is weakness itself against
> The immortal unrecorded laws of God.
> They are not merely now: they were, and shall be,
> Operative for ever, beyond man utterly.[11]

Unwritten moral laws proclaim ties to her dead brother. These ties of love are timeless, originating "beyond man." To disobey the higher law would lead to a moral pain worse than death.

> This death of mine
> Is of no importance; but if I had left my brother
> Lying in death unburied, I should have suffered.[12]

Despite the justifications of Antigone and the wrath of his son, Creon sentences Antigone to be sealed in a stone vault where death may come in its own time. By this passive means of execution, Creon seeks to isolate Antigone and to absolve himself of responsibility. Antigone is left alone, imagined by Creon to be autonomous in her fate:

> You know your orders: take her to the vault
> And leave her alone there. And if she lives or dies,
> That's her affair, not ours: our hands are clean.[13]

The tragedy wrought by this clash between obedience to the law and commitment to the connection of human lives goes beyond the death of Antigone. Having lost his bride-to-be, Creon's son takes his own life. Hearing of her son's death, Creon's wife follows suit.

Antigone and Creon embody a conflict of moralities. Creon is correct that unbridled subjectivity endangers social order and opens the possibility for arbitrary conduct. At the same time, Antigone is right that untempered rule of law itself becomes arbitrary and obscures the interdependence of human relationships. Ironically, Antigone's allegiance to relationships and her defiance of the law precipitate enforcement of the law and the loss of human relationships; Creon's stubborn insistence on the law as a barrier against anarchy results in the chaos of death. Standing alone, neither Creon's view nor Antigone's adequately undergirds a moral, stable, and healthy society.

Like Sophocles, we write about these contrasting ways of comprehending the world – a way that focuses on attachment and relationships and a way that centers on rights and equal application of laws. Like him, we examine institutional morality and personal morality, the imperative to follow rules and maintain order and the necessity to avoid harm and protect relationships. Sometimes these differences are complementary, and sometimes they are in conflict.

Developmental psychology: morality of care and rights

In both what they see and how they see it, psychologists are a product of a world in which women, at least historically, have operated largely in the private realm of the home and family while men have been major players in the public sphere of commerce, politics, and law. Consequently, psychologists have written about gender-based moral differences that align with the public and private spheres. Following the pattern presented by Sophocles, these differences reflect a female morality attuned to relationships and affection, and a male morality based on abstract principles expressed in laws and rules. For example, Freud wrote that women's superego was never "so inexorable, so impersonal, so independent of its emotional origins as we require it to be in men." As a result, Freud thought that women "show less sense of justice than men, that they are less ready to submit to the great exigencies of life, that they are more often influenced in their judgments by feelings of affection or hostility."[14]

More recently, developmental psychologist Lawrence Kohlberg likewise linked gender and morality. Kohlberg identified moral perspective as a developing cognitive trait which can be understood in terms of successive levels of attainment. Based on interview data, Kohlberg constructed a hierarchical scheme of moral plateaus which we call the morality of rights.[15] Moral superiority is gauged in terms of the relation of the self to the rules of society, with highest attainment emphasizing rights and obligations, rules and principles, and questions of justice, fairness, reciprocity, and equality — all concepts familiar in the American legal system. Kohlberg's earlier studies found that women more often reason at an intermediate level of moral development, where judgment is influenced by relationships and concrete human concerns.

Both Freud and Kohlberg make the value judgment that women's relationally attuned morality is less developed, less valuable than the male morality with which it is compared. They interpret a female emphasis on relationships and contextual reasoning as an indicator of immaturity and an inability to develop autonomy and independence. In this negative evaluation, psychological theories reflect the view of a wider society which regards women's moral orientation as a limiting characteristic particularly appropriate to traditional roles of wife and mother.

As a colleague of Kohlberg's at Harvard, Carol Gilligan agreed with the observation of gender-linked moral differences, but rejected the negative judgment placed on women's morality. Discovering that Kohlberg's early work involved no female subjects, Gilligan questioned whether he might have described exactly what he saw — the moral structure most often followed by men in our culture. From her interviews with women, she traces an alternative developmental path in which the centrality of relationships is crucial to personal and social well-being. Women's development leads to what Gilligan calls the morality of care,[16] an imperative to avoid harm and preserve relationships. She argues that an ethic of care represents a positive and indispensable aspect of moral maturity.[17]

Gilligan, Nancy Chodorow, and other relational feminists[18] believe that traits traditionally associated with gender arise out of early childhood social, psychological, and cognitive processes. Chodorow asserts that intimate childhood relationships with the mother, most often the primary caretaker in our culture, affect girls and boys differently. Because they are of the same sex as their mother, girls form their sense of gender through identification, while boys must establish a masculine identity through separation and differentiation from femaleness. The differing psychological tasks required for gender development lead to certain personality traits and moral perspectives in women and men. Although relational theorists differ about the primary cause of differences between women's and men's senses of self, they all agree that "feminine personality comes to define itself in relation and connection to other people more than masculine personality does."[19] Further, these theorists argue that because of different social contexts and developmental paths, women develop distinct ways of knowing and problem solving.[20]

Growing out of women's sense of self as connected to others is a different vision of the social and moral world. What Freud and Kohlberg describe as women's less developed morality, Gilligan reinterprets as a morality attuned to the specific contexts of people's lives, a morality of responsiveness to the needs of others. Thus, what is seen from a traditional perspective as women's lack of independence and assertiveness Gilligan reinterprets as a strength valuable to community and essential to human survival.

Avenues of psychological development correlate with two contrasting perceptions of social reality – the perspective of care and the perspective of rights. From a care point of view, society is an interconnected, interdependent web of life.[21] The social fabric is woven of human relations and kept whole through responsiveness, empathy, and unmediated personal interaction. By contrast, those with a rights orientation experience society as composed of autonomous, separate individuals. A hierarchy of rules, rights, and obligations mediate human interactions and help preserve independence. Safety from aggression is found not in connection with others but in rules protecting individuals from infringement.

Each of these perceptions of social reality incorporates the values and identity of those who adhere to it. Each viewpoint potentially threatens the other, and each evolves its own strategy for self-perpetuation. Because men's identity is most often rooted in autonomous individuality, risk lies in intimacy of relationship, which endangers separateness and curtails freedom. If value and identity reside in atomistic separation, means must be found to safeguard the boundaries, to protect against intrusion. Rules of noninterference and rights of self-determination serve this purpose well. To maintain distance, relationships are conceived in contractual terms and are subject to negotiation. In this way, those of a rights persuasion at the same time protect their identity and their place in society.

Women, on the other hand, often describe themselves in terms of relationship with others.[22] Isolation threatens both the self and the network of relationships. If identity and social value reside in the interconnectedness of life, ways must be found to keep the fabric of relationships intact. Rather than employ defensive tools to protect themselves, those with a care orientation actively reach out to make contact, to show concern, to mend hurt. Responsiveness to the needs of others serves the community and the individual's sense of self. Because harm to anyone endangers the whole, responsibility requires an engaged, vigilant extension of self on behalf of others.

From a rights perspective, responsibility has a very different meaning. Moral relationships are preserved through fair resolution of conflicts between separate individuals and through maintenance of rules and rights that protect autonomy. Responsibility is discharged by restraint from interference with the separateness of others. As the founding fathers did in the Constitution, rights thinkers seek safety in checks and balances and separation of powers. Since people are separate, such thinkers tend to abstract or separate relationships from the human context. The atomistic individual, rather than an individual in social connection, is the primary point of reference. Social rules in fact guard against too much interaction; both morality and justice are defined in terms of rights.

For those with a rights orientation, intimacy and interdependence can threaten the right to be free, autonomous individuals; from a care perspective, the morality of rights may appear callous, uncaringly destructive of community. Rather than rely on abstract, hierarchical thinking, care-oriented people seek solutions that consider the full range of human context. Rather than focusing on rights and duties, the morality of care inquires about outcome. Who will be harmed? How seriously? What will happen to relationships? For any given moral decision, these questions can be answered only with attention to the particulars of the specific situation. No formula will work.

Norms such as continuity of relations and prevention of hurt take precedence over rules and rights, fair process, and equal treatment. For the ethic of care, attention rests on avoiding harm, maintaining relationships, responsibility to others, and a contextual, empathetic understanding of individual differences. The flavor of this difference can be sampled by imagining how different the Declaration of Independence would have been if, instead of "all men are created equal . . . with certain unalienable Rights," Thomas Jefferson had written "all people are created interdependent with mutual responsibility to aid others."

A society composed of discrete individuals created as equal encourages competition and dominance if resources are unequally distributed and positions in society hierarchically arranged. The ideals of equality speak to the right to run in the race but say nothing about distribution of rewards at the finish. Each person strives to secure a place in the social order, and because the places at the finish line are far from equal, competition abounds. The goal is to win; rules protect only the fairness of the contest. If community well-being is not a primary concern, and if individual achievement is thought to be largely isolated from the welfare of others, little inhibits the desire to race ahead. Only a sense of interdependence and community restrains competition and changes the goal from individual to group success. A vision based on a network of interdependencies encourages compromise and cooperation, for your gain is also my gain.[23] The world looks very different for those who see themselves as competing for a place in the lifeboat than for those already in the lifeboat working together to keep it afloat.

In some ways morality of rights describes the ethics of a game of chess – each piece has a place, and each moves according to the rules. The chess pieces are hierarchically rated, and each has its own distinct role. The pieces remain separate and cannot occupy the same space. Rules and rights designate interaction and protect the identity of each piece. As long as conduct is fair and rules are followed, elimination of pieces is simply part of the game, a game which produces winners and losers.

By comparison, morality of care governs a mountain-climbing expedition whose members are connected by a web of rope. They are interdependent and committed to the responsibility of safeguarding each other. Each new situation must be understood in its own terms and evaluated to determine how the community of climbers will be protected. Whether on a belay or in moving supplies from one camp to another, each person gains value by relationship to the group. Achievement occurs through community success. The accompanying table gives a schematic view of the two moral orientations.

When we describe a care or a rights perspective, we are not talking about clear dichotomies but about tendencies, in both how a person is likely to think and which gender is more likely to think that way. These moral perspectives take many forms. Rather than designating a homogeneous point of view, the labels are merely shorthand for a propensity to adhere to certain values and assumptions and for a prominence of certain ways of assimilating and assessing experience. Each individual reflects a special blend of moral understanding which is affected by culture, ethnicity, social and economic class, and historical experience.

As we discuss the moral perspectives of care and rights, it is impossible to avoid the language of dichotomies in an effort to etch clearly lines of difference and to avoid endless qualifications. Because we do lapse into the language of dichotomies, we make our qualifications here to be carried by the reader throughout the book. These qualifications blur easy distinctions and fuzz the edges of categories. (1) Although there is a significant likelihood that women will have a care orientation and men a rights orientation, these moral worlds are reversed for a number of men and women in our society. There are men who use primarily a care viewpoint and women who tend to see the world in terms favored by Kohlberg.[24] (2) Nearly everyone combines some degrees of rights- and care-oriented moral thinking. When we say that someone is rights- or care-oriented, we mean that one orientation guides that person's perception and resolution of moral issues more strongly than does the other perspective in the

Two moral orientations

	Morality of rights	Morality of care
Social world	Autonomous, separate individuals	Interdependent web of community members
Driving social force	Competition, winning	Cooperation, compromise
Moral problem	Conflict of rights and duties between separate individuals	Conflict of responsibilities in network of relationships
Moral goal	Fair resolution – maintenance of rules	Avoid harm – maintenance of relationships
Responsibility	Restrain from interference	Active response to others
Values	Rights, duties, fairness, due process, equal protection	Harmony, empathy, community, caring responsiveness, integration
Reasoning	Formal, abstract, hierarchical, objective	Personal, contextual, holistic, engaged
Symbol	Balanced scales of justice	Ecosystem in harmonious equilibrium

specific situation under consideration. (3) The categories of rights and care themselves often overlap, particularly at the higher levels of moral thinking. Each incorporates elements of the other. These caveats notwithstanding, the two models have broad explanatory power in our attempt to understand how men and women interact with the worlds of social and moral decision making.

While Gilligan's work has provided a critical corrective to dismissal of women's moral orientation as inferior to men's, it runs the danger of idealizing women's morality and overlooking the historical and social contexts within which it develops. Critics assert that Gilligan revives an essentialist, ahistorical understanding of women's traits.[25] Nonetheless, her work has substantial explanatory power and resonates with experience. For many, her thinking has helped clarify and order recurring events in their lives. Listening to lawyers' descriptions of moral conflict with Gilligan's description of care and rights in mind allowed us to make sense of what lawyers were saying without judging either approach to be superior and without seeing gender links as inevitable or restrictive.[26]

Nonanatomical gender differences arise out of particular social and historical realities. Because of the complexity of their origins, generalizations about gender differences admit many exceptions. In a culture of inequality, the danger is that sex differences are used to justify the relegation of women to secondary status. This danger is acute if conceptualizations are mistakenly understood as normative rather than as descriptive, as the way things should be rather than simply as the way things have been. The trick is to examine gender differences constructively without falling into the pit of stereotyping and discrimination. This is especially true, if, as we believe, moral maturity in women and men requires having care and rights perspectives integrated and in balance, with the balance struck for each person a function of cultural experience rather than gender. The need for integration and balance comes from a search for identity both through autonomous individualism and through being part of a community.

How best to rule: laws and philosopher kings

Developmental psychologists were not the first to identify the moral world views described by Kohlberg and Gilligan. Psychologists have explored the psychological origins of these perspectives, but the moral viewpoints themselves have persisted over time as themes in literature and political philosophy.

It is not surprising that moral developmental psychology and political philosophy reflect the same insights, for both attempt to understand how people can and do relate to one another. One begins with the psyche of the individual, and the other with the structure of social organization. Ultimately, however, both engage the same value questions: What is the proper place of rules in ordering social relationships? Is individualized, contextual responsiveness or objective, delineated law more likely to produce fair and enduring results? How is it possible to blend the two to get the virtues of each? Answering these questions may be the primary task of both individual morality and political philosophy. Following the rules has the advantage of treating everyone the same and thus achieving fairness. Contextual responsiveness has the advantage of treating unique individuals differently and thus achieving fairness. The paradox unravels only if we can set up ways of judging when people should be treated similarly and when differently.

In a democracy the preeminence of humanly constructed rules would seem most easily accepted, because the authority of the rules derives from those governed by them. At least theoretically, laws are legitimate because we have the opportunity to participate in the process by which they were made. Even when we disagree with the rules, we have traded our right to ignore them for our right to participate fairly in a democratic process. Yet, despite this argument for the authority of social rules, the question of how to respond to a given law remains alive. This is true, in part, because of issues about fairness and participation in the rule-making process but, more important for our purposes, because of a tradition of higher or natural law such as was envoked by Antigone. Whether derived from God, the natural environment, or human nature, the natural-law tradition tells us that there are values and principles more important than human-made law, or what philosophers call positive law. Despite epistemological problems about the origins and content of natural law, many continue to believe, with Thomas Jefferson, that there are "certain unalienable Rights," values we will not allow to be encroached upon no matter what the legislature might enact. In recent times, racial segregation, the Vietnam War, abortion, and environmental degradation have elicited such a response. Natural-law tradition sets the stage for tension between transcendent moral beliefs and positive law.

Herman Melville dramatizes the conflict of natural and positive law in the court-martial of Billy Budd.[27] Arguing for the death penalty, Captain Vere confronts "natural Justice" in the form of the "private conscience" of the officers convened to try Billy for innocently striking a fatal blow to a superior officer who had deceitfully sought to destroy him. Though he shares their ambivalence, Vere urges, "These buttons that we wear attest that our allegiance [is not] to Nature [but] to the King." In the tight society of a British ship in time of war, there is no room for diluting the rules, for "in receiving our commissions, we in the most important regards ceased to be natural free agents." Making the ultimate appeal for the power of positive law, Vere asks, "Would it be so much we ourselves that would condemn as it would be martial law operating through us? For that law and the rigor of it, we are not responsible."[28] Vere recognizes that his officers are bothered not just by compassion "but also the conscience, the private conscience. But tell me whether or not, occupying the position we do, private conscience should not yield to that imperial one formulated in the code under which alone we officially proceed?"[29] For Vere, and finally for his officers, social role defined by the positions they occupy determines how they regard the law of England, a law that has wrought consequences for which they are not responsible. The relations among role, rules, and responsibility are a theme to which we will return in subsequent chapters.

While Vere represents one response to positive law, the possibilities sketched by moral philosophers are boundless. Clustered at one end are relativists, situationalists, and opportunists who ascribe little importance to obeying the rules. They are goal-directed and find rules useful only in support of their goals. At the other extreme are moralists or absolutists who see compliance with positive law as an ultimate value. Such unquestioned obedience to rules, like wholesale disregard, limits social possibility. A common view in our society falls between the extremes, in what philosophers call rule utilitarianism. Following the rules has inherent value. Most people will benefit most if everyone follows the rules most of the time. In extreme circumstances, however, a rule may be ignored when it clashes with a higher value or principle. This requires long-range calculations. Determination must be made not only that the higher value is more important than the positive law but also that it is sufficiently important to justify both the consequences of breaking the legal rule and whatever risk the breach poses to the ordering system of rules itself. Rule utilitarians span the distance between little and absolute regard for law. They vary in what it takes to push them beyond the rules and into the realm of higher law and private conscience, the realm where they act as philosopher kings. Even though lawyers occupy the social role of keeper of the law, all with whom we talked were rule utilitarians. They all held the rules in high regard and varied in the catalyst required to tempt them outside the framework of law and into what they frequently referred to as "playing God."

This issue — whether governance should rely on the wisdom and flexibility of a philosopher king or the certainty and generality of law — is of central interest to Plato. In the *Statesman*, Plato affirms his conclusion from the *Republic* that "the political ideal is not full authority for laws" but, rather, the ideal lies in rule by a philosopher king, a person "willing and able to rule with moral and intellectual insight and to render every man his due with strictest fairness."[30] Governing by laws is "second best" because the legislator must act "for the generality of his subjects under average circumstances," using what Plato calls "a 'bulk' method rather than an individual treatment."[31]

Law can never issue an injunction binding on all which really embodies what is best for each; it cannot prescribe with perfect accuracy what is good and right for each member of the community at any one time. The differences of human personality, the variety of men's activities, and the inevitable unsettlement attending all human experience make it impossible for any art whatsoever to issue unqualified rules holding good on all questions at all times.[32]

Plato finally opts for a system of rules, not because philosopher kings are inferior but because they are so hard to find. In the absence of those who could be trusted to apply deftly the art of statesmanship, Plato accepts the governance of laws, which "represent the fruit of experience," as the best we can do. Despite the limitations of "strict laws," to breach the law is a greater shortcoming, "for such transgression, if tolerated, would do even more than a rigid code to pervert all ordered activity."[33] Whereas the philosopher king represents particularized response to human experience, laws are a generalized response which must always fall short because "it is impossible . . . for something invariable and unqualified to deal satisfactorily with what is never uniform and constant."[34] However, once reality necessitates reliance on rules, Plato, like Sophocles, recognizes that defiance of law threatens social order.

The different political forms considered by Plato and the conflicting moral voices of Antigone and Creon produce distinctive meanings of justice and social order. In the appropriate cultural context, both the morality of care, focused on interdependent community and contextual analysis, and the morality of rights, centered on the assumptions of autonomous separateness and the universality of rules, can provide a basis for functional concepts of justice.

Aristotle describes one such concept that, like the American legal system, is based on rights and exalts equality as an ideal. He identifies separate kinds of justice, each with its own particular form of equality. Guided by principles of equal treatment of equals and unequal treatment of unequals, distributive justice dictates the fair allocation of honors and wealth. Distribution is in proportion to merit or what Aristotle called the "equality of ratios." Corrective justice, on the other hand, is administered not proportionately but in accordance with the direct equality of arithmetic – one for one, an eye for an eye. Payment or punishment is used to correct or to rectify in equal measure to the wrong. Reciprocity is the touchstone.

Societal understanding of civil and criminal applications of corrective justice has diverged little from the Aristotelian model:

> For it makes no difference whether a good man has defrauded a bad man or a bad man a good one, nor whether it is a good or a bad man that has committed adultery; the law looks only to the distinctive character of the injury, and treats the parties as equal, if one is in the wrong and the other is being wronged, and if one inflicted injury and the other has received it. Therefore, this kind of injustice being an inequality, the judge tries to equalize it.[35]

Aristotle's description of the role of the judge emphasizes a mechanical equality and presupposes an atomized social world in which individuals exist as separate, equal integers. Since justice depends on equality, the job of the judge is to balance a mathematical equation by shifting interchangeable parts:

> Now the judge restores equality; it is as though there were a line divided into unequal parts, and he took away that by which the greater segment exceeds the half, and added it to the smaller segment. And when the whole has been equally divided, then they say they have "their own" – i.e., when they have got what is equal. The equal is intermediate between the greater and the lesser line according to arithmetical proportion.[36]

Equal treatment in corrective justice is one of the rules that helps safeguard distribution in proportion to merit, or equal opportunity to compete in the arena of distributive justice. Equality here pertains only to the chance to compete and not to the result of the competition.

Anthropologist Laura Nader portrays a culture where justice differs markedly from Aristotle's model of mathematical precision, where the standard is not a rights-oriented equality of treatment but a care-oriented restoration of relationships.[37] The phrase "to make the balance" describes an underlying goal of dispute settlement among the Zapotec Pueblos of Ralu'a, Mexico. "Balance is an ideal in many systems of law, but the definition of balance differs among cultures. The Zapotec ideal is not 'an eye for an eye,' but rather what restores personal relations to equilibrium."[38] A Zapotec judge seeks the balance of a system in harmony rather than the mechanical equilibrium of an Aristotelian equation. Zapotec justice presupposes a social world of interdependent human beings rather than an atomized society.

The Zapotec cases Nader describes are presided over by the *presidente,* who is drafted by the local people on the basis of experience and skills. He knows the community and uses a historical and contextual understanding of a dispute in restoring harmony. There is no fiction of judicial ignorance. In his own realm, he is Plato's philosopher king. Each dispute is looked at individually, and the parties are given latitude to indicate what is relevant in resolving their differences. Subjective truth as perceived by a person in a particular context takes precedence over a search for objective truth. People's understanding of what happened overshadows what actually happened. Because the process looks to the future rather than to the past, little effort is spent establishing facts or fault. Because the Zapotecs "prefer peace to justice, harmony to truth," the goal of the process is "restoration of relations to a form or condition of equilibrium, a condition when conflict was absent."[39] The path to this goal is through compromise, which will restore the balance and allow people to continue to live together in a constructive community.

Whereas the Zapotec court system seeks to restore balance, the model embodied in law schools and the attorney role is a win–lose, zero sum game. Often, adversary adjudication results in exacerbation of conflict. We litigate rights and obligations on the basis of a search into the past for objective truth. The Zapotecs look to future restoration grounded in a reality defined by the subjective experience of the disputants. The parties are prime participants in a free-flowing process where they define relevant consideration in their own terms. For

us, procedural formality and rules of evidence structure the courtroom, often focusing on marginally relevant issues which are difficult
for the disputants to comprehend. In our system the parties are mute
for most, if not all, of the trial. Our goal is justice defined as a fair
and equal application of universal rules with procedural safeguards.
For Zapotecs, the goal is restoration of balance in the life of a community. Whereas our symbol for justice is the goddess Themis, blind-
folded to be unaware of individual differences and holding scales in
Aristotelian balance, the image for the Zapotecs is an ecosystem in
harmonious equilibrium.

Each system has strengths and faults, and in reality neither is
devoid of elements of the other. Both reflect the needs and assumptions of the culture, or at least of those in the culture who structure
and dominate the legal system. According to anthropologist Max
Gluckman, societies develop dispute-resolution processes that match
the value they place on relationships. In societies where the disputants have integrated, continuing relationships and a stake in community stability, the dispute-resolution process is usually arranged to
maintain those relationships and to restore harmony. This is true of
the Lozi society along the Zambezi River in southern Africa.

The Lozi disapprove of any irremediable breaking of relationships. . . . The judges
try to prevent the breaking of relationships, and to make it possible for the parties to
live together amicably in the future. . . . Therefore the court tends to be conciliating;
it strives to effect a compromise acceptable to, and accepted by, all the parties. . . .
This task of the judges is related to the nature of the social relationships out of which
spring the disputes that come before them. In order to fulfill their task the judges
constantly have to broaden the field of their enquiries, and consider the total history
of relations between the litigants, not only the narrow legal issue raised by one of
them.[40]

In our culture, business people often forgo litigation, preferring
instead to arbitrate or simply to absorb losses, because of their long-
term dependence on healthy continuing relationships within the business community. Of such relationally oriented legal systems, anthropologist E. Adamson Hoebel concludes, "The common quality
that is found in these disparate legal systems stems not from like
systems of social structure but rather from general similarity of basic
values – values which place the maintenance of group solidarity first

and transactional rights and duties second."[41] Thus, what the Zapotecs, the Lozi, and commercial arbitration systems have in common is a value shared with the morality of care – the importance of continuity of relationships.

Native American culture likewise places a premium on relationships and community.[42] Several years ago at Window Rock on the Navajo reservation, we were told of a young Navajo attorney trained in a white law school. A Navajo judge warned him that if he did not stop competing so hard and pressing every advantage for the victory of his client, he would no longer be welcome to practice in tribal court. He was violating a taboo of community. As Laura Nader explains,

Scarcity or perceived scarcity has an effect on how people behave. In terms of law, scarcity of land and other property crucial to subsistence leads people to use forums and procedures that will allow them to win, regardless of what it does to relationships. However, if there is a desire to continue relationships, there is a strong likelihood that compromise will be preferred to a winner-take-all solution.[43]

By "perceived scarcity" Nader means there is not enough for all people to have as much as they would like, a condition that now pertains to almost everything, including air and the oceans.

This situation recalls the social model assumed by a rights-based legal system. Autonomous individuals vie for limited resources (oil, power, prestige, home runs), and rules protect the fairness of competition. Under this scheme, Hoebel's "transactional rights" are valued more highly than continuity of relationships. Where an ethic of community prevails, the problem of scarcity is handled very differently. The desired outcome is set – continuation and welfare of the group. Means of distribution are adjusted to that end. In contrast, under a rights system, no particular end is envisioned. Given the autonomy of individuals, the fairness of the race is what matters. Competition inevitably strains relationships, and in a society in which relationships are primary, competition will be controlled and outcome and distribution accomplished at least in part by means that do not so tax human bonds. This analysis raises a number of large and perplexing questions. Has our legal system ignored a preference for relationships shared by a substantial but largely disenfranchised segment of the population? Is our culture gaining increasing awareness and appreciation of the interdependent quality of our existence? How much change in what Hoebel calls "basic values" is required to kindle change in an institution as set in its ways as the legal system? How much does investment in the legal system restrict recognition of our interdependence as a basis of social decisions and ultimately as a basis for our survival?

In our legal system, contrasting moral assumptions have created a tension between contextual, individualized treatment and blind justice applying the letter of the law equally to all. Individualized application has the virtue of recognizing uniqueness of individuals in particular circumstances, and it tailors the law accordingly. The pitfalls of this approach lie in abuse of discretion and in distinctions based on prejudice rather than reason. In comparison, strict application of unbending rules can be a safeguard against arbitrary conduct and discrimination.

While these concerns led to the prominent placement in the Constitution of the rights to due process and equal protection, the legalistic approach incurs its own liability. Rules may be applied in circumstances that make neither sense nor justice, and little room is left for compassion. We have opted for a competitive, adversary model based on rights, duties, and, at least ideally, equal application of both procedural and substantive rules. At the same time, pockets of individualization and discretion persist to temper the dominant legal philosophy. The jury system and a periodic return to individualized sentencing of criminals are examples of the ambivalence of our society toward devotion to a strict morality of rights.

The morality of practitioners: divergent orientations

Questions about the moral world view of attorneys are relevant to anyone who cares about the shape of our society – who it rewards, who it penalizes, who it extols, and to whom it distributes its benefits. The law is a social construct which reflects dominant cultural beliefs. We create the law in our own image, and then the legally ordered society reflects and reinforces our perceptions and values – or at least the values and perceptions of those who share in its creation and upkeep. Those who have been excluded from structuring and nurturing the legal system may not find their aspirations and world views mirrored there. For instance, American Indians' religious beliefs find little comfort in the white man's law.[44] As that term implies, women also have been routinely excluded from molding the legal system, but that exclusion is now being dramatically reversed.

In addition to psychological studies of gender differences in moral reasoning, our thoughts were originally sparked by the phenomenal increase of women in law school, the gateway to the legal profession. The route to law practice has not always been open for women. In 1893, United States Supreme Court Justice Bradley invoked nature, family, God, and destiny in upholding the decision of the State of Illinois to exclude Myra Bradwell from the legal profession:

The civil law, as well as nature herself, always recognized a wide difference in the respective spheres and destinies of man and woman. Man is, or should be, woman's protector and defender. The natural and proper timidity and delicacy which belongs to the female sex evidently unfits it for many of the occupations of civil life. The constitution of the family organization, which is founded in the divine ordinance as well as in the nature of things, indicates the domestic sphere as that which properly belongs to the domain and functions of womanhood. The harmony, not to say identity, of interests and views which belong or should belong to the family institution, is repugnant to the idea of a woman adopting a distinct and independent career from her husband.

The paramount destiny and mission of woman are to fulfill the noble and benign offices of wife and mother. This is the law of the Creator. And the rules of civil society must be adapted to the general constitution of things, and cannot be based on exceptional cases.[45]

As social mores changed, so did governing legal principles; rules barring the Myra Bradwells from law practice gave way. By 1963, legal obstacles were down, but only 877 women began law school compared with 19,877 men. Women constituted less than 4 percent of the total enrollment. Since then, the number of women in law school has grown constantly. In 1986, 16,491 women entered law school. A total of 47,920 women enrolled made up 40 percent of law school students.[46] More and more women are becoming lawyers, and in the near future nearly as many women as men will be practicing law.

Insights into gender differences and the rapid increase of women in law school take on particular significance against the backdrop of defining postulates of the American legal system. Constitutions, statutes, administrative codes, and case law enunciate rules as to permitted and prohibited conduct. They prioritize claims to social resources. We have rules concerning rights to air space above property, rights of minorities bidding for government contracts, the right to be represented by an attorney even if we cannot afford one, the right to watch certain kinds of movies but not others, rights of creditors and debtors and of landlords and tenants, the right to have one's spouse keep confidences, and the right to an abortion so long as the pregnancy has not entered the third trimester. Rule 1.6 of the American Bar Association Model Rules of Professional Conduct comments, "Almost without exception, clients come to lawyers in order to determine what their rights are."

This system of rights and duties is expressed in rules and promotes adversary relationships between theoretically autonomous and legally equal people. Institutions and individuals compete to assert their rights and resist the imposition of obligation by others. All this occurs within a labyrinth of procedures that presumably help ensure fair and uniform application of law. Organized around a complex set of duties, obligations, rights, and procedures, the law circumscribes a universe more reflective of Creon than Antigone. This is only one way to structure relations, a way closely resembling that preferred by the predominantly male morality of rights. With accelerated entry of women into law practice, the voice of care is increasingly heard along with the voice of rights in interpreting the legal system and responding to its mandates.

When we spoke to practicing attorneys for the study described in the preface, they often expressed two different views of social reality and their attendant moralities of care and rights. In response to a hypothetical situation in which a person has confessed to murder but the attorney is convinced that the confession could be excluded from the evidence presented at trial, attorney Brent Stephens experiences little conflict with obligations of the lawyer role:

You're the hired gun for this guy and you have the duty, obligation to represent him, which includes preparation of a defense to the charges. If there's a chance of excluding the confession, then you've got to do that. The other side of the dilemma I see is this, the dilemma of his dangerousness to society. I've never had too much trouble with that fact situation, because I didn't make the rules that you play by. The government did. . . . And you're the hired gun there to take advantage of those rules on behalf of your client. I've never had any qualms about defending and getting off a person who is guilty. I don't have bad feelings afterward. The fear that that person may commit more murders – for some reason that never affected me a great deal either. . . . You have to look at the system you're working within – as an attorney, what parameters have been set up for you, what your role is. Your role isn't to be the protector of society. It's not to insure that guilty guys go to jail, that murderers go to jail. In our system of criminal justice, you're there to represent the interests of this defendant and to do whatever to obtain the best possible result for him. So if you look and examine those parameters, the obligations you have, the very reason for your presence on that case, you don't have a great deal of difficulty in resolving the dilemma.

In contrast, talking about the same hypothetical situation, attorney Frances Andrews feels a commitment to protect others from hurt, an obligation that reaches beyond rules and professional role:

I have an overriding obligation to see he is not released, or that he is not released without safeguards. . . . I have a duty to see that my fellow mankind, including my family, are not murdered in their beds if I can do something to prevent it. . . . The bottom line is that I would not let him be released without safeguards if I had a deep abiding conviction that by doing so I was placing other persons in jeopardy. No matter what the consequences to me professionally would be, I could not do that if in my own mind, and based upon my own sincere beliefs, there was a problem. . . . I have a moral obligation to the people he might harm in the future. Once I am convinced, if I am convinced, that there is a good probability that he will do what I believe he will do, at that point my moral obligation steps in, and I have a duty to do whatever is in my power to see that he is not allowed to do that.

These two lawyers illustrate opposite ends of a spectrum – one following social rules and role, the other responsive to a personal ethic of protecting people from hurt. Brent Stephens frames his duty in legal and societal terms, explaining how the ethics of the situation have already been decided by institutional rules. These rules define his actions in regard to other people and separate him from ethical concern for the consequences of his professional conduct. Frances Andrews immediately focuses on possible harm to people in the future. Her responsibility does not arise out of the lawyer role; rather, it stems from a personal sense of connection with others, an affirmative duty to protect others.

In a second instance, lawyers reacted to a situation in which a client seeks custody of two young children. The client accidentally reveals to the attorney information that indicates the client would be a poor parent for the children. After discussing the situation, attorneys were asked whether they would respond differently if the inadvertently revealed information indicated that the client was likely to harm the children physically. Again from Brent Stephen and Frances Andrews, the voices of rights and rules and of care and responsiveness are heard. For Brent the adversary system and client confidentiality permit abstraction from human context so that quandary is avoided:

It's an adversary context on this custody decision, and the other client has a hired gun and you're a hired gun for your guy. Do I ever ask myself what is best for the children? Should you be working as the attorney for the best interests of the children? I don't think you are. That's the judge's decision after he's sifted it all out. What you're working toward is the presentation of the most effective case for your client, and if you can build a super good case that your client is the best parent or it's in the best interests of the children that he have custody, great.

(Element of physical harm added.)

Maybe it would weigh a little more heavily on me. But I think that I would undertake the same decision-making process.

For Frances Andrews the situation seems more complicated. As threat to life escalates, responsibility to the children takes precedence over rules and the professional obligations of guns for hire:

I would like to think that the needs of the children should be placed first and foremost, but also I want to insure that my client will have confidence and trust in me. . . . I don't feel, on the one hand, in that situation I would be justified in revealing his secret, his confidence, but on the other hand, I would have concern for the children. . . . Where there is no threat of harm to the children and it's just a question of which one is better suited to raise them, I don't feel that I can reveal the letter. That's what he's hiring me for. That's what he paid me for. That's what the ethical code is there for. He's got a right to have his confidences respected. . . . I would do everything possible up to the line that I have to hold as an attorney to see that the rights of the children were protected, even if that included keeping an eye on the children after the custody proceedings were finalized and keeping in contact with my client. But, no, I would not reveal the information.

(Threat of physical harm to the children introduced.)

Yes, I would reveal it. Because my right to respect the confidence, the right of my client to have the confidence respected, only goes to the point where I know that those confidences will not harm someone else. . . . At that point my duty to children would override my ethical duty to the client. (*Where does your duty to the children come from?*) There's a duty to everyone in society. . . . The children certainly have the right to have their lives protected, and since they do not have the capability to do that, then they have to be; they have the right to expect that people who can protect them will do so.

Again these two lawyers sharply diverge as allegiance to different ethical imperatives takes them down separate paths. Seeing the custody dispute as a duel of hired guns, Brent Stephens relies on his role as attorney to excuse himself from concern for the children. The judge looks out for the children; for the lawyer it is a contest.

From Frances Andrews's perspective, needs of the children conflict with obligations of role. When being a good attorney threatens harm to someone else, personal moral imperative to prevent hurt overrides ethical duty as a lawyer. In a reversal of Brent's position, her responsibility to specific people takes precedence over conformity to role. Like that of Antigone, Frances's commitment to the network of human relationships challenges the rule of law.

Both Frances Andrews and Brent Stephens are capable attorneys. The perspective of each has its advantages and its limitations. Brent's approach ensures that a time-tested system will work in accord with expectations. Rules of evidence designed to achieve fairness are honored, and clients' rights are protected. Discrimination and arbitrariness are minimized. But the end result may be that concrete, critical considerations are ignored and innocent people are hurt. This is where Frances's perspective becomes a valuable safeguard. Preference of these lawyers for one moral focus over another is not simply a matter of taste but has an impact on institutional structures and power relationships.

How lawyers view morality has implications for relationships, for all morality is basically a matter of relationships: How *should* we relate to others? Much the same can be said for law. It is essentially a matter of structuring how we relate to one another. This underlying kinship of law and morality is critical. Both indicate basic assumptions and values about the social world and human relationships.

Law begins by reflecting and reinforcing decisions about relationships and then becomes in itself a determinant of how we relate. Even the most intimate of relationships become subject to legal interpretation — sex with an AIDS sufferer becomes an assault, prenuptial agreements are negotiated, and children with birth defects sue for wrongful birth. Under the dominion of law, relationships in our culture come to exemplify peculiarities of the legal system, with its emphasis on arm's length negotiations, procedural fairness, and uniform application of rules.

2 The lawyer's role: partisanship, neutrality, and moral distance

More than any other people in history, Americans rely on the legal system to define who they are and what they may, must, and must not do. Lacking common history, shared mores and traditions, a unified religious background, or identifiable kinship lines, they depend on their legal system as a primary instrument for creating social order. Through law they specify status, wealth, and power. Some kinds of conduct are forbidden; claims to limited resources, delineated; personal autonomy, protected; balances of power, erected; hierarchies of rights and obligations, sanctified. Formal procedures are elaborated for adjudication of conflicting claims.

Law creates reality, a social world in which all participate. Whether the issue is abortion, the rights of corporations, or the continuation of slavery, law undertakes so basic a task as to define who or what qualifies as a person. This reality-creating function of the legal system was discussed with unusual candor by the highest court of New York State in the case challenging a liberalized abortion law.

Conceptually, . . . a conceived child may be regarded as a person, albeit at a fetal stage. It is not true, however, that the legal order necessarily corresponds to the natural order. That it should or ought is a fair argument, but the argument does not make its conclusion the law. . . .

What is a legal person is for the law, including, of course, the Constitution, to say, which simply means that upon according legal personality to a thing the law affords it the rights and privileges of a legal person. . . . The process is, indeed, circular, because it is definitional. . . . That the legislative action may be wise or unwise, even unjust and violative of principles beyond the law, does not change the legal issue or how it is to be resolved. The point is that it is a policy determination whether legal personalities should attach and not a question of biological or "natural" correspondence.[1]

Given this freedom from "biological or 'natural' correspondence," a legal system of entangling complexity emerges, a complex-

27

ity made legendary by Kafka and Dickens. Difficulty in traversing this labyrinth without special knowledge and special skills supports the legal profession. As Supreme Court Justice Sandra Day O'Connor observed, attorneys are "provided with expertise that is both esoteric and extremely powerful."[2] Like those who cross the desert without a guide, only the foolish venture "before the law" unattended. For all practical purposes, lawyers monopolize access to one of the three branches of government. As owners of the keys to the courthouse, they jealously guard their exclusive right to practice law. Whether by accident or by design, the legal system has grown increasingly inaccessible to the uninitiated. In a sense, lawyers are like guardians for their clients; however, they act not because of the incapacity or disability of their clients but because of the arcane environment in which clients are required to do legal business. Within this environment the attorney plays an indispensable role, itself a highly structured product of legal creativity.

Speaking the client's words: the lawyer as mouthpiece

Whether mechanic, ballet dancer, senator, circus clown, or attorney, social expectations and institutional structures define the conduct and affectations of the roles one assumes. In a very real sense people merge with the roles they play. What begins as a role becomes part of a person's identity. Existentialist Jean-Paul Sartre was an insightful observer of the power that roles exert in our lives. For him, human consciousness was characterized by freedom – the capacity to define oneself independently by action. When following the norms and demands of social roles, a person is simply acting according to expectations of others. Sartre argued that personal authenticity is threatened by allegiance to an externally defined role, and that a role is assumed as a guise for attempting to absolve ourselves of personal moral responsibility for our conduct.[3]

Because they are so comprehensive and time-demanding, professional roles tend to be particularly dominant and threatening to personal identity. In an initial social contact, people are often identified by their profession. That first question "Who are you" often takes the form "What do you do." Many people become their professional identity and thus give up some of their power for self-definition and some of their obligation for personal responsibility. This risk is particularly acute for those who play the role of lawyer.

Whereas most professional roles relate to a specific task – to design a bridge or to heal a patient – the lawyer's role encompasses and intrudes. As defined by tradition and by professional code, the job of a lawyer is to represent vigorously the position and interests of a client, to take a client's place in the legal process. In a service-oriented society, many pay for services, but few consumers make so comprehensive a claim on the total person as a client does on an attorney. A lawyer becomes the voice and presence of a client, perhaps advocating things the lawyer regards with distaste. A client who wishes to build a shopping center hires an attorney who not only advises what is legally possible but also helps structure the project, advocates it before public agencies, speaks on its behalf to the newspapers, and defends it vigorously against attack – all this regardless of the lawyer's own feelings about the project. In a sense, the client has purchased more than a hired gun. The client has also acquired a piece of the attorney's integrity, credibility, mind, and soul. The lawyer stands in the client's shoes, thinks the client's thoughts, speaks the client's words, advocates the client's position. The attorney is the client's mouthpiece, the client's alter ego.

Susan Constans, one of the attorneys we interviewed, recalls a comparison of the way doctors and lawyers relate to those they serve: "The physician does an examination, makes a diagnosis, prescribes medication, or some kind of therapy, and the person walks out the door with their disease. When somebody comes to see an attorney, they bring their disease in, lay it on the desk, and they leave and you've got it." The client walks out unencumbered, for the lawyer has assumed the problems on the client's behalf. To a varying but always substantial degree, a client gives up power, judgment, and control to an attorney; and in return, an attorney assumes a client's concerns, values, and intentions. It is not surprising that when we empower someone to stand in our place and to act on our behalf, we call it a power of attorney.

A role that entails such a dramatic shift of power and personality and demands so much time and commitment will leave an imprint on whoever assumes the role. Where a role invades our being, our patterns of thought, our allegiances, our definitions of moral relevancy, it is difficult to limit the extent of identification with that role. Indeed, it may be psychologically and professionally imperative for lawyers to become their role and to identify with their clients in order to maintain sanity, commitment, and professional competence. It is much easier to argue effectively on behalf of the insurance company seeking to deprive a widow of death benefits if the attorney is convinced that the insurance company wears the white hat. But because tomorrow the lawyer may be defending the widow against an insurance company, it is also important to have malleable convictions.

This very malleability becomes part of the role definition of a legal advocate. Charles Curtis, a prominent Boston attorney, describes the chameleon-like quality lawyers must adopt:

It is profoundly true that the first person a lawyer persuades is himself. A practicing lawyer will soon detect in himself a perfectly astonishing amount of sincerity. By the time that he has even sketched out his brief, however skeptically he started, he finds himself believing more and more in what he says, until he has to hark back to his original opinion in order to orient himself. And later, when he starts arguing the case before the court, his belief is total, and he is quite sincere about it. You cannot very well keep your tongue in your cheek while you are talking. He believes what he is saying in a way that will later astonish himself as much as now it does others.[4]

Dexterity or lack of apparent principle in adopting the cause of another becomes a prime professional asset. "A lawyer is required to be disingenuous. He is required to make statements as well as arguments which he does not believe in. . . . And he must never lose the reputation of lacking veracity, because his freedom from the strict bonds of veracity and of the law are the two chief assets of the profession."[5] Susan Constans, an attorney we interviewed, attests to this need for adaptability: "I have to be flexible enough to really throw myself into whatever role I have in a particular case, and a lot of time those positions are antithetical. . . . It's like I have to contradict myself depending upon what role I'm taking, but I think that's absolutely essential if you're going to do a good job for your client." Not knowing who will walk into the office on a given morning, the lawyer must be ready to provide committed representation to either the widow or the insurance company, judging the legality but not the morality of the cause.

Role identification: the system depends on it

Placing limitations on a lawyer's role identification is complicated by the "fight theory" of dispute resolution.[6] Like sports and the American economic system, the model is competitive. Because specialized knowledge and skills are required to compete in the legal system, individuals may hire or be furnished with specially trained gladiators to compete in their place. In any legal transaction or dispute, attorneys are likely to be not only most vocal and visible but often exclusively so. While it is possible to conceive of a different legal system without attorneys at center stage, imagining the American legal system without lawyers as virtuoso performers is not possible.

Within this interlocking system, two rationales justify attorneys acting as unfettered advocates. First, the role and the system are so intertwined that an attorney who does not fulfill the obligations of professional responsibility threatens the fair, effective functioning of the legal system. In support of this justification, "the bar assumes both transient and transcendent responsibilities: to serve clients and to serve justice. . . . Lawyers equate these, and assume that they do one when they do the other."[7] The lawyer is the linchpin in a system of interdependent parts. A network of countervailing forces is designed around the assumption that the lawyer role will be fulfilled without reservation. To tamper within the linchpin is to endanger the whole.

The second, and less apparent, justification for untempered advocacy derives from the protection a lawyer provides for the personal freedom, autonomy, and dignity of the client by enabling the client to use the legal system competently. This argument begins with the postulate that individual autonomy is a prime moral value. Because the legal system mediates rights and obligations in our society, it is essential to autonomy and freedom that an individual have the means to participate effectively in this process. Given that effective participation depends on representation by an attorney, legal counsel is morally obligated to assist the client in exercising autonomy. Under this reasoning, a breach of partisanship, such as a betrayal of client confidentiality, is in itself a moral breach. Commitment to client becomes an overriding moral consideration, rather than just a fulfillment of a professional, institutional role.

For adherents to this second position, moral obligation to clients is a kind of higher claim which overshadows any conflict between professional and personal morality. From this reasoning flows a moral rather than structural justification for neutral partisanship and an answer to the perplexing question, "How can it be that it is not only permissible, but indeed morally right, to favor the interest of a particular person in a way which we can be fairly sure is either harmful to another particular individual or not maximumly conducive to the welfare of society as a whole?"[8]

Partisanship and neutrality: virtues of an advocate

Underlying the facile identity of lawyer and client are the principles of partisanship and neutrality.[9] These principles describe the traditional conception of an advocate operating within the adversary system — a familiar role to all of the attorneys with whom we talked.[10] Partisanship requires uncompromised devotion of an attorney to serving a client's interests. The loyalty of an attorney to a client is exclusive and aggressive. A client has powerful ethical and even constitutional claims on the unyielding partisanship of an advocate. The unflagging devotion of partisanship resonates in the words of Lord Brougham in his 1821 defense of Queen Caroline's divorce case before the House of Lords:

An advocate, in the discharge of his duty, knows but one person in all the world, and that person is his client. To save that client by all means and expedients, and at all hazards and costs to other persons, and, among them, to himself, is his first and only duty; and in performing this duty he must not regard the alarm, the torments, the destruction which he may bring upon others. Separating the duty of a patriot from that of an advocate, he must go on reckless of consequences, though it should be his unhappy fate to involve his country in confusion.[11]

Neutrality, the second foundation block of the lawyer's role, requires an attorney to represent a client without passing judgment on the character of the client or on the moral merits of the client's position. Once representation is undertaken, suspension of moral assessment becomes part of the job; thus, a lawyer stands as the partisan for a cause about which the lawyer cannot pass judgment. How can someone be both neutral and partisan? The lawyer-client relationship is the key to the puzzle, for it supplies the essential piece lost to partisanship when neutrality is imposed. Commitment is necessary for partisanship, and in the vacuum of neutrality, the lawyer-client relationship identifies the object of commitment needed by partisanship to function.

The strange notion of judgmental neutrality in the context of advocacy was the point of Baron Bramwell in 1871:

A man's rights are to be determined by the Court, not by his attorney or Counsel. It is for the want of remembering this that foolish people object to lawyers that they will advocate a case against their own opinions. A client is entitled to say to his Counsel, "I want your advocacy, not your judgment; I prefer that of the Court."[12]

Brooke Johnson, a lawyer in our study, summed up the posture of a neutral advocate: "You're retained to represent another person. You are their spokesperson and their representative. You're not there to impose your own values on that person's life, whether or not they're better than that person's values."

According to this traditional conception of the lawyer's role, an attorney must further the objectives of a client while acting within the bounds of the law. Thus, the sole determinants of conduct in the lawyer's moral universe are the law and the interests of the client. Besides a narrowly circumscribed obligation as an officer of the court, a lawyer need not, and as a professional, must not, go beyond these two considerations. Adherence to legal rules and to the objectives of a client defines moral responsibility without regard to the well-being of others. From a strictly professional point of view, the lawyer for an insurance company forsakes all others and is not even allowed the compassion that the insurance company itself might display. Charles Curtis describes the morality that arises from the vicarious conduct of an attorney:

We are not dealing with the morals which govern a man acting for himself, but with the ethics of advocacy. We are talking about the special moral code which governs a man who is acting for another. Lawyers in their practice – how they behave else where does not concern us – put off more and more of our common morals the further they go in a profession which treats right and wrong, vice and virtue, on such equal terms.[13]

Role-determined morality: the problem of moral distance

Richard Wasserstrom introduced the term "role-differentiated behavior" to describe how a given role reorients or distinguishes a person's moral vision.[14] This concept of role-determined perspective is useful in understanding how a lawyer takes on the odd combination of partisanship and neutrality. Role-differentiated behavior means that it is appropriate, and perhaps obligatory, for a person in one role to value and attend to certain factors that might reasonably be ignored by a person in another role. The term "moral world" describes the moral considerations relevant to a person in a given role.[15] A physician's moral world differs from that of a prosecutor. A doctor in the emergency room acts to save a life without regard to whether the patient might be a criminal whom the state will eventually kill. For the doctor, the relevant considerations are different from the professional concerns of the prosecutor. The moral perspective circumscribed by role not only tells us how we ought to act and what we ought to value; it also excuses our omissions. Seemingly oblivious of concern for unemployment in the logging industry, an indignant environmentalist seeks to protect the old growth forest habitat of the spotted owl; a school board member lobbies for more money for education at the expense of facilities for the elderly.

Professional conduct is a type of role-determined behavior in which the defining attributes of the role specify how a professional relates to other people. Partisanship and neutrality delimit the moral world of a lawyer and focus nearly exclusive attention on client concerns. The role of the neutral partisan both requires and justifies an attorney's preference for the interests of the client over those of all others. Although everyone else in town may favor the interest of the widow, an attorney's job is to favor the interest of the insurance company. It is as though Polonius's admonition to his son were turned on its head – This above all: to thine own client be true, and it must follow as the night the day . . .

For clarity we emphasize the limited and rarefied nature of the professional moral world of the legal advocate, but its exclusivity is more apparent in concept than in the lives of most attorneys with whom we spoke. Despite the power of comprehensive and invasive roles to define who we are, few lawyers, even in their professional lives, ignore all considerations beyond legal compliance and client representation. Questions of personal self-interest, such as financial success and peer group acceptance, undoubtedly compete for attention as a lawyer makes decisions about unqualified partisanship and blind neutrality. Another and, for our purposes, more relevant consideration that may directly challenge traditionally defined professional role is the personal morality that each attorney brings into the practice of law. Personal morality provides a second set of relevant concerns which the attorney must reconcile with the moral dictates of professional responsibility. Despite the attractiveness of the relatively simple and unambiguous moral world of client allegiance and the code of professional conduct, only a few lawyers in our study succeeded in avoiding tension between personal and professional moral considerations.

The gap between the relevant concerns of professional ethics and the relevant concerns of personal morality is called "moral distance."[16] In the interest of the client, professional role requires an attorney to consider as morally insignificant certain factors that a lay person might consider crucial, and vice versa. Our interviews indicate that moral distance also occurs within individual attorneys to the extent that role identification separates lawyers from their own personal morality.

Although at the time he did not have a name for it, moral distance is illustrated by an experience early in the legal career of one of the authors, Rand Jack:

While an associate in a large metropolitan law firm, I was asked by a partner to work with him representing an insurance company that was refusing to pay the life insurance claim of an elderly widow. A policy had been purchased shortly before her husband's death to secure continued ownership of a small restaurant, the only means of livelihood available to the widow. Claiming that the policy had been obtained through misrepresentation, the insurance company denied coverage. The husband had disclosed that he had heart problems at the time he applied for insurance, but made no mention on his insurance application that he also had diabetes. The company claimed that at the time of application, the husband knew that he had both a heart problem and diabetes, a fatal combination which would have caused the insurance company to refuse to write coverage. The physician who examined the husband as part of the insurance application was also the family doctor.

I was asked by the partner in charge of the case to take the deposition, or pretrial sworn testimony, of the doctor to determine whether he knew of the diabetes at the time he filled out the medical portion of the insurance application. After a few minutes of questioning, the doctor admitted that he had learned of the husband's diabetes a couple of days before the insurance medical examination. Presumably because of a combination of factors – long years of service to the family, the importance of this policy to the future financial well-being of the wife, and the coincidence of the knowledge of diabetes coming a day or two before the insurance physical – the doctor mentally postponed the arrival of this information to a less disastrous date. Once the admission was in hand, I terminated the deposition, for the case was effectively over. We had won. The widow would not get the money; in all probability she would lose financial security; and justice was done.

When I went back to the office with an account of what had happened, I was warmly congratulated. Fraud had been uncovered; money would be saved for a valuable client. While I understood that what the doctor and husband had done was wrong and that the insurance company had a legally legitimate reason for refusing to pay the claim, I did not feel like celebrating. Despite pressures to the contrary, I wanted to hang on to my feeling of ambivalence. Whatever the legal rules and shades of moral wrongdoing, a vulnerable, elderly person had been hurt and would feel the hardship for the rest of her life; and yet, the insurance company had done nothing wrong, legally or morally. The complexity lies both in the relationship of the widow and the insurance company and in my role as an attorney.

I had played the specified lawyer role and had secured justice according to the rules of the legal system, but my personal morality flinched at the hurt caused by this particular application of a generally sound legal rule. There was a substantial distance between the relevant concerns in my personal moral sphere and in my professional moral sphere. My personal morality told me that the hurt to the widow mattered and that it should affect my reaction to the situation. My professional role told me that the hurt was irrelevant and that vigorous, effective representation of my client was the prime consideration in determining the ethical quality of my action.

A major concern of this book is to understand this idea of moral distance and to explore how attorneys deal with the gap between personal and professional morality when it stretches and threatens to tear the fiber of individual personality.

Ethics of advocacy: license to act as others may not

The distance between professional ethics and personal morality opens at least in part because an advocate is required by role to do things that would be morally unacceptable if done by anyone other than a lawyer. This difference is captured with stark bluntness in the quip: "If you want to take dough from a murderer for helping him beat the rap, you must be admitted to the bar."[17]

Although there has been some scholarly disagreement regarding the ethical limits of advocacy, William Simon asserts persuasively that the argument is not about whether lawyers must act beyond the general bounds of moral constraint, but rather where to draw the line between permissible and impermissible advocacy. It is generally acknowledged that "the lawyer will employ means on behalf of his client which he would not consider proper in a non-professional context even to advance his own ends."[18] Seeing someone approach peril, most people would feel morally bound to give warning. An advocate not only watches with glee as an opponent moves toward danger but will do everything possible to lubricate progress, including setting and, if feasible, disguising the trap.

Testimonials are plentiful as to the special dispensation given to lawyers acting as advocates. Where else in society would the conduct described by Supreme Court Justice White be condoned?

> If he can confuse a witness, even a truthful one, or make him appear at a disadvantage, unsure or indecisive, that will be his normal course. Our interest in not convicting the innocent permits counsel to put the State to its proof, to put the State's case in the worst possible light, regardless of what he thinks or knows to be the truth. Undoubtedly, there are some limits which defense counsel must observe, but more often than not, defense counsel will cross-examine a prosecution witness, and impeach him if he can, even if he thinks the witness is telling the truth.[19]

This same countenance of deception and concealment is central to Judge Jerome Frank's critique of the adversary system:

> What is the role of the lawyer in bringing the evidence before the trial court? As you may learn by reading any one of a dozen or more handbooks on how to try a lawsuit, an experienced lawyer uses all sorts of stratagems to minimize the effect on the judge or jury of testimony disadvantageous to his client, even when the lawyer has no doubt of the accuracy and honesty of that testimony. . . . If such a witness happens to be timid, frightened by the unfamiliarity of court-room ways, the lawyer, in his cross-examination, plays on that weakness, in order to confuse his witness and make it appear that he is concealing significant facts.[20]

Lawyers in our study likewise elevated professional responsibility in a way that lay persons might find difficult to accept. Discussing a rape situation in which the lawyer knew the client to be guilty,

George Willis was asked if he would put the victim on the stand and discredit her.

A: I'd do it. I'd make her look as despicable as I possibly could.

Q: How would you feel about that? Would that create a tension between your own personal sense of right and wrong and your professional responsibility?

A: No.

Q: Why not?

A: Because the state's got the burden to prove my client guilty beyond a reasonable doubt.

Q: And if you can block that by tearing her up—?

A: Absolutely, that's my job.

Professor Simon observes that the ideology of the adversary system rationalizes the peculiar ethical orientation of an attorney — "his explicit refusal to be bound by personal and social norms which he considers binding on others."[21] The unique quality of this ideology stems from the combination of neutrality with partisanship. While physicians and ministers are neutral in deciding who they serve, they do not take on and advocate the causes of those they assist. On the other hand, environmentalists and conservative Republicans are partisans, but they only ally with those whose values they share. It is the strange plight of the lawyer to be both neutral and partisan.

In dealing with confidentiality, the Rules of Professional Conduct practically equate partisanship and neutrality with attorney responsibility. The requirement of confidentiality can lead to a split between normal social expectations and proper attorney conduct. As a basic principle, an attorney is prohibited from revealing confidences of a client. After repudiating attempts to dilute the strictures of client confidentiality, the House of Delegates of the American Bar Association in 1983 affirmed rules that require disclosure by an attorney only when necessary to avoid assisting a client's criminal or fraudulent act in a proceeding before the court. Attorneys were left discretion to reveal confidences in order to prevent further crimes likely to result in imminent death or substantial bodily harm. Thus, the rules permit, and perhaps require, lawyers to hold confidences in the face of highly undesirable consequences.[22] A substantial number of attorneys in our study reach precisely this conclusion. Although most lay people would quickly divulge information to prevent harm to a child, most attorneys we talked to understood their ethical obligation to the contrary, except perhaps in extreme circumstances.

A case from New York State[23] illustrates the distance between societal and professional morality, seemingly confirming Charles Curtis's controversial statement that under proper circumstances "one of the functions of a lawyer is to lie for his client."[24] While preparing defense for a criminal trial, attorneys learned from their client that he had been responsible for other murders unrelated to the pending case. The lawyers confirmed the client's story by visiting the site where one of the bodies had been hidden. At issue was the right of the client to have confidences respected despite claims of innocent persons to information of great importance to them. Faced with inquiries, the attorneys maintained confidentiality and refrained from disclosing knowledge of the deaths or the location of the bodies to authorities or to the families of the missing victims. What is unusual about this case is not that the attorney's conduct was vindicated but that it was challenged at all. Who else in our society could conceal such information with impunity?

For most people this New York case points to an agonizing break between professional responsibility and personal morality. Some attorneys respond to situations such as these with relative ease; for others, personal morality competes with professional responsibility to reveal a disquieting breach between them. At some point, a lawyer may be tempted to ignore the rules and respond as a philosopher king. Many factors undoubtedly influence the experience of conflict between external and internal commands — how lawyers perceive and identify with their role, how they rationalize and justify what they do in terms of constructive contributions of the legal system to social welfare, and how much their personal morality and role morality coincide from the outset.

Role identification: stoic detachment and constriction of moral vision

In his famous moral inquiry about whether "to be or not to be," Hamlet was concerned only with his own personal conflicts. In comparison, a lawyer's moral problem is compounded by the perplexity of the "difference between acting for another and acting for yourself." "You devote yourself to the interest of another at the peril of yourself. Vicarious action tempts a man too far from himself. Men will do for others what they are not willing to do for themselves – nobler as well as ignoble things."[25] Jim Smallwood, an attorney with whom we spoke, echoed this sentiment: "I'll do certain things in negotiations for somebody that I'd never do for myself, because I just don't feel good, I just don't feel right about it. . . . You're trained to do that. I guess you have to do it."

Because a lawyer speaks and acts for another according to externally prescribed rules, it is logical to disavow responsibility for the position taken on behalf of a client and for its consequences. An advocate psychologically separates the self from words and thoughts that in fact belong to someone else who has purchased them. This attitude of detachment itself becomes a part of the lawyer's professional role. To ensure moral and psychological well-being and to facilitate effective client representation, the neutrality of a hired gun may be an irresistible part of being an attorney.

Charles Curtis believes detachment makes the practice of law a Stoic rather than a Christian pursuit. To serve the client and to protect the self, a lawyer must emulate the commitment of the Stoic, which is characterized by fervent detachment rather than involved empathy. Attorneys we interviewed spoke of the need "to assume a distance" and used terms to describe client relationships such as "detached concern." As Larry Smith said, "the best thing you can do for that individual is to be terribly concerned on a professional level but not too concerned for them on a personal level." Curtis puts this posture in historical perspective: "The practice of law is vicarious, not altruistic, and the lawyer must go back of Christianity to Stoicism for the vicarious detachment which will permit him to serve his client."[26]

Although stoic detachment is part of the classic, and perhaps necessary, definition of an attorney's professional role, a price is paid when detachment translates into a moral skepticism and reservation of commitment. For the person who easily wears the lawyer's role and accepts its specifications without question, there is a danger of limiting moral vision. If this happens, a lawyer loses the ability to bring a wide and diverse world of moral considerations to bear on important questions, and may suffer decay of moral instinct. For many clients the result is a narrowing of advice they receive since only moral considerations relevant to professional perspective are brought to bear. When this occurs, a society that depends heavily on law and legal counsel is also poorer.

Despite these concerns, the intense, encompassing nature of the attorney role encourages extremes – either full adherence to role or, less frequently, dissociation. There are tremendous pressures for tight role identification. Conformance to role helps define professional competence and integrity. Since the role establishes the rules of the game, close identification increases the likelihood of success in the legal occupation and simplifies the spectrum of moral considerations. Because of the comprehensive structuring of the legal role, the question "What should I do" in the daily decision making of most attorneys involves tactical considerations rather than questions of moral ought.

Even with pressure for role identification, if the gap between role and personal morality is too wide, divorce from role may be less traumatic than identification. Yet failure to embrace the role carries its own problems. To remain apart from the institutionalized identity may impair ability to act effectively in the legal system. Psychologically, it may leave the attorney divided between the pervasive requirements to act like a lawyer and a differently attuned inner agenda. Both extremes of identification and dissociation "have in common the unwanted consequences that practical deliberation, judgment, and action *within* the role are effectively cut off from ordinary moral beliefs, attitudes, feelings and relationships – resources upon which responsible judgment and action depend. This consequence is very costly in both personal and social terms."[27]

As a number of attorneys in our study suggest, the long-range interests of everyone might best be served not by the total detachment of Creon or the passionate ardor of Antigone but by some middle ground – by a "more ethically reflective form of legal practice."[28] Our interviews indicate that those searching for a middle ground often use the morality of care to temper the stoic detachment inherent in a morality of rights. Most of the lawyers we interviewed avoid the pitfalls of overidentification and dissociation. Despite the either/or demand of the role, most live with the benefits and tensions of a position somewhere in between. To varying degrees, they keep their own personal morality as a viable faculty in their professional lives. However, those who most successfully maintain a broad moral landscape and stave off atrophy of personal moral sensitivity pay a price. They live with continuing tension created by trying to meet fully the demands of the lawyer role while at the same time not letting professional dictates overwhelm their identity.[29]

Moral costs: more than "getting our moral sums right"

One of the dangers of overidentification with role is that the lawyer occupies a constricted moral universe where ethical correctness is closely identified with representing client interests. Not only are substantive moral considerations limited, but the process and complexity of moral thinking are artificially restrained. The subtlety of moral reasoning as a way of reaching conclusions becomes confused with a system that measures correctness by victorious outcome. Unlike the adversary system, "morality is not merely a matter of getting things right – as in solving a puzzle or learning to speak graciously – but a matter of relating to people in a special and specifically human way."[30] This broadened moral vision suggests one way of occupying the middle ground, of avoiding both the tunnel vision inherent in total role identification and the alienation that accompanies rejection of that role. An attorney may be able to fulfill essential attributes of the professional role, and yet retain an acceptable level of loyalty to personal morality by paying particular attention to the way in which moral decisions are made and by recognizing and accepting responsibility for the consequences of those decisions. Taking responsibility corresponds closely to the notion of moral costs[31] – the price paid when a moral decision leaves some legitimate interests unsatisfied.

Moral dilemmas arise in the context of conflicting obligations. When all moral obligations cannot be met, some will be slighted. Moral uncertainty may involve a choice between competing rules or principles so that the choice of one diminishes the integrity of the other. For instance, in the Watergate affair certain participants were forced to choose between allegiance to the president and telling the truth. Another type of dilemma happens when any decision hurts someone, and the problem is to determine who should bear the harm.

The classic illustration is the lifeboat with less capacity than the number of people in distress. A third type of conflict occurs if personal moral imperatives to avoid harm clash with institutional rules to which an individual is committed. When the rule against stealing conflicts with the moral necessity of feeding children, any course of action registers moral costs. If a person steals, an important rule for social order is encroached; if restraint is exercised, children suffer hunger. This type of conflict between institutional rule and personal value is the most common moral dilemma described to us by attorneys as exacting moral costs. Almost invariably, the institutional rule in the conflict is a requirement dictated by professional role.

Because morality includes relationships as well as rules, moral correctness must go beyond a formalistic balancing of principles, beyond "getting our moral sums right."[32] By taking responsibility for the consequences of our actions and adjusting conduct to moderate undesirable impact on others, we acknowledge that even morally proper decisions sometimes involve moral costs. To assess the full dimensions of a moral dilemma requires breadth of moral vision. An attorney who recognizes the moral costs of a decision acknowledges the legitimacy of competing interests and the concerns of others. Attention to moral costs allows a lawyer to serve primary professional obligations while at the same time maintaining a vital personal moral concern.

We found many attorneys in our study moderating the extremes of total role identification by recognizing and assuming responsibility for the moral costs of their conduct. Taking responsibility was manifest either inwardly as emotional distress or outwardly as action to mitigate the consequences of fulfilling requirements of the lawyer role. Whereas moral cost is the unavoidable harm inherent in some moral choices, responsibility is the individual's engagement with that harm. The meaning of "responsibility" resides in the root of that word – the ability to respond to harm that a choice causes. In the face of a moral dilemma, harm may be inevitable; but responsiveness to that harm is discretionary and depends on the moral quality of the actor.

An actual murder case, which became the basis for one of our hypothetical interview questions, illustrates an attorney taking cognizance of moral costs. Representing a dangerous, crazy confessed murderer, the defense lawyer knew that he could exclude a confession and set his client free. This role-prescribed conduct threatened harm to the community and perhaps ultimately to the client. Recognizing the moral cost to the community of excluding the confession, the attorney had the defendant's mother appointed his guardian. The lawyer then convinced the mother that it was in her son's best interest to plead not guilty by reason of insanity rather than risk the consequences of going free and killing again. The plea was accepted after a pro forma hearing, and the defendant was institutionalized without the matter of the admissibility of the confession being considered by the court. The attorney moderated his strict ethical obligation as an advocate and in so doing mitigated probable harm to a potential innocent victim and to the client. To understand and to take responsibility for moral costs required defense counsel to maintain a moral vision that enabled him to see beyond the ethical imperatives of professional role.

Law school: professionalization of the lawyer

When initiated into the profession, most people are not detached, neutral, partisan stoics who think like lawyers and share the assumptions of professional ethics. Although some undoubtedly are born to be lawyers and readily take on the professional garb, a large number require indoctrination and a rite of passage. Only through training do most lawyers develop an "indifference to a wide variety of ends and consequences that in other contexts would be of undeniable moral significance."[33] The process of distancing the personal self from the newly emerging professional self happens most dramatically in law school. Virtually every new lawyer passes through the gates of law school on the way to receiving the keys to the courthouse door.

John Bonsignore provides a conceptual framework for understanding the distancing process as it occurs in law school.[34] He begins by asking why the venerable law teacher Carl Llewellyn introduces his book of lectures for first-year law students with a nursery rhyme, "The Bramble Bush."

There was a man in our town
And he was wonderous wise
He jumped into a bramble bush
And scratched out both his eyes —
And when he saw that he was blind,
With all his might and main
He jumped into another one
And scratched them in again.

What did the man jumping into the bramble bush have in common with students beginning law school? How is it that the brambled environment that took sight away then gave it back?

Bonsignore argues that law schools have the ability to dominate participants and to crowd out competing values. Each person enters law school with a "home world," a set of successful experiences that confirm a workable self-concept and way of relating in the world. Almost without exception, beginning law students are bright and articulate. They have enjoyed substantial achievement in academic settings prior to law school. The more those entering an institution can keep the proved strategies of the "home world," the less influence the institution has in altering values and identities of the participants.

Law schools systematically cut individuals loose from "psychosocial anchoring points" that have proved beneficial in the past. Normal relationships, habits, and activities are sharply curtailed. Through mortification and competition, through an awakening of what pays off and what does not within the institution, the "transformation in attitudes that law students have about themselves and the worth of their past" gradually takes place. "Much of the first year's struggles may be traceable to the unwillingness of law students to accept the legal world view, the kinds of questions asked in law, and the way lawyers answer questions." For many, "at stake, behind this contest of wills is nothing other than the paradigm of law, from world view through technique." Often at the expense of personal morality, law school instills the new role morality of the attorney. The emerging professional is "learning to see the world as a lawyer and to use legal techniques to the exclusion of other organizing principles."[35] Like the bramble bush, law school extinguishes the old vision and replaces it with a new and perhaps radically altered perception of the world.

In a firsthand account of his initial year at Harvard Law School, Scott Turow dramatizes this replacement of one vision with another by professors he calls "brain thieves": "'They're turning me into someone else,' she said, referring to our professors. 'They're making me different. . . . It's someone I don't *want* to be,' she said. 'Don't you get the feeling all the time that you're being indoctrinated?'"[36] Susan Constans, one of the lawyers in our study, likewise uses a term associated with the experience of prisoners of war: "When you enter law school, they tell you that you won't be the same person when you leave, and you think it's a crock of shit. But it's true. . . . It's some very wicked form of brainwashing." Another attorney, Kathryn Colby, put it even more bluntly: "I turned to my friends and said, 'They're fucking with your brain; can't you feel it?'" Rather than just new knowledge and skills, an alternative world view is ingrained. A new paradigm of thinking, assessing, and valuing comes to compete with the pre–law school version of the world. Attorney Peter Oran told us, "Law school reoriented my brain waves." This theme of transformation dominates Turow's description of law school:

I *feel* a lot of things about prostitution and they have everything to do with the way I *think* about prostitution. I don't want to become the kind of person who tries to pretend that my feelings have nothing to do with my opinions. . . . I heard similar comments [from classmates], all to the effect that they were being limited, harmed, by the education, forced to substitute dry reason for emotion, to cultivate opinions which were "rational" but which had no roots in the experience, the life they'd had before. They were being cut away from themselves.[37]

With the development of moral distance and growing role identification comes the danger of eroded moral sensitivities. Tension exists as new ways threaten the old: "It was a grimly literal, linear, step-by-step process of thought that we were learning . . . an immensely useful technical skill, but I feared it would calcify my approach to other subjects."[38] In our interview, Leon Gilder echoed this sentiment: "Law school can limit, and for some people it really severely limits their view of the world, as if the world is some narrow, logical thing that ends up in resolutions that are right or wrong."

Turow speaks of the power of law to define reality and the training in mental dexterity that comes through participation in that process. Skepticism is reinforced by unprincipled commitment:

So on one hand you believed nothing. And on the other, for the sake of logical consistency, and to preserve long established rules, you would accept the most ridiculous fictions – that a corporation was a person, that an apartment tenant was renting land and not a dwelling. What all of that showed me was that the law as a way of looking at the world and my own more personal way of seeing things could not be thoroughly meshed; that at some point, somehow, I would have to *learn* those habits of mind without making them my own in the deepest sense.[39]

The press to ingest new habits of mind can be disconcerting, as attorney John Crowell observes: "At first I felt that law school and the practice of law were so emotionally desensitizing that it was an occupational hazard to be a lawyer." Like John Crowell and the other lawyers we spoke with, no one who attends law school for three years completely escapes the thorns that excise prior vision and implant new. For some the bramble bush cuts deeply and surgery is radical, while for others the learning of a new perspective does not entail loss of the old.

Responsiveness and care: ambivalent accommodations in the law

While for the most part American culture has followed Plato's wisdom and adopted a system of laws rather than search for a philosopher king, some legal institutions reflect ambivalence in this choice. Some matters just do not seem amenable to rules based on generalization of experience. The American legal system, though in a minority position, has always contained substantial elements of care morality as a check on the harshness of rule by law.

For instance, in early English legal history, courts of equity emerged "to be the 'correction of the law where, by reason of its universality, it is deficient.'" The purpose of equity courts was "to do complete justice in a case where a court of law is unable, because of the inflexibility of the rules by which it is bound, to adapt its judgment to the special circumstances of the case."[40] The concerns of eighteenth-century law commentator William Blackstone focus specifically on those attributes of equity jurisdiction that give rise to it. Because equity depends "upon the particular circumstances of each individual case, there can be no established rules and fixed precepts of equity laid down." There is danger in this:

The liberty of considering all cases in an equitable light must not be indulged too far, lest thereby we destroy all law, and leave the decision of every question entirely in the breast of the judge. And law, without equity, though hard and disagreeable, is much more desirable for the public good, than equity without law; which would make every judge a legislator and introduce most infinite confusion.[41]

The history of sentencing convicted criminals and the power of a jury to disregard the law are other examples of ambivalence between rule-bound decision making and discretion that responds to particular circumstances. Over the years, sentencing policies have oscillated between strict rules that prescribe specific punishments for particular crimes and almost unfettered discretion that allows a judge to mold punishment to the situation of the individual accused. The perennial question is whether the punishment should fit the crime or the criminal.

Americans are likewise a bit uneasy with regard to the authority of jurors to ignore the law and to impose the judgment of their consciences. Although juries are told what the law is and instructed to follow it, there is an "unreviewable and unreversible power in the jury to acquit in disregard of the instructions on the law given by the trial judge."[42] In the face of unpopular laws and illegal acts of conscience, in extending leniency and equity, juries are said to exercise the conscience of the community by disregarding or nullifying the law as applied to a particular case. Nevertheless, courts have shied from informing juries of this "prerogative-in-fact," because "its explicit avowal risks the ultimate logic of anarchy."[43]

Writing in 1922, Roscoe Pound recognized the importance for a healthy legal system of accommodating both individualization and generalization in application of the law. He distinguished between fixed detailed legal rules and legal standards that "involve a certain moral judgment upon conduct," that call for common sense or trained intuition rather than legal knowledge, and that are "relative to times and places and circumstances and . . . recognize that within the bounds fixed each case is to a certain extent unique."[44]

Philosophically the apportionment of the field between rule and discretion which is suggested by the use of rules and of standards respectively in modern law has its basis in the respective fields of intelligence and intuition. . . . Likewise rules, where we proceed mechanically, are more adapted to property and to business transactions; and standards, where we proceed upon intuitions, are more adapted to human conduct and to the conduct of enterprises. . . . In the law of property and in the law of commercial transactions it is precisely this general element and its relation to past situations that is decisive. The rule, mechanically applied, works by repetition and precludes individuality in results, which would threaten the security of acquisitions and the security of transactions. On the other hand, in the hand-made as distinguished from the machine-made product, the specialized skill of the workman gives us something infinitely more subtle than can be expressed in rules. In law some situations call for the product of hands, not of machines, for they involve not repetition, where the general elements are significant, but unique events, in which special circumstances are significant.[45]

Like the individual attorneys we interviewed, the legal system simultaneously entertains the moralities of care and rights, but with rights and rules in overwhelming dominance. It is the degree of that dominance that an influx of care-oriented attorneys could challenge. We talked to practical, practicing lawyers who recognize that, given our culture, it would be impossible to follow the Zapotec model. None of them suggested abandoning the rule of law, but many questioned to what extent a focus on universality of rules, on abstract questions of fairness and equality of distribution, precludes consideration of the "breadth of what is possible in the law."[46] Some of these attorneys are very comfortable in their role and feel little tension between personal and professional morality. The world of philosopher kings exercises little pull on them. Others, however, experience stress between their personal morality and the role expectations of an attorney. Despite law school, they hold on to substantial remnants of the past. These lawyers seek a fuller integration of care and rights, both to preserve their own integrity and to serve their clients and the legal system better.

To varying degrees, attorneys occupy two moral worlds – the complex, multifaceted world of personal morality and the more rarefied, eccentric domain of the practicing attorney. Like all of us, lawyers in their nonprofessional life must use their personal morality to deal with family and friends, poverty, suffering, and inequality.

However, lawyers also have a special moral province reserved only for them. In an attorney's moral world, there are peculiar procedural rules and normative principles that may contradict ways of thinking and acting generally approved as morally correct. Differences of rights and care sometimes coexist in the everyday personal morality of an attorney; sometimes they occur when lawyers face the role assigned them by the legal system. We are now ready to examine further the relationship between moral perspectives and the legal system.

How do attorneys understand joint occupancy of these incongruent moral worlds? How often do they find themselves embodying both Creon and Antigone, with an ensuing conflict between their personal and institutional lives? When this happens, how do they sort out, balance, affirm, and deny their personal morality and the professional morality imposed by the title attorney-at-law? Given the limited hospitality for care values in a male-dominated legal system, will the influx of female attorneys bring a significant new influence to bear on the practice of law? To what extent does self-selection, law school, and professional socialization affect moral orientation and the way individual attorneys relate to their professional role? As women enter the legal system in increasing numbers, how likely are they to bring with them a moral orientation in serious tension with some of the presuppositions of that system? Will the institutions of law simply remold anyone who seeks to enter with contrary ways of valuing and thinking, or will the tension persist, either at the expense of those who experience it or with slow modification of the legal structure? If the quotient of care thinking in the legal system increases substantially, how will this affect individual lawyers, the system, society? How will lawyers understand professional role? Can the tension between professional obligation and morality of care contribute to a constructive revitalization of the legal system?

3   Personal morality: the orientation of lawyers toward rights and care

Law institutionalizes the morality of our culture. By this we do not mean to join the discussion of whether it is possible or wise to legislate sexual mores and consumption habits. We are concerned with a broader understanding of morality – how we should relate to one another (landlord and tenant, husband and wife, employer and employee), how we should act (honor oral agreements, label poisonous products, pay child support), what rights we should have (to move about freely, enter into contracts, run for public office), in what proportions we should share in the wealth and power of society (investment tax credits, farm subsidies, collective bargaining). In this broad sense, the legal system articulates, sanctifies, and enforces our values. Because the legal system is itself a moral system which intimately affects our lives, there is reason to be concerned about the moral world view of lawyers who are its chief guardians and manipulators. Since the legal system and lawyers are inseparable, the moral orientation of lawyers has greater impact on the general public than the moral orientation of most others. To put it simply, the moral perspective of attorneys affects a system that in turn affects all of us.

How each lawyer influences the legal system is complicated and varies from case to case. For any given lawyer the effect is not system-wide, but subtle and localized. Cumulatively, however, the moral orientation of attorneys has structured the legal system and will continue to mold it. The impact comes about through the interplay of a lawyer and the legal system in the daily course of business. The moral vision a lawyer brings to the law affects how that attorney relates to clients, perceives problems, formulates solutions, makes decisions, and evaluates results. An attorney with rose-colored glasses will tend to see things with a rosy tint. The effect is in hue and shade, not in black and white.

51

If an artist and an engineer go to a carnival, they share approximately the same experience, but the particular perspective of each determines how they interpret what they see. When watching a Ferris wheel, the artist perceives form and flow, the integrity of composition; the engineer notices gear ratios and stress factors, the integrity of mechanical systems. Both function well within the carnival environment, but each has a different understanding of the experience. Except for the most artistic of artists or mechanical of engineers, there will also be an overlap and complement of perspective.

Our interviews with lawyers indicate that, like the artist and the engineer, attorneys bring differing perspectives to their work. Whether lawyers perceive through a morality of care or of rights influences their experience in the law. Attorneys with either orientation function well as practitioners, but the moral glasses they wear clearly affect the hue and tint of how they see the system and interact with it. In this chapter we discuss the extent to which practicing lawyers reason with a care orientation. Do women in our sample use a care focus more often than men? How are care and rights thinking manifested as lawyers talk of their work?

The interview: format and response

A number of pressures tend to foreclose expressions of care among practicing attorneys: self-selection into a system with compatible values, socialization through law school and the norms of practice, and the efficacy of a rights perspective in producing professional success. We assumed that these forces would be felt strongly by women entering a primarily male environment where their conduct is closely scrutinized and rigorously evaluated. Presumably, women with a highly developed morality of care would be under pressure to relinquish their divergent perspective and to take on a posture designed to facilitate the professional success so long denied their gender.

A second set of factors tending to silence voices of care among the lawyers of our study was the interview situation itself. A male attorney interviewed the lawyers during the regular business day in their professional offices. The environment placed them in their lawyer role. Also, the letter requesting participation in the study said we were interested in exploring moral choices of attorneys, not of people in general. The format of the interview suggested repeatedly that they were being interviewed as lawyers, and not as PTA members or tennis players. We asked, "How do you, as an individual lawyer, think about this problem?" Many of the questions were such that only an attorney could respond, and thus the message was unequivocal that a lawyerlike response was called for. To the extent that the role of lawyer carries with it expectations of a morality of rights, those expectations were inescapable in the interview. Nonetheless, statements of care were woven into the responses of nearly every attorney we talked with, and for a substantial number of attorneys, that orientation was dominant, at least at some point in the interview.

For purposes of analysis, we divided the interview into three sections:

1. *General moral orientation.* This segment of the interview consisted of broad questions about an attorney's experience practicing law and the primary responsibilities that the person feels as an attorney. We explored the lawyer's understanding of justice and morality, the person's sense of self, and how personal relationships and sense of self are affected by legal training and practice. This part of the interview allowed maximum opportunity to step out of the role of attorney and to insert personal moral perspective unencumbered by the demands of professional role.

2. *Real-life dilemmas.* We asked all of the attorneys if they had ever confronted situations in their practice where they faced moral conflict, where they were uncertain what they should do. Lawyers were free to define what they perceived as moral conflict and to discuss it in their own terms, but the question clearly fixed them in their role as an attorney. Sixty-three real-life dilemmas were described, with only six attorneys declining to identify a situation of moral conflict in their practice.

3. *Hypothetical dilemmas.* With two hypothetical dilemmas we placed the lawyers inescapably in their professional role and specifically defined the situation of conflict. Any attempt to express personal morality had to overcome the demand to consider requirements of role.

The three parts of the interview imposed a hierarchy of control over the attorney being interviewed. In the general section of the interview, a lawyer had wide latitude to define both the subject of response and the standpoint from which reply would be made. Personal morality was easily introduced here. In a real-life dilemma, an attorney had discretion to select the topic of response, but the professional perspective was definitely suggested by the interview format. Presumably personal morality would enter here in the lawyer's selection and discussion of situations of moral conflict. But because the person was specifically being asked to respond as a lawyer, that role asserted a proper point of view from which to reply. Finally, the hypothetical dilemmas left the least leeway for an individual to insert a personal perspective. These were definitely legal problems that carried the expectation for an answer from a professional vantage point. The first hypothetical dilemma, concerning the crazy killer and suppressible confession, provided the least room for an expression of conflicting personal morality. The overriding clarity of the constitutional mandate that a lawyer play the role of neutral partisan makes a professional perspective difficult to escape. The second hypothetical dilemma, the child custody case, gave more room for conflicting personal morality to surface, but still the position and expectation of reply were those of a lawyer's world view.

Data from our study show that a significant number of lawyers in the sample had strong care concerns in their personal morality.[1] (Statistical findings and analyses are in endnotes and Appendix II. See Appendix I for Coding Manual and for interrater reliability.) As the interview format moved to situations of greater imperative for response from a professional perspective, the percentage of care responses decreased while the expression of rights orientation correspondingly increased. For instance, care thinking was most often expressed in the general moral orientation and real-life dilemmas portion of the interview, and rights reasoning was overwhelmingly relied on in responding to the hypothetical confessed-murderer dilemma. The more the interview fixed attorneys in their legal role, the more they talked like lawyers and the less care thinking was visible.

Our data also indicate that of the lawyers showing strong care concerns in their personal morality, a disproportionate number are women. In the general moral orientation, women evidence a significant morality of care whereas men's perspective is dominated by a rights morality. With the exception of the confessed-murderer dilemma, women as a group expressed strong care concerns throughout the interview relative to men. In fact, everywhere except with respect to the first hypothetical dilemma, the women's percentage of care responses was more than twice as high as the men's. The compelling role commands of this dilemma had a leveling effect, so that there women displayed a definite rights orientation and their percentage of care statements dropped slightly below twice those of men.[2]

Looking at the percentage of women's care statements across the interview, we see a pattern that matches exactly the decreasing latitude allowed for the expression of personal morality and the increasing demand for conformance to the morality of rights inherent in the attorney role. In comparison, men tended to keep a relatively constant care response throughout the interview. Perhaps because their personal morality is already aligned with the lawyer role, men are little affected by the increasingly confining structure of the interview format. Pressures to assume the lawyer role and voice the moral expectations of rights merely push most men toward a position they already occupy. On the other hand, given that women exhibited a much stronger general moral orientation of care, the rising demands for speaking from the perspective of professional role made it increasingly difficult for them to voice their personal morality. In the care responses to the two hypothetical dilemmas, the difference is striking. When, as in the first dilemma, the rules of the game are clear and emphatic, women reason according to the rules of rights morality. But where clarity is less and the danger of harm more personalized, where role morality does not so completely exclude personal morality, women's care orientation reemerges to guide perception and response.[3]

General moral orientation: the tint of the attorney's glasses

The color of moral glasses affects attorneys' perception of, and response to, the legal environment. What moral language do lawyers use to describe their experience of the legal system? What do morality and responsibility mean to practicing lawyers? How do moralities of care and rights affect lawyers' judgments about the nature of what may be accomplished by a moral decision, about the course of conduct most likely to achieve the desired end? In the general moral-orientation aspect of the interview, we found that a significant majority of responses from female attorneys reflected care concerns and more than three-quarters of the male responses came from a rights perspective.[4]

MORALITY AND RESPONSIBILITY

The orientations of care and rights posit alternative models for understanding morality and responsibility. From a perspective of interdependence, goodness is measured by the effects of one's actions on others. Relationships provide the reference point for moral thought and moral action. Morality requires an active commitment to individual people, to healing and preserving relationships. From the perspective of individual autonomy, goodness is measured by standards of conduct. Lack of a defined standard threatens fairness, equality, and order. Concern with both harm and rules emerges in reply to the questions, "What does morality mean to you?" and "What makes something a moral problem or dilemma for you?"

Jane Triminger: I guess I decide what's good on the basis of things like that it's not selfish and that it helps others or makes a difference in other people's lives. Or it lends something to the human species along the lines of being cooperative and working with other people and keeping in contact with other people rather than tending to drive you into isolation. Being mindful of others around you. Things like that, and the things that aren't those I would put in the bad category.

William Moresby: Morality is a sort of general term that applies to those standards of conduct and behavior by which you can determine rightness. It, of necessity, incorporates an external standard. I guess I could define morality by saying morality is being honest and telling the truth, and obeying the law. Morality is just doing what's right, you know. (*What makes something a moral problem for you?*) When it bumps into an area that I haven't defined, where I don't have a sense of a defined standard of behavior.

Lois Halley: It seems to me [morality is] anything that raises to mind hurting other people or taking things away from other people or some sort of monetary gain for oneself. I think if one is really coming into some sort of windfall, it's got to be coming from somewhere, and I think that raises a moral issue of looking round and seeing where it is coming from and is somebody else getting shortchanged because they're getting this extra goody. And I suppose just how we interact with each other, if there's a contentiousness or bad feelings or bad blood between some people, that raises some moral issues because I guess I see us all as having a little bit of a moral obligation of being nice to each other and to get along.

Larry Smith: I think that everyone has their own individual morality that's largely the result of the society that we're brought up in and the family and the social circumstances. I think it would be perhaps too simply defined as the standards of conduct below which they do not wish to sink and they often do, that's part of being human. As far as absolutes, I think there are certain absolutes that I'm really not ready or qualified to define in terms of morality. But I think morality is largely consistent. I think that the standards are basically consistent for most people. The application of the standards might differ.

To show how moral orientation organizes perception of responsibility, we follow Lois Halley and Larry Smith, the last two lawyers quoted, through part of the general section of the interview. Both these lawyers are in civil practice, handling small business and estate planning matters; both have been practicing law for three to four years.

We asked Larry Smith, "What do you see as your major responsibility or responsibilities in practicing law?"

Doing the best job for my client that I can. Somebody has a dispute and they need a hired gun, and I step in, keeping in mind my responsibilities to my client and to the profession, the court, things like that — my ethical obligations. I think my responsibility is to try and get the best result I can for my client. (*What is your ethical obligation?*) I think that would include my obligations as an officer of the court. My obligation is to follow the law, both the code of professional responsibility and the law, and, I think I have to say, within that I would probably have to inject whatever my own personal ethics might be. I'll tell clients, when they come to me, that if they want somebody that will play by the rules, use the rules aggressively, yet not break the rules, then they've come to the right person. If they want somebody that will get the result by breaking any of the rules, I'm not the one. . . . I'm representing the individual, and I'm not representing what I think about the individual. It's a matter of me working for them aggressively and zealously and all that.

This response regarding a lawyer's responsibility is almost stereotypical. As described previously, ideals of partisanship and neutrality are fulfilled by aggressive advocacy. When asked, "Does legal practice present you with any moral dilemmas or moral problems?" Larry Smith is protected by clear standards that dictate his course of action: "I could see how it could, but it hasn't. . . . Again, it comes to a question of what I can and cannot do within the bounds of representing my client."

As long as standards are clear, a lawyer need only "play by the rules, use the rules aggressively" in order to fulfill professional responsibility. A problem arises only when the rules lack firmness. "It is all a question of line drawing. What is using a rule aggressively as opposed to, say, bending a rule, and then where does it become breaking a rule? Some rules don't break; they just bend, and I guess those are judgment calls." He further explains that his lack of moral dilemmas arises from

the way that I approach some things. What my criminal law professor once told me is that the secret to practice in criminal law is to play the thing as if it were a game, and you're just trying to beat the prosecutor. Obviously you have to read into that all the ethical obligations and things like that; but he said you should take the stance, if you have a problem representing a criminal defendant: Just pretend he's your brother, and then think of what you would do.

Seeing the legal contest as a game, Larry Smith understands that goodness is achieved by playing within the rules. Since the rules sanction his functioning as a hired gun, he is comfortable in that role, a role that guarantees smooth running of the institutional machinery.

A critique of Larry Smith's position is inherent in an alternative view of morality that spawns a different understanding of responsibility. For Lois Halley, responsibility is more encompassing and less mechanical:

I feel I have an obligation to society, to be the best lawyer I can be, be as honest as I can be, and to practice law in keeping with what I consider to be my moral fiber. And to myself I have the same obligations so that I won't later feel I've compromised my values by developing some attitudes to justify decisions I've made along the way rather than thinking them through. And I have an obligation to my family . . . to not let my career, as I expect from him [her husband] also, not to let his career have an adverse impact on our marriage and life together.

She describes a conflict that arises from this understanding of responsibility that keeps both society and the client in view:

If you take on a client, everybody's entitled to the best representation they can get, and that whole idea. Then, how does that balance if your client's wishes go contrary to what you really consider to be the better resolution of the problem? And so I guess it's always that tension of working with those two, but I think it would determine how one framed one's arguments, and also what limits one would go to before saying to the client, "I just can't go any farther for you." I think it's important not to get to the point where a person won't draw a line as to how far they'll go to win.

Both Larry Smith and Lois Halley describe ethical limits in terms of drawing a line. For Larry, the problem of line drawing arises because of the vagueness or malleability of rules. He wants to win following the rules but must determine the boundaries they prescribe. Lois's creed of winning within the rules is tempered by broader considerations. For her, drawing the line consists in striking a balance between care and rights considerations:

What are the costs to the various people involved? Who's going to be hurt the most? Who's going to gain the most? . . . Also, how much societal waste will be involved? Is this really worth litigating in the first place? . . . Is this person bringing a suit because they're mad at the guy for something else, or is it because there's a real – is the lawsuit really about the issue they say it's about or is it just bad blood?

Lois's assumptions about social interdependence pushes game and hired-gun metaphors toward the margins. Waste, hurt, and costs are more difficult to assess than rule compliance, but their impact is real and cannot be ignored by anyone who sees integrated community as the basic social unit. Scanning legal careers from law school to the top of the profession, Lois continues her de facto critique of more conventional professional perspectives:

They teach you this in law school, if nothing else, to get caught up in the idea of winning, and that it be seen as a sport rather than what's the best resolution, not only for these parties, but the broader societal resolution. You know, what's best for all of us, and what's best for the parties in front of us, rather than who's got the better attorney and the larger resources to do more discovery and throw out more road blocks, et cetera. . . . I just think that we lose sight of the importance of the issues at hand, especially as lawyers caught up in wanting to win and have everybody think we're top dog because we're so great that we were able to pull this one off when everyone knew all the equities were on the other side. And I don't want it to develop in me.

THE GOAL OF MORAL ACTION AND HOW TO ACHIEVE IT

In posing the questions, "Is the concept of justice important to you as a practicing lawyer?" and "How would you define justice?" we asked attorneys to reflect on the moral goals of the law. Those with a strong rights perspective usually define justice in terms of fair application of rules. With rules so integral to the achievement of fairness, equal application of rules becomes the primary determinant of justice, and maintenance of the integrity of rules an end in itself. By comparison, lawyers with a strong care orientation perceive justice through a different filter: The moral good of the law is not so much fairness as the avoidance of harm. This skeletal comparison takes on flesh in the words of Forrest Hill and Phyllis Travis.

Forrest Hill insists on maintaining rules for the general good, despite their adverse impact on particular people:

When I talk about when something is right or when it's wrong – the guy loans the old lady money on a terrible investment at 24 percent, and she dissipates all of her savings – it is purely a contract situation. Right or wrong, you look at the result. If she was competent and she wasn't defrauded at the time of the original transaction, what's right is that she's got to pay it. You've got to be responsible at some point. To me, that's right, even though I kind of find the guy out there loaning money to people in those circumstances a little offensive morally. But from my perspective that's a right result when the judge forecloses on the mortgage or whatever.

Rather than see the conflict as interpersonal, Forrest defines justice in terms of the legal issue and the rules that govern it. By characterizing the situation as "purely a contract," he shunts aside the fact that a contract is only the legal formalization of a relationship that, like any other relationship, is surrounded by issues of trust, inequity, hurt, and mutuality. Legalization of the relationship and of his perspective permits Forrest to ignore these factors and still remain well within the bounds of professional ethics. Although he finds the loan shark "a little offensive morally," his major concern is with adherence to rules that create order, consistency, and predictability – all preconditions to individual autonomy.

You've got to play by the rules, and I find it very offensive – judges tearing up contracts because they just sort of feel there's something wrong with them. . . . Obviously a court of appeals a lot of times makes very bad law because of the fact situations. They look at a fact situation and say, "Jeeze, we've got a rule here but it just doesn't seem to fit. We'll carve an exception or ignore it, just write around a previous opinion." Well, people made decisions in advance based upon these guys pronouncing what the law is, and to me that's very, very unfair. It's kind of like changing the rules after the game has been played, and I just don't like that. I find that really offensive. So, from that standpoint, I guess right is consistency, so that, as troops in the field, we know what to do when we're advising somebody.

Although couched in practical terms, the underlying concern of Forrest Hill is with fairness, a uniform, consistent application of laws. Rules order the collective game, and one player cannot change them without affecting everyone. What makes a rule change unacceptable is his perception that the rules are a social contract on which people rely to play the game. Altering the rules unilaterally violates the social agreement. As long as the rules are intact, autonomy and fairness are safeguarded by restraint on interference with individual activity. To this lawyer, the villain is the judge who interferes by going behind the rules to create an exception, thus threatening the reliability of the rules and freedom of contract. This goes to the heart of the matter, since no legal right is more sacred to rights reasoners than the authority of autonomous individuals to define their own duties and claims through private agreements.

Dealing with a criminal law situation, Phyllis Travis enunciates a very different understanding of moral good in the legal system and the impact of adhering to rules. Her driving concern is not compliance but hurt to specific people, hurt that happens within the bounds of the rules. She senses a compelling need for an alternative to strict application of law:

I don't get my sense of justice from anything I learned in law school or from the professional codes. It's just that I react to certain things as being unjust. I can give you an example. . . . A boy who had recently turned eighteen had an incestuous relationship with his younger sister. Though it hadn't happened for a year and a half, the counselor of the sister reported the incident to the sheriff. My client was summoned in to talk to the sheriff, and he was very cooperative. He asked for the number of the treatment center because he realized that there was something wrong with what he had done – psychologically wrong – and that he needed to deal with it and that his younger sister did too. She's two years younger than he is. . . . I was working with him and with the sheriff's department to get him into treatment and also for them not to go out and arrest him at the high school. If they were going to file charges, to let me know about it ahead of time so that the least hurt and upset to the family that was going to be caused could be caused. . . . The prosecutor filed in adult court first degree felony charges against this kid. That is an example of what I think is unjust. I stayed up all night – I was so upset and outraged that they would do that. It makes me want to cry even thinking about it. . . . It's just the idea that this prosecutor has the nerve to do this when there's a better way to resolve this problem.

I think that when people are treated unfairly, when they're not given the courtesy that we all deserve as people, when the prosecutor's office goes on a big power trip, or another attorney does that, I think that's unjust. I'm sure to that prosecutor who filed this charge, it's just because the kid committed a crime and, no matter what, he committed a crime, and it has to be— you know, it's a crime against society and all this other stuff. But to me it's not that black and white. I think that's a case that could have been resolved a different way morally, and I do think that that has to come into play.

The whole concept of law is a moral concept, and I think this client is being treated within the bounds of the system, yes. He was within perfect rights to file those charges, but morally wrong. . . . These kids made a mistake in their personal lives, and it didn't hurt anybody except themselves. I just feel that there should be some alternative – there should be some human compassion, some feeling for this kid who made a mistake. They're both very young, and putting them through this is a terrible thing to do. . . . And I think that he's [the prosecutor] hurting a lot of people, whereas if we'd handled it a different way, we'd have the same result, which would be to get this kid into treatment, but we would not have hurt as many people in the process. And that's what I think is morally wrong.

Phyllis Travis equates injustice with causing unnecessary harm through the literal, strict application of law. In this specific context and with these particular people, she sees rules as destructive to the network of relationships: "It's costing him a lot of money; it's costing his family money; it's costing them anxiety. People know about it. And they're dealing with it within the family." In contrast to that of the prosecutor, her goal is "that the least hurt and upset to the family . . . could be caused."

Like Antigone, Phyllis tries to force the powerful state to recognize possible harm from a blind application of law without regard to individual situations. On the other hand, Forrest Hill shares Creon's concern for order. He rejects exceptions to the rule, and envisions social breakdown if the rules of order bend to accommodate specific situations. Both lawyers are concerned with societal welfare, and both deal with vulnerable people – the old and the young. Their moral filters, however, affect their understanding of the source and nature of harm. To one it is long-term and structural; to the other, immediate and personal. For Forrest, the harm to be avoided is inequality and unfairness to people in general. Protection is secured by uniform and equal application of rules. The goal of moral action is achieved through abstract, principled reasoning. Concern for the integrity of a system of rules eclipses the worry over individual hurt caused by a slightly offensive loan shark. Phyllis asserts different ends and different means. She wants to avoid harm to specific people;

protection is secured by active responsiveness to young people in trouble. As she reasons toward what constitutes justice in this case, Phyllis takes into account the motivations and responses of the parties involved and considers future consequences.

For Constance McElroy, just as for Phyllis Travis, the goal of moral action is defined by contextual reasoning which individualizes understanding of legal problems. Despite the letter of the law, Constance implements her own sense of morality – "caring for other people . . . kindness, you know, in being considerate and that sort of thing, helping other people, being useful."

I had a case where a set of parents severely beat their eleven-year-old child. She had bruises all the way down her back and all the way down her buttocks and her legs to her knees. . . . If you look at it purely from the advocate's position, I could go into court and say these people deserve six months apiece in jail. This is absolutely outrageous. I didn't take that position, and I don't think it would have been right for me to take that position.

Constance employs a historical perspective on how this situation came to be in order to decide on her response to the needs of the people involved:

The child is Laotian, the mother is Laotian, and the father is white. They are very different people. He is an extremely authoritarian ex-sergeant who sees things totally in black and white. She's a mail-order bride who didn't say anything about this child before she came. This child is very difficult because she was abandoned in Laos and raised in an abusive situation. When she was seven years old, she was publicly shamed for doing something wrong. Now how wrong could she have been at seven years old? They don't have much money. She's a part-time housemaid, and he's unemployed and does the babysitting.

For Constance, an appropriate understanding of context can help structure a resolution to restore relationship and minimize harm. Immorality resides in violent assault on relationship; the goal is to enter the context and restore connection. Her response to the situation is inseparable from her perception of the specific problem.

We want the family to get back together. They were unrepresented by an attorney, and I felt that the important thing is that these people are going to be together for a long time. The child is going to go back soon. I only recommended a week in jail apiece, and that was only more to educate them as to what was coming if they didn't comply. . . . They're going to have to go to two kinds of parenting classes, plus going to counseling, plus make sure the kids go to counseling. . . . I called a pastor of their church and said to look out for them. If you look at it just in terms of the amount of time in jail and fines, they got nothing. But they didn't really get nothing, and, on the other hand, you've got to put the family back together again. And I think that is the important part of my job. It just would be stupid and it would be irresponsible to go in and say each one of them gets six months in jail. For one thing, where are those kids going to go? And how are they ever going to be able to put anything back together again after that?

This contextual resolution seems soft compared with an Aristotelian calculus of equality between punishment and crime; worse yet, it may smack of Antigone's lawlessness, threatening rather than mending the social order. On the other hand, Constance's action can be viewed as providing the humane resolution which best promises long-term healing and the hope of nonabusive social stability. Whether Constance's solution is in fact humane depends on the soundness of her conclusion about the impact of bringing the family together again. We examine only the structure of how she thinks, and are in no position to assess if she has made an error in judgment within that structure. In our interpretation of her reasoning, Constance is concerned with underlying attributes such as interdependence, support, and responsiveness to need – values traditionally associated with family and care morality. However, our society is becoming increasingly aware that any relationship, including that of the family, can be a sanctuary for abuse as well as for love. Reconstituting a relationship does not necessarily avoid hurt; it may actually provide an opportunity for violence. The touchstone of care morality and of Constance's thinking is not the external formality of relationships but the qualities that make for healthy relationships and constructive social units.

For principled reasoners, considering specific contexts and consequences to individuals creates a diversion, an impediment to the general application of law. Personal relationships operate as a pull from the objectivity and clarity of principled thinking. As in our earlier example of the widow and the insurance company, vulnerability and suffering must be overlooked as an unfortunate consequence of maintaining order. The care reasoner rejoins that relationships constitute not a liability but, rather, the very substance of morality. Moral problems arise out of the fraying and breaking of connections and can be resolved only in the context of relationship.

To prevent harm is the moral good, and this can be accomplished within the legal system only through a contextual understanding of the requirements for reconstituting the network of personal relationships.

Real-life dilemmas: where to draw the line

We asked each lawyer, "Has there ever been a situation in your work where you faced a moral conflict, and where you were uncertain what was the right thing to do?" Of the 36 attorneys interviewed, 30 described at least one dilemma and 17 discussed more than one.[5] These dilemmas disclose the content of their moral concerns as well as the orientation used to guide reflection on these issues. Unlike the carefully structured hypothetical dilemmas, the real-life dilemma question gave attorneys latitude to discuss their own experience. In describing these real-life dilemmas, nearly 60 percent of the women used care reasoning in their responses, whereas more than 75 percent of the men reasoned with a rights orientation in their replies.[6]

Most real-life moral dilemmas involve role requirements for partisanship and neutrality, individual values of truth and honesty, or adherence to rules causing personal harm.[7] Ethicist Sissela Bok identifies the core of many of these conundrums: "The strain on lawyers within the adversary system becomes evident precisely at this point – where the principle of confidentiality collides with the necessity to stay 'within the bounds of the law.'"[8] Attorneys in these circumstances must often solve the line-drawing problem introduced earlier by Larry Smith and Lois Halley.

Central to many dilemmas is the question, "How far do I go to present the client in the best light." Leon Gilder outlines the problem, echoing the concern of maintaining standards of truth while fulfilling responsibilities as an advocate:

The one area that comes up is whether the person you are representing is not telling the truth – even if you don't know it factually, you know it emotionally. And basically they're willing to go up and perjure themselves and you're aware of that. The general rule is, as long as you don't know as a fact that they're doing it, you can do it. But if you know as a fact that they're doing it, the rule is that you can't present that. Often in criminal situations you know your client is not telling the truth. You know it on an emotional level and a centered level, but you don't know it on a factual level. . . . It's a dilemma because every lawyer has to decide where they're going to draw the line. (*What is the conflict in that situation?*) Well, the conflict is, again, building a case around something that you know is not true, that you deeply believe is not true. The dilemma is drawing those lines between advocating your client's position and getting in a position where you're building up a case that you know is not true but that you might be able to sell. And actually, in the criminal area, I'm not so sure that society doesn't expect you to go up there and do that. And certainly your client expects you to do that.

Leon's problem of where to draw the line between "advocating your client's position" and "building a case around something that you know is not true" is illustrated by a recent case in Florida. Lawyer Ellis Ruben found himself in jail because he refused a court order to represent a client who, he strongly suspected, was fabricating an alibi defense. Ruben was caught between two clear dictates of professional ethics – the prohibition against knowingly putting a witness on the stand who plans to lie and the requirement to respect client confidences. In terms reminiscent of Creon, the president of the local bar association thought that Ruben's duty was clear once the court had spoken: "It's a lawyer's duty to act in accordance with the rules of law as pronounced by the courts. Otherwise, we would have anarchy."⁹

Where to "draw the line" is affected by a lawyer's understanding of the function of truth in ethical decision making, an understanding in turn influenced by personal morality. From a rights orientation, truth operates as a standard for moral conduct: Never lie. From a care perspective, truth is not a rule of conduct but a means of taking into account everyone's needs. To care thinkers, truth is functional and demands allegiance primarily because it provides the best way to assess and meet needs.

The differing functions of truth and their relation to an advocate's role are highlighted in the real-life dilemmas described by Janice Orens and Spencer Jones. Janice speaks with a strong morality of care. When asked what creates a moral problem for her, she responds, "When doing what I want to do will harm other people, will hurt them in any way."

Janice describes how legal practice posed a problem of "shading truth." She gives an example of a "disadvantaged client," for whom "sometimes it's not the best idea to tell everything that you know in a hearing." Occasionally, she chooses to leave facts out "in order to help this client get some desperately needed support: money, food, medical care, housing." Caught between the rule of law and her own compassion, she would like to find

some impartial judge that you could take this moral dilemma to – how to allocate resources in a society – and say, "Here is my needy person. Here are the things for the needy person; here are the things against the needy person. Please decide and be fair or wise." It's not going to happen. The prejudices stack the system against low-income people, minorities, women, et cetera.

Janice holds to truth as a way of understanding and meeting needs, and wants to put this quest into the formal structure of judicial decision making. The absence of a philosopher king and a realistic assessment of how the rules work force her to shade the truth in order to help her client.

Turning to another situation, Janice tells of a client with "limited ability to communicate, because of low intelligence." She reiterates the theme of tension between truth telling and avoiding harm within the context of the legal system. Once again she wishes for a system like the Zapotecs', where the full truth of the person can be spoken and where the balance struck harmonizes a community of needs. In an administrative hearing, Janice withheld unfavorable information about her client. Even though she acted consistently with professional ethics, she felt "sleazy," as though she were "cutting the truth." She did this because "it was very important for this lady to get some money; she didn't have any money. She could have starved and was going to have to leave her housing." Given the dire needs of her client, "it was easy to make that decision," although it made her uncomfortable to "hide" the truth.

To Janice, truth operates not as a standard to ensure fairness in the race but as a mechanism for shared resolution of problems and for the inclusion of everyone's needs in the calculus of adequate distribution at the finish line.

It's really difficult to be open, and to be truthful. It's very very hard. There are lots of penalties. . . . But in fact, the more open you are about what's needed, about what you feel, about what's happening, the more the other person can identify with, and make a resolution of, the problem that will include what you need in the resolution.

That's not the way the system works. It's not the way most things work, but I still want it to be more that way. I want it to be more that way — oriented toward openness, oriented toward communication, toward shared resolution of problems.

For truth to be an effective problem-solving tool, authorities must hear and act on it. Janice is concerned that "the system doesn't have as much fairness for some people as for others." If everyone pursued "this idea of truth which I respect, this idea that if all things were said out loud and a perfectly fair person were to be listening to them, then maybe we wouldn't have to shade anything. But that's not the way reality is."

From Janice's point of view, truth in the legal system does not help meet the needs of disadvantaged people, and so she opts for the survival needs of her client over loyalty to the adjudicatory process as a search for truth. What her client may get under the rules of the legal system is not adequate. The appropriate question is, What does the client need to alleviate hurt? She is at once mindful of the morality of rights and aware of the dangers of her own contextual relativism. "You're doing a morally reprehensible act in order to get a morally positive benefit." The danger of having the "means serve the ends" is that "it's too easily twisted the other way. You know, a lot of things that happened in the Holocaust were like that." Janice acts on the imperative to protect those who cannot help themselves, but with a recognition of the moral risk associated with a world where the ends justify the means. For her, within the legal structure, truth becomes an obstacle to achieving moral ends.

Spencer Jones understands dilemmas of truth very differently. He has a strong rights orientation and sees truth as the best guarantor of fair application of the rules. Having defined morality as "attempting to treat other people . . . as you'd like to be treated yourself, to do what is fair and be fair to the people you're dealing with," Spencer describes the same problem of truth which confronted Florida lawyer Ruben:

Some of the moral dilemmas that I run into frequently are cases where you're going to put a witness on the stand and you want to present the witness as best you can, obviously, but also ethically. Really, the witness should be up there to tell his own story in his own way and not in a way that's going to impress the jury the most and is going to look the best as far as the case is concerned.

Calling this a problem of where to draw the line, Spencer says that "if you tell the witness what the answer should be, you're not only immoral but you're illegal and unethical. But then again you can get into the situation where you're not telling the witness what the answer should be but how he should present the answer." Even though "I think that's legal and it may be ethical," this lawyer still has "some problem with the morality of that; it gets to be a fine line."

When asked where the moral dilemma lies, Spencer points to the conflict between permissible conduct of the advocate and his belief that "the jury or the judge should be able to hear the evidence in a natural state." The practice of "rehearsing it" and "telling the witness" impedes the determination of guilt or innocence. "I think your fact finders are better able to find out things if the things can be presented naturally." As for Janice Orens, the truth here plays a functional role, but the goal for Spencer is not meeting individual needs but, rather, ensuring that rules for determining guilt and innocence are fairly and efficiently applied. His conflict is between facilitating a trial as an untampered-with search for truth and advocacy of his client's case.

Spencer describes a specific incident in which his client, accused of rape, tried to lie about ownership of a watch found at the victim's house. He recounts telling this client, "Whether it's your watch or not, since your watch fits perfectly well into our theory of the case and into what you've told me before, then I don't think you ought to go before the jury and tell the jury it's not your watch, because then they're going to think you're lying there, and your whole defense is going to fall apart." The defense had been structured around admission of ownership of the watch, and now the client was ready to change his story. Spencer feels this instance is "even more so of a moral dilemma because I'm telling my client how he ought to testify where he's saying . . . this isn't my watch." Asked why this is a moral dilemma rather than a practical one, the attorney responds, "It's moral because . . . I think the jury is entitled ideally to hear whatever he's going to say . . . and [I should] not shape that testimony to fit what other things he's said and what the theory of the case is." In the moral world of this and other lawyers, shaping testimony presents a collision between duty to client and commitment to finding objective truth in the courtroom.

For both Janice Orens and Spencer Jones, truth is an impediment to full representation of client. For one it obstructs personal morality, and for the other, professional obligation. Janice cannot make full disclosure in a legal context and still meet her moral obligation to avoid harm to a needy client. A judge who does not take sufficient notice of context and personal differences cannot be trusted to administer to individual needs. Spencer cannot encourage truth and still discharge his obligation as a partisan advocate, but at the same time truth is essential to his personal moral goal of fair resolution. A court denied full access to the truth cannot be expected to administer justice fairly and equally.

To some extent the legal system itself shares this irresolution of the relationship between truth and advocacy which challenges Spencer Jones and Janice Orens. In a recent Supreme Court decision, Chief Justice Warren Burger ruled that refusal by an attorney to cooperate in a client's commission of perjury had not denied the client adequate legal counsel. Burger drew the line on the side of truth at the expense of partisan advocacy. Though the conclusion of the Court was not controversial, some of Burger's language describing the limits of an advocate's duty questions traditional roles in the adversary system: "Plainly, that duty is limited to legitimate, lawful conduct compatible with the very nature of a trial as a search for truth."[10] Burger's expansive language seems to undermine the usual assumption that lawyers participate in the search for truth by fulfilling their role as advocates rather than by acting as independent agents for the discovery of truth.[11] "The responsibility of an ethical lawyer" to a client is qualified by the lawyer's duty "as an officer of the court and a key component of a system of justice, dedicated to a search for truth."[12]

Where to draw the line often implicates the neutrality of a lawyer. How certain must an advocate be that testimony is false before refusing to present it in court? Burger suggests that tempering partisanship and neutrality "is consistent with the governance of trial conduct in what we have long called a search for truth. The suggestion sometimes made that a 'lawyer must believe his client, not judge him' in no sense means a lawyer can honorably be a party to or in any way give aid to presenting known perjury."[13]

In addition to the effect of moral perspective on problems of truth and line drawing, real-life dilemmas also illustrate that the orientation of a lawyer is not fixed but may shift to accommodate new conditions. Most lawyers possess some elements of both care and rights thinking, and under the proper circumstances either may emerge as a prevailing perception. Even strongly rights-oriented attorneys may reject uniform application of rules if a particular case is sufficiently compelling. George Willis, for example, has an almost flawless rights perspective throughout most of his interview. He speaks of the system as an article of faith:

Are you going to say in some cases you've got the right to an attorney, but if we think the crime sufficiently heinous or we think everything points to the fact that you're guilty, in those cases are we going to say you don't have the right to an attorney? What kind of system of justice is that? You've got to believe in the system or you don't believe in the system.

In a striking reversal, this highly role-identified advocate describes a real-life dilemma where he perceives that the even-handed application of law causes undue hurt. From the same lawyer who said of clients, "You're just another case to me," the needs of an individual client can elicit a perspective of care. For George, a rights orientation, with its assumption of equality among people, reaches its limits with the realization that, in fact, life's circumstances make people unequal. The recognition that some are less fortunate than others leads him to temper equality with equity.

I have a situation where I'm representing this old gaffer. He just picks a succession of felonies – goes into somebody's house, usually a relative. The guy's got some mental problem. Puts on a cowboy hat, cooks himself something to eat with about four pounds of butter and fills the house up with smoke. . . . What's happened in the past is he's committed a burglary like that, and the prosecuting attorney doesn't have any place to put him; I don't have any place to put him, so we run him in on a guilty plea, credit for time. Sheriff will kick him back out on the street. Well, whamo zamo, he goes out and commits another burglary. Now the prosecuting attorney wants to put him in prison. I don't want to see this old guy die in prison. . . . I say– well, I guess I call myself a nice guy. I just ain't got it in me to look that old gaffer in the eye and say "Jeeze, I think you ought to plead guilty and go to the institution." What I've been doing is trying to find out whether there is some sort of geriatric placement for this guy. I suppose it's moral questions you ask there. The guy's got no brains for himself, so it's kind of your responsibility. (*Is that something different from your responsibility as a defense attorney?*) Well, that's probably a pretty good question. . . . I think in mental cases I see my obligation as being somewhat different. I see myself as somewhat more concerned with the actual welfare of the client than I do in a criminal case. If I get a guy back out on the street that's nuts, and he ends up killing himself or throwing himself in front of cars or something like that, that would bother me because he's not dealing with a full deck. And he's kind of counting on me to make those kinds of decisions for him. So I look at my obligation a little bit differently.

George still talks in deontological terms of duty and obligation, yet his reasoning has shifted from complying with rules and maintaining the system's integrity to caring for someone in need. This change occurs through an altered conception of the obligations of role when dealing with "mental cases." An even-handed application of the law stops with a perception of such human vulnerability.

Like George, most lawyers we interviewed reported moral dilemmas, but a few did not. They explained this omission by reference to the dominance of professional role, which compels setting personal standards aside when entering their law office. Using a metaphor of masks, Tom Wooding describes how he appears as someone else when practicing law:

You know, I've never had that [moral conflict], because I used to tell people I could defend the person who killed my brother, because I think I'm very good at changing masks – putting on my advocate mask and taking off my mask as a person. I have to stay within the bounds of the law. I work damn hard to be an attorney. I've got to make sure that I don't violate anyone's sense of what's right and wrong as far as an ethical standpoint, but I represent them within the bounds of the law. I don't really give a damn about it, about what they did or what they didn't do. If they've got certain rights, they're going to get those rights. It doesn't matter if they kill fifty little children or whether they spit on the sidewalk. . . . So morality, as long as I stay within the bounds of the law, I don't even think about it.

Depicting an extreme neutrality, this lawyer's personal concerns are hidden behind an advocate mask, shaped by parameters of profession. His own sense of morality is ignored in order to pursue being an attorney according to the governing rules of neutrality and partisanship. In the next chapter we review in more detail this dominance of role that forecloses the interplay of personal morality.

First hypothetical dilemma: professional command performance

The hypothetical dilemmas posed in the interview were designed to elicit moral reasoning in two contexts – in criminal law, where the

Constitution, Supreme Court decisions, and professional obligations align to command an easily discernible professional response, and in domestic law, where rules are less clear and competing considerations more prominent. The first dilemma juxtaposes a responsibility to defend the client and a personal concern that if the client is released, he might kill again.

Suppose you are representing an accused murderer who has confessed to the crime in such detail that no one, including you, has the slightest doubt that he committed the murder. Without the confession, there is not sufficient evidence to prosecute, much less convict, your client. A psychiatric examination and the bizarre speech and behavior of your client convince you that he is very crazy. In fact, you are sure that you could have the confession excluded on the grounds that he was incompetent to waive his right to an attorney when given his *Miranda* warnings prior to confessing. You also have every reason to believe that your client continues to be very dangerous.

This hypothetical dilemma presents a compelling case for strict adherence to the obligations of professional role. It incorporates three critical constitutional norms: right to counsel, privilege against self-incrimination, and obligation of the attorney for vigorous representation. The right to representation by counsel in a criminal case is clearly announced in the Sixth Amendment to the United States Constitution and has been vigorously affirmed in many Supreme Court cases.

From the very beginning, our state and national constitutions and laws have laid great emphasis on procedural and substantive safeguards designed to assure fair trials before impartial tribunals in which every defendant stands equal before the law. This noble ideal cannot be realized if the poor man charged with crime has to face his accusers without a lawyer to assist him.[14]

The right of an accused to refuse to self-incriminate without a knowing, intelligent decision to do so is also well grounded in constitutional law.

The privilege against self-incrimination – the essential mainstay of our adversary system – is founded on a complex of values. . . . All these policies point to one overriding thought: The constitutional foundation underlying the privilege is the respect a government – state or federal – must accord to the dignity and integrity of its citizens. . . . In sum, the privilege is fulfilled only when the person is guaranteed the right "to remain silent unless he chooses to speak in the unfettered exercise of his own will."[15]

The obligation of the attorney to suppress the confession is likewise firmly embedded in constitutional law and the adversary sys-

tem. In *United States v. Wade,* Justice White described the responsibilities of a defense attorney:

> But defense counsel has no comparable obligation to ascertain or present the truth.
> Our system assigns him a different mission. He must be and is interested in prevent-
> ing the conviction of the innocent, but, absent a voluntary plea of guilty, we also
> insist that he defend his client whether he is innocent or guilty. The State has the
> obligation to present the evidence. Defense counsel need present nothing, even if he
> knows what the truth is. . . . As part of our modified adversary system and as part of
> the duty imposed on the most honorable defense counsel, we countenance or require
> conduct which in many instances has little, if any, relation to the search for truth.[16]

While the lawyer's responsibility in the first hypothetical dilemma
derives directly from the loftiest authority in the legal hierarchy, it is
reinforced by a practical analysis of the vulnerability of a defendant
in the criminal justice system. Generally speaking, a criminal defense
situation presents the most telling argument for an advocate with
unflinching commitment to client representation at the expense of
other considerations. The full authority and resources of the state are
brought to bear upon a defendant, who often has but one ally – an
attorney. Procedural rules such as the presumption of innocence, the
right to jury trial, and the right to have tainted confessions excluded
recognize this imbalance of power and seek to rectify it. Such procedural rules, however, generally require the expertise of an attorney
if they are to be placed effectively at the disposal of the defendant.
The responsibility of an attorney to a client led Chief Justice Earl
Warren to make a statement in the *Miranda* case that might equally
be applied to the lawyer in the first dilemma: "This is not cause for
considering the attorney a menace to law enforcement. It is merely
carrying out what he is sworn to do under his oath – to protect to the
extent of his ability the rights of his client. In fulfilling this responsibility the attorney plays a vital role in the administration of criminal
justice under our Constitution."[17]

This constitutional mandate is reflected in an exception to the
general rule against advocating a groundless position. The exception
embedded in the Rules of Professional Conduct allows a criminal
defense lawyer to "put the prosecution to its proof even if there is no
non-frivolous basis for defense."[18] Other factors in the first dilemma
that press for uncompromising commitment to a client's cause are

the mental incompetence of the client and the lack of a specific victim threatened with harm. Taken together, the conditions of this hypothetical dilemma make the conduct required to meet professional obligations as unambiguous as possible. At the same time, factors that elicit a morality of care, such as certainty of harm, are left vague and amorphous.

All lawyers initially construe this dilemma in terms of rights and duties – the right of the client to procedural safeguards and the duty of an attorney to protect that right. Although everyone recognizes the danger to the community in releasing a murderer, some find a dilemma while others do not. The situation usually elicits rights reasoning and excludes care focus because of the clarity of the lawyer's obligation and the lack of specific potential harm. Despite this pull toward rights, some attorneys with a strong care orientation risk breaking the rules in order to stave off further violence. However, even most attorneys with a dominant care perspective do not withstand the strict legal formulation of this hypothetical dilemma. Both men and women respond to the dilemma with a high percentage of rights statements.[19]

In assessing lawyers' responses to the hypothetical dilemmas, we used the following four questions: (1) How is the problem perceived? (2) What is the goal of moral action? What is the good to be served? (3) What is the process of decision making? How does the person decide what to do? (4) How is the decision or act evaluated?[20] While it is usually impossible to divide narrative responses into such neat categories, they nonetheless prove a useful analytic tool as the following examples illustrate.

Presented with the first hypothetical dilemma, Leon Gilder sees it as involving legal issues, not people. His perception of the problem immediately centers on questions of rules. "I guess the reason that doesn't present me with a dilemma is that I think there are major social issues involved on both sides apart from the individual. This presents the whole dilemma of the exclusionary rule, which has become a major dilemma in our society at this time." Framing the problem in terms of the rule that prohibits admissibility of involuntary confessions, Leon states his goal as the limitation of government interference with individuals, including the confessed murderer:

I very strongly support the exclusionary rule because of the value I have on limiting social impact on individuals through the Bill of Rights. . . . Obviously releasing a crazy man to do something again is very negative. But I also see the other aspect of it as controlling the behavior of government, which I sincerely believe needs to be controlled.

For Leon, protecting the individual from intrusive government is more important than the potential harm of criminal conduct. His responsibility is to act as an advocate for the client, not as a general caretaker for the public. "As an attorney, your initial and the biggest responsibility is to your client." From this vantage point, the correct moral response is to ignore individual circumstances and protect a rule that guards personal autonomy. Leon evaluates his decision to exclude the confession in the light of relevant legal rules: "I would not have a problem within the Bill of Rights and within the exclusionary rule . . . having someone released on those grounds."

In contrast, John Crowell locates the moral problem of the dilemma within the interpersonal situation. With this shift, the dilemma changes from one of significant social issues to one of conflicting needs of people for protection from the possibility of harm. The goal of moral action is to safeguard both the accused and the public.

I would feel a great personal responsibility if that person went out on the streets and harmed anybody again. . . . The dilemma to me appears to be that if you represent the person as they would like to be represented, they'll want to go free. They want to have no punishment or penalty for what they did, and you could accomplish that probably. On the other hand, what they really need for themselves, in my opinion, might be psychiatric treatment that would keep them out of trouble in the future, protect them. And what we all need is to be protected from them, so that's a very big dilemma.

John seeks to prevent harm, but the problem is complicated by conflicting claims; responsiveness to the desires of the client holds the threat of harm to the community. This lawyer perceives himself as part of the community, and in this context, responsibility calls for active intervention rather than restraint. The process of making a decision involves an empathetic assessment of the client's position. Equating moral good with the prevention of harm, John says, "I would be a lot more comfortable protecting other people than I would be protecting my client's rights."

In the course of his reasoning about the dilemma, John explicitly invokes the authority of his personal morality: "I'm enough of an individualist to believe that the ultimate thing that you have to do is either reconcile the work that you do with yourself or not do it." He then proceeds to examine the specifics of his responsibility to prevent harm to his client and the conflicting responsibility to potential victims. The more certain he is that the client will "harm a particular person," the less bothersome the dilemma and the more urgent his obligation to protect the community. Always lurking behind the dilemma is the feeling of being personally "responsible if he went out and harmed somebody." The goal of stopping violence carries with it the responsibility to act in order to achieve that goal.

In describing how to evaluate conduct in this situation, John begins with a standard statement of professional responsibility:

It's a rule that's comfortable for me to have, I think, because it gives me some defensible guidelines for my conduct. If a nonlawyer asked me how in the world could you do what you just did in this case, I could say my standards as an attorney require me to represent my client zealously within the bounds of the law, and that's why I do it. And because I'm an attorney and I accepted those rules, that's comfortable for me to fall back on. It doesn't require me to search my moral conscience to decide whether what I've done is right or not.

In this case, however, a conventional response is not adequate for John. The conclusive criteria for evaluation are whether harm is successfully avoided and whether you can "be proud of yourself and satisfied with who you are," which "requires you to have a developed conscience of your own and to follow that conscience." For John, avoidance of harm is more important than role identity or rules of the system.

I would be very upset if that person went out and harmed someone else, and it would probably make me question very deeply whether even though that's what my role as an attorney required, whether that was a morally defensible position or not. If I got this person— got the charges dropped by having the confession excluded, and the person went out and harmed someone else, that probably, I would hope, would shock my conscience enough that it would make me question very deeply whether or not that was a good system.

This lawyer's difficulty with the murderer dilemma reflects an ongoing tension in the law — how to reconcile the rights of the individual with the needs of the community. Leon Gilder sees the danger in the hypothetical dilemma as the threat that rules will not be followed. For John Crowell the risk is potential hurt to individual people. For one the problem is abstracted from interpersonal considerations, whereas for the other it is located squarely in human relationships and the threat of harm. Integrity of rules contrasts with integrity of relationships. On the one hand, responsibility is specified by role as requiring restraint and, on the other, responsibility is defined by conscience as an imperative to act. Leon Gilder assumes a world of autonomous individuals who need protection by rules against government interference; John Crowell perceives a society of interdependent people who must be protected in their relationships by the outreach of care.

Second hypothetical dilemma: the pull of responsiveness

Our second hypothetical dilemma presents a conflict between welfare of children and loyalty to client.

Suppose that you are an attorney in a divorce proceeding, and your client seeks custody of the two young children of the marriage. In the course of your representation your client gives you a bundle of documents that inadvertently contains a letter bearing on the fitness of your client to have custody of the children. The information in the letter is not known and is not likely to become known by the other side. Without disclosure of the letter, you believe your client will win the custody battle; you're equally confident that the other party will prevail if the letter is revealed. In your own mind the information clearly makes your client a marginal parent and the other party a far superior parent.

Midway through the discussion of the second hypothetical dilemma, the interviewer amended the facts so that the letter contained the threat of serious bodily harm to the children. Thus, the dilemma actually presented attorneys with two differing sets of circumstances calling for response.

Several considerations from the Model Rules of Professional Conduct are pertinent to analysis of this situation. In a section entitled "Preamble: A Lawyer's Responsibilities," attorneys are told that when the opposing side is represented by counsel, "a lawyer can be a zealous advocate on behalf of a client and at the same time assume that justice is being done. So also, a lawyer can be sure that preserving client confidences ordinarily serves the public interest." In this hypothetical custody dispute, it should be noted, the children are not parties and are not represented by an attorney, though their welfare is at stake.

Faced with this dilemma, nearly all lawyers interviewed sought, at some point, to withdraw from representation. In the Rules of Professional Conduct, Rule 1.16 (b) (3) allows for this in a number of circumstances, including when "a client insists upon pursuing an objective that the lawyer considers repugnant or imprudent." However, Rule 1.16 also requires that the attorney continue representation when ordered to do so by the court. We regularly invoked this latter provision to keep attorneys in the case and confronting the moral conflict. Rule 3.3 requires attorneys to disclose relevant legal authority, such as controlling statutes or court decisions, and to refrain from offering false evidence, but it imposes no obligation to disclose factual evidence such as the letter in question here.

Central to an analysis of our second hypothetical dilemma is Rule 1.6, which prohibits a lawyer from revealing confidential information obtained from a client, except under certain narrowly defined circumstances. The lawyer "may reveal" such information "to prevent the client from committing a criminal act that the lawyer believes is likely to result in imminent death or substantial bodily harm." Two things should be noted about this exception to the general rule of confidentiality: First, it is permissive; the lawyer may reveal but is not required to reveal. Second, the conditions under which disclosure is permitted are filled with what lawyers call weasel words: "believes," "likely," "imminent," "substantial." How certain must the lawyer's "belief" be; how probable is "likely"; is "imminent" nearly certain or very soon; and how serious is "substantial"? These words allow what appears a firm rule to become slippery and elusive. We blocked use of this rule as an easy out by saying that the attorney felt personally convinced of the impending harm but did not think that the conviction rose to the level of belief and likelihood required by the rule.

The second hypothetical dilemma is further complicated by the general solicitousness of law for children. The broad standard to be applied in cases such as this requires the court to decide in the best interests of the children. Can the court really do this if the letter is not disclosed? Are considerations of procedural justice as compelling here as they were in the criminal case, or do consequences now weigh more heavily on what constitutes justice? Would response to this question be affected if the children were independently represented?

Under court rules attorneys are allowed to discover from each other factual information, such as the letter at issue here, by written questions or by oral examination. However, in keeping with the adversary system, if the other side does not ask, a lawyer does not have to answer. Combining the rules of discovery, the best-interests-of-the-child standard, and the rules of professional conduct produces less clarity and authority than the constitutionally grounded guidelines of the first hypothetical dilemma. There is also a tempting invitation to go beyond the strictures of professional responsibility in search of guideposts that will lead to safety for the children. For most attorneys the second dilemma is more perplexing, the course of ethical conduct less clear. A lawyer's responsibility as an officer of the court to help achieve a result in the best interests of the children opposes a lawyer's responsibility to a client; thus, relevant moral considerations for fulfilling professional role obligations are in conflict. Compared with the situation created by the first dilemma, what it means to be a good lawyer is more vague. Although the first dilemma also carried with it the probability of harm, here hurt is immediately tied to the attorney's conduct and the threat falls on specific vulnerable individuals.

In the second dilemma, a traditional hired-gun approach would almost certainly result in injury to children. For this reason, 89 percent of the lawyers felt that the circumstances presented a moral dilemma, and only five attorneys, four men and one woman, used no care considerations in addressing the situation. In rights responses, male reasoning declined about 8 percent from the first to the second dilemma. In comparison, women's loyalty to a rights perspective dropped by more than 21 percent between the two dilemmas. The reasoning of men and women attorneys was fairly close in the first dilemma, but a substantial difference opens between the genders in the second dilemma.[21] In the criminal law case of the first dilemma, the rules are clear, both in terms of the professional role of the lawyer and in terms of the rights of the client. Lacking the clarity of role dictates inherent in the first dilemma, attorneys discussing the custody case expressed more ambivalence as to how they should proceed.

When role expectations and legal rules fail to chart the way adequately in the second dilemma, room opens for increased influence of personal morality. To those with a morality of care, the imperative to prevent harm became a beacon shining through the fog of conflicting obligations. For those predisposed toward a morality of rights, principles of neutrality and partisanship showed the way. Many found no distinct path. Unclear mandates of role and of concern for children who would be harmed as a consequence of effective advocacy left a feeling of discontent. James Grant discusses this difficulty in relation to community expectations:

I'm saying it's easier to represent the criminal defendant, because when you take on that role, society has already told you it's okay. With respect to this other guy, when you took that case on you didn't agree that he should necessarily get the kids just because he wants them. He has a right to custody if he's a qualified and fit parent. I see that as being a distinction. We've already agreed that a guy that's a known criminal and all that is entitled to this representation. And he can be a real jerk and a creep and a bad guy, but he's still entitled to get off on a technicality if it's there. And when you take on those cases, you take it on with the knowledge and with the moral decision having been reached. Whereas, when you take on the guy in a custody case— when I take them on, I take them on from the point of view that I want to see a just result here.

In a domestic relations setting, universal application of general rules only compounds the difficulty of finding a just result. As Forrest Hill says, "What's right and wrong . . . is impossible to generalize. It's just based on the individual fact situation. I can't think of any objective criteria to apply to it." A lack of objective criteria threatens the rule of law, often leading attorneys to complain that the adversary system is inappropriate for resolving custody disputes. At the root of this complaint is puzzlement over the advocate's proper goal.

When Justice Burger sought to enlist criminal defense lawyers directly in the search for truth, he confounded traditional notions of partisanship and neutrality. The role of an advocate becomes even more problematic when the best interests of children are at stake. What constitutes the children's best interests is not only subjective but also may be directly contrary to the interests of a client. This led one attorney to say, "I just perceive my role to be different in this process than the traditional role." Whereas some lawyers use the latitude of this situation to enlarge the possibilities for response, others stick to their legal guns.

Advocates who approach the dilemma from a rights perspective structure their responses in terms of conflicting legal obligations. Resolution calls for analysis by a legal tactician rather than consultation with an ethicist. By contrast, care-oriented attorneys see not legal issues but hazard to a child.

Jim Smallwood: Well, it's not a moral issue for me, it's a legal issue for me. . . . On the one hand I've got a client privilege to protect, and on the other hand, the law says that I've got the best interests of the child to protect. I mean it's not even a moral issue anymore. It becomes a legal issue what you do in that circumstance. You've got two competing issues. . . . I guess most of the time that things are falling in favor of the fact that I have a legal and ethical responsibility to a client, and that's the position I take.

Constance McElroy: Well, the moral issue is I don't want to participate in increasing the hazard to a child; the ethical issue is whether you perpetrate fraud on the court. And I find that I can resolve the two very well together. I mean, it's not money we're talking about here. We're talking about people, and you can't undo it. When you're talking about money and maybe it's damages, people will sort it out and pick up and go on; they can redo. You can't undo an incidence of violence. You can't undo something like that for a child. You can't undo what's going to happen for the rest of their lives.

As an amoral technician, Jim establishes his neutrality by discounting moral aspects of the situation. Even though the best-interests-of-the-child standard brings the children's needs into consideration, his framing the situation as a legal issue frees him from the necessity of moral response. In comparison, Constance examines both her professional ethical duty to the court and her personal moral responsibility to the children. She evaluates the central issue as one of lasting harm, and thus as necessitating a moral response. Moral and ethical responsibilities align to give clear direction that the children must be protected. While Jim stands apart and imposes objectivity on a problem of conflicting rules, Constance burrows into the specifics of the situation. From this contextual vantage point, she responds to the children's need out of a sense of responsibility for how her action or failure to act affects them. In Jim's thinking, we see no similar concern for context, consequences, or responsibility. For him, the best interests of the child represent a legal rule to be balanced in an Aristotelian equation with other legal rules.

Two other interviews illustrate how perception of the problem determines response. Mack Harris is one of the few attorneys for whom the children are absent from consideration; but for Marlene Rivers, the well-being of the children is so central that it affects her perception of role. Both lawyers talk about responsibility – the traditional responsibility of the advocate and a reformulated responsibility that goes beyond winning.

Mack Harris: You've got the necessity, just about absolute, of representing your client's best interest, who has apparently expressed custody desire. . . . I would probably have no problem in concealing the letter. . . . How important is the moral issue of disclosure, disclosing this possible future problem? If you disclose that, the client is probably going to discharge you anyway. . . . Let's say you do disclose it, and the client doesn't discharge you and you can actually ease the client into a full disclosure mode and convince them [the Court] that his reasons to want custody are separate from this, and they're good. . . . Argue it. You know, a good argument would be that they brought it in to disclose it to you. . . . You could turn that into something.

Marlene Rivers: I'd get my client into my office and tell him that I had run into the letter, and if he did not drop seeking custody, I would tell him that if he wants me to continue to represent him I would disclose the contents of the letter. . . . I think that when you're dealing with family law, your responsibility is not just to win for your client. . . . You're dealing with the lives of children in a very, very direct way, and if I felt my client . . . not capable of parenting those children, I would not, I could not represent him in a custody fight. . . . I would discuss it with him, and I would try to have a very good understanding of what was going on. And if I felt anywhere along the line that it was not in the best interest of the children, I would make sure there was an evaluation for the children's benefit . . . because in a situation like that a lot of times the interests of the children sort of get lost.

Mack Harris affirms an absolute duty to his client. As required by his perception of role, he is an advocate all the way, and plots to turn the disclosure itself into something advantageous. When the lawyer's vision goes beyond the interest of the client and encompasses the children, a moral response becomes more complex. For Marlene Rivers, action is not mandated by loyalty to client but must be explored incrementally. The process is complicated, subjective, and contextual.

While Mack Harris relies on the traditional role of the lawyer for a secure and proved perspective, Marlene Rivers redefines her responsibility without reliance on institutional assistance. Seeking "to make the balance," she plots her course: "I'd try to weigh things out in my own mind – how bad it would be for the children if he got custody, and what the chances of that harming them would be, and the chances of rectifying it in the immediate future. If I couldn't get any satisfaction from my client, I might talk to the other lawyer."

In assessing the custody dilemma, nearly every attorney at one point or another sought to withdraw from the case. We responded that if the lawyer withdrew, the next attorney would probably never learn of the letter, and thus the harmful consequences would still result. Lawyers with a strong rights orientation felt that their moral obligation ended with their own withdrawal. Having played their lawyer role, responsibility stopped. For example, after being reminded that "in this case, if you withdraw, then the guy gets custody," Spencer Jones comments, "I wouldn't feel bad about that, because first of all I couldn't disclose it. It wouldn't be ethical, but that's not a factor. You know it would just come into my own personal feelings of do I want to be involved in this scumbag getting custody of the kids." When questioned, Spencer acknowledged that his involvement and not the result matters. Concern centers on his own integrity and the ethics of role. The impact of his conduct on the children falls outside his consideration. His professional neutrality constricts a sense of personal responsibility. Neutrality implies "I make no judgment"; responsibility has been assumed by the legal system.

In comparison, lawyers with a care orientation feel a sense of responsibility to protect the children in the second dilemma, even after having withdrawn from the case. For example, Phyllis Travis struggles initially with the issue of client confidence. Concerned about the adequacy of the client's ability to parent, Phyllis describes how she would "approach her from the point of view of . . . look this indicates to me that there are some real problems here. And you need to solve these problems before you get custody of these kids because if you don't, you're going to hurt your children and there are going to be problems all the way down the line." If her client would not cooperate, or if the letter was "that horrible," then "I may have to turn it over to somebody else." Yet Phyllis's sense of responsibility does not end with transfer of the case. Saying that "it wouldn't absolve me," she describes a continuing sense of obligation: "But what it would mean would be, I would always worry about those kids, and I would probably say to the other attorney, you need to talk with the client." If circumstances warranted, "I would have to bring the letter to the attention of the authorities and then just take my medicine when it came." While the ethics of role protect Spencer Jones from feeling responsibility, Phyllis Travis's sense of obligation to the children transcends the role and pushes her to take personal risks.

Rights and care: competition and integration of perspectives

Moral perspectives of rights and care have roots deep in childhood. Growing up, we all experience traumas of inequality and bonds of attachment. Children always lack equality with adults in strength, knowledge, and authority; equality is a constant battle with siblings and peers. At the same time, attachments occur with special adults, other children, animals, and familiar objects. Certain vulnerabilities coincide with these experiences of inequality and attachment. With inequality comes the danger of domination; attachment raises the specter of desertion. In many ways, our culture teaches children that fairness can be a remedy to oppression, and care an antidote to abandonment. These concerns are brought forward into adult life and help form the basis of moral understanding.

The justice perspective draws attention to problems of inequality and oppression and holds up an ideal of reciprocity and equal respect. The care perspective draws attention to problems of detachment or abandonment and holds up an ideal of attention and response to need. Two moral injunctions – not to treat others unfairly, and not to turn away from someone in need – capture these different concerns.[22]

Most of the examples in this chapter illustrate the difference between moralities of rights and of care; therefore, we have used excerpts from either end of the moral spectrum where one or the other orientation dominates. In these instances, a guiding moral orientation appears to overwhelm or even to exclude the other perspective.

Yet, when we examine each interview in its entirety, reliance on a single moral orientation is the exception.[23] Despite socialization, role expectations, and institutional pressures, most lawyers express a spectrum of moral reasoning that includes both rights and care concerns. While one orientation usually dominates, in other instances the two coexist as competing or as integrated perspectives.

Where the orientations coexist, lawyers generally recognize that each orientation carries its own validity and serves a social purpose. Fairness, equality, protection from harm, and harmony of relationships are all important moral considerations. Sometimes they are compatible, sometimes one must be chosen over the other. For lawyers who use both perspectives, choosing between duty and responsiveness can create a moral dilemma. Faced with such a choice, attorneys follow one of two approaches in making moral decisions. They examine each perspective and choose the one that appears most compelling under the circumstances, or they integrate the two perspectives to allow for both rights and care concerns to guide action. For attorneys in whom moral orientations compete, the less preferred perspective is not dropped from view but remains present as a check or moderating force. If circumstances change, the nondominant orientation may gain ascendancy.

Speaking of the second hypothetical dilemma, Darcy Andrews illustrates this tension between moral concerns and how changed conditions effect a shift in perspective. If a lawyer keeps both the morality of care and of rights as live options, the problem is to determine which approach is appropriate in a given situation: "I don't feel on the one hand that in that situation I would be justified in revealing his secret, his confidence. But on the other hand, I would have a concern for the children." Darcy Andrews talks of competition between the perspectives in the face of changing circumstances: "If the client is adamant in the situation that's being posed, where there's no threat of harm to the children, I don't feel I can reveal the letter. That's what he's hiring me for, that's what he's paid me for, that's what the ethical code is there for. He's got a right to have his confidences respected." Yet, when we stated that the letter reveals a threat of physical danger to the children, traditional role recedes and a different moral vision takes control. The well-being of children becomes a decisive consideration: "The right of my client to have his confidences respected only goes up to the point where I know that those confidences will not harm someone else. You know the old cliché, my right to swing my arm ends where your nose begins. . . . At that point my duty to the children would override my ethical duty to the client."

Susan Constans also brings both moral perspectives to her understanding of the second hypothetical dilemma. As she frames the issue, she confronts an either/or moral choice: "How would I describe the dilemma? Well, I have a duty to my client on the one hand, and I have – I don't know what the word would be – I have a caring for the children on the other hand. . . . I think what I would do in that case is I would not disclose the letter." Explaining her decision, rights and care considerations operate in tandem:

I have a real strict duty of confidence . . . it's no different than somebody giving their confession to a priest. You know, he or she might turn out to be an okay parent. I wouldn't make an entire judgment on that one letter, to say that these kids are going to die in this person's custody, whereas they're going to flourish in the other person's custody. How do I know that the other side doesn't have a letter to the same effect?

When asked to describe how she would choose between her obligation of confidentiality and her caring for the children, Susan uses the metaphor of a balanced scale. She compares this situation with the first dilemma, where she opted to protect the potential victim from harm at the expense of her client's rights.

It's some kind of an internal, intuitive balance. It's like for your other example, there was a balanced scale that was real obvious to me, and in this example there is a balanced scale that's real obvious to me, and they're opposite. In one case I felt the duty to society was much greater than to do the A-1 perfect job for that client. In this case, it just feels like my duty is to keep client confidence.

Articulating why her duty to the client prevails over her concern for the children, she reasons contextually in comparing the certainty of harm in the two hypothetical cases. Keeping a range of moral concerns in view, Susan's balanced scale is more the ecological balance of the Zapotecs than the blind scales of justice. Rights and care values compete in her thinking as she evaluates factors specific to each situation to determine which approach is more appropriate.

In the first place, you're talking about a crazy person who allegedly has already committed one heinous crime, and who if freed will undoubtedly do something similar. In the second case you're talking about children in a "maybe" situation as opposed to a nonmarginal situation. But then you've got the judge, a judge who's going to listen to all the witnesses and who's going to make an independent judgment and size those people up, and decide in the custody trial. . . . If it turns out that the children are not being well cared for you can always get a change of custody or a modification. If that lunatic goes out and kills somebody you can't go out and resurrect them. They're just very different kinds of problems.

The first hypothetical dilemma pulls Susan from her traditional role because of the certainty of harm from a freed murderer; in the second instance, she remains in the role of advocate because she is not sure that "there's absolutely nobody but me to protect those children." She lists others who are available to look out for the children, thus leaving herself leeway to meet institutional expectations. "The children always have a right to a guardian. They've got an attorney on the other side. There's a judge, there's Child Protective Services. If they were truly in danger, I would hope that somebody would intervene." After a careful assessment of the circumstances, this lawyer chooses "the duty of client confidence" because she is satisfied that others are responsible for concerns of care.

For Ed Abrams both perspectives are also present, but in a more integrated than competitive fashion. Rather than care concerns vying with rights concerns in an either/or fashion, they converge in a synthesis which preserves both. The attorney stands outside of the conventions that characterize each perspective and formulates an inclusive moral world view. He describes the murderer's case in terms of care and rights considerations:

I think everyone has an obligation to society to prevent harm. It sounds like from this fact situation that the person could be acquitted on the facts. And if that were the case, then he would be out at large in the public. Maybe, as an alternative, one could do that and immediately have him taken into custody by civil mental health officers, I don't know. What you're dividing is the lawyer's duty to his client and his duty to society as a human being. And that's tough, because, what I believe is that lawyers' duty to their clients is a very serious duty, very serious.

Ed puzzles over the difficulty of measuring and comparing harms. If someone is going to be hurt no matter what the decision, how do you decide who? He explores this problem by analogizing the dilemma to a situation where if "you have to shoot one person to prevent ten persons from being killed, is it all right if you shoot the person?" Following this care characterization of the dilemma, he moves to the imperatives of rights and duties in the criminal law context: "If I were his lawyer, I would press his rights as a defendant to have the matter suppressed, because . . . I think that any lawyer who is defending a criminal has an especially accentuated duty to follow the letter of the law. That's exactly why criminal law is the way it is — for the preservation of certain rights."

Into this compelling, duty-bound situation, Ed integrates care considerations: "And I don't think that I would attempt to have the person acquitted unless adequate steps had been taken to make sure that he wasn't going to be released into the public at large." The integration, which requires some compromise, a "minor betrayal," culminates in his response to the question of whether he has infringed on responsibilities to his client. "I don't think so. I think that the obligation to the client is to have him released in the criminal matter. To follow through in the criminal matter, to represent him zealously in that. It may be a sort of a minor betrayal to release him and have him confined again in a different proceeding, but I think it is legally justifiable and morally justifiable." To meet legal and moral ends, Ed protects the rights of the client and then tries to safeguard the community by having the client taken into custody by mental health officers.

A final example of moral integration concerns Robert Whitfield, a business lawyer who lives in the community where we interviewed attorneys but who was not part of the original study. The case involves the dissolution and purchase of business assets of a partnership, a threatened lawsuit over the transaction, and the sale of a piece of commercial real estate. From another point of view, the case is about family turmoil, strife between a father and son-in-law, breakup of relationships, and hurt and alienation felt by three generations.

Johnson, the owner of a well-established family business which bears his name, brought in Warren, his son-in-law, as a partner and manager of the business. Johnson and Warren soon had a falling out and Fred, an old friend of Johnson's, helped them to reach a settlement whereby Johnson purchased all of Warren's interest in the business. The experience left Johnson "gruff and embittered." Shortly after the settlement, Warren and Johnson's daughter went through an angry divorce, which added to the hostility between the two men.

Several years later, Johnson told business lawyer Robert Whitfield that he had been "raped" in the partnership settlement and that he intended to sue both his former son-in-law and his old friend, Fred. Johnson was working on the lawsuit with another attorney, described as "mercenary, cold-blooded." Several months later Johnson again met with Robert Whitfield and told him he was about to unleash his lawsuit but was feeling ambivalent. Upset, Johnson talked about his "family's affair" with Warren and his betrayal by his friend Fred. As Robert recalls,

At the end of the story he asked me what I thought. I asked him whether he really wanted to know. He said that he did. I told Johnson that he seemed seriously agitated, and that the litigation would exaggerate his agitation and continue it far into the future [and that] threats are ineffective with Warren. I judged Warren a lonely and hurt person, who would respond a lot more to care and understanding than to ultimatums.

Robert also told Johnson that the lawsuit had little basis, that Fred may, in fact, have been of great service to Johnson in avoiding a long, acrimonious and public airing of family laundry, and that the litigation would be both trying and exposing for Johnson, his family, and his business. Johnson did not enjoy hearing these things. "Johnson interrupted me several times while I spoke. More than twice we raised our voices at one another. At the end I told him to think about it and that if he wanted to talk to me more he could contact me next week."

I thought constantly about the people and my strategy for resolving the problem over the weekend. The more I thought, the more I wanted it to work and believed it could. I wanted it to work for Johnson because I felt that a man whose entire past impelled him to vengeance might be setting that aside. . . . I wanted it to work for Warren for the sake of his children, who must be suffering from the bitter enmity which has existed between their father and their grandfather for several years now.

Johnson called on Monday and again rehearsed his grievances. Robert told him he could either spend the rest of his life stewing about it or he could move on. Begrudgingly Johnson enlisted Robert's help,

and Robert set out to find all that he could about the history of the
relationship between Johnson and Warren, about their current financial situations, about the original settlement, and about a piece of
commercial property still owned by them jointly which was a continuing point of contention. In the process, Robert secured Johnson's
promise to call off the lawsuit, thus substituting a process of compromise for one of conflict. In this new process, assertion of rights would
be secondary to accommodation. This suited Robert, for in his words,
"I am not a street fighter."

Robert then developed a shuttle negotiation strategy to disengage
Johnson and Warren from joint ownership of the commercial property and to settle financial matters between them. Robert contacted
Warren and told him of the conversations between him and Johnson.
Despite a substantial gap between what Warren wanted for his interest in the commercial property and what Johnson was willing to
pay, Robert told Warren that he wanted to work out a settlement so
that everyone could get on with their lives and relationships. Robert
also informed Warren that he wanted to deal with him directly and
not with another attorney.

Robert decided to try to negotiate an agreement in one day. He
sensed that both men wanted to get the conflict behind them and that
the pressure of settling affairs quickly might overcome their reluctance to compromise. This strategy also served Robert's personal
need not to prolong the emotional stress.

Meeting at eight in the morning, Robert told Warren that he represented Johnson but that he "was not employing the tactics of an
advocate." To gain Warren's trust, Robert carefully disclosed all that
had transpired since his first conversation with Johnson, including
his advice that the threatened lawsuit lacked substance. The disclosure was complete. "I told Warren that I wanted to clean up
everything so that their relationship would have the best possible
chance of restoration some day."

I spent quite a bit of time at the beginning of lunch talking with Warren about his
business. We also talked about the failure of his second marriage and the psychiatrist
that he was seeing. After that I brought up the subject of the settlement. I told him
that I was exhausted and that I wondered why I was in this business. I did not say it
for effect – I meant every word of it. I was weary and losing my optimism.

Aware of both Johnson's and Warren's financial and emotional situations, Robert helped Warren structure an offer that Robert was confident would not shut down discussions.

After several meetings first with one party and then with the other, and after a number of intervening complexities that threatened collapse of discussions, a settlement was finally reached. At one point, with $1,690 separating the parties, Robert told Warren that the deal was set. When asked how he could be so sure, Robert said he would bill Johnson that amount and use the payment to cover the difference if need be. The deal done, Robert reflected:

I have accomplished nothing more satisfying in the ten years of my practice than this. If I were not paid a penny for the work, I would have no complaint. . . . I hope this brings Johnson some peace and that it purges him of his obsession with the financial losses that he suffered in 1983, coupled with the betrayal which he believes was perpetrated by Warren and Fred. I hope that Johnson and Fred can restore their friendship and that Warren's children can forget, over time, the hatred which has existed between Warren and Johnson as their relationship possibly recovers.

What Robert did was both courageous and risky. Neutrality had little place in the role he played. He at least flirted with a number of conflicts of interest and breach of confidence violations. Any of these could have caused Johnson to question seriously Robert's partisanship and zealous advocacy. Robert's felt need to keep negotiations personal and thus a one-lawyer process could easily have been misconstrued. As he moved away from neutrality and partisanship, he extended the reach of his moral responsibility. The full business and personal context of everyone involved gave play to a wide range of ethical considerations. Without abandoning notions of property, contractual, and partnership rights, an overlay of care concerns for relationships and harmony guided Robert's conduct of himself as an attorney.

Given the personality of Johnson, the history of acrimony, the underlying divorce, and the decision of Johnson to engage an adversary-oriented litigator, many lawyers would judge Robert's conduct as bordering on foolhearted. In the hands of someone less skilled and self-confident, the situation abounds with pitfalls. Threats of collapsed negotiations, loss of client, and ethical violations circled the whole proceeding like vultures. Was Robert's course of action inherently dangerous, or does it only appear so because it was unusual and contrary to expectations? How would it look if the rules promoted rather than discouraged this kind of morally responsive lawyering? Giving this much independence and authority to an attorney risks hegemony, and perhaps even arrogance. In relationship to the client, a lawyer's position is already inherently powerful, with the power held in trust for the client. Any change in the rules to encourage such active moral intervention would also have to safeguard against over-reaching and abuse.

Most legal problems, like this one, have a human dimension in which relationships are usually involved. A rights orientation tends to focus on the legal issues while care requires looking at the particular situations of people and their relationships. Robert understood that the human and legal aspects of this situation were so intertwined that to ignore one would be to do injustice to the other. Believing correctly that he could serve both relationships and rights, Robert Whitfield risked becoming a more active moral agent than the law usually allows.

Our interviews and the case described by Robert Whitfield reveal how personal morality finds expression within the legal world. For both women and men, a care orientation may remain hidden when procedural fairness and equal treatment are central issues, and when the rules guiding professional conduct are authoritative. But when confronted with a situation of probable harm, where rules are less adamant and role expectations less emphatic, care morality emerges in women attorneys with whom we talked on roughly equal terms with a morality of rights. When describing their own values or dilemmas they have encountered in law practice, care reasoning becomes strongly dominant in their responses. Where the adversary process is most justified and issues of fairness and equal treatment central, these women follow a traditional advocate's role within the legal system. In situations where other concerns are more compelling, attorneys with a strong care orientation often use both rights and care approaches in understanding and resolving a problem.

In its divergence from historical premises of the legal system, care morality is a potentially innovative force to temper the increasingly contentious nature of law. A lawyer's attempt to keep both moral viewpoints alive and active in decision making creates the possibility that the concerns of both rights and care will be weighed. When this happens, a client receives humane counsel and attorneys need not mask a portion of their identity. Entertaining two perspectives requires moral maturity and tolerance for ambiguity in concrete situations. The tension between rights and care reflects the problem of how to balance separateness and interdependence. For the attorney, the client, the legal system, and society, the presence of both moral perspectives allows more flexibility in approach and permits more compassionate consequences.

4   Personal morality and attorney role: changing perceptions of professional obligation

According to conventional wisdom, full adherence to the lawyer's role is mandatory for the legal system and for attorneys. Proper functioning of the system presupposes lawyers who fill their roles according to the letter of the law. Likewise, if lawyers expect professional success, they will abide by the rules that govern professional conduct. Rules of the role are carefully defined and powerfully communicated in law school, in the code of professional conduct, and in the daily practice of law. These rules specify correct action, duties and responsibilities, normative values, and the proper way to relate to others involved in the system, especially clients.

Moral terrain: a spectrum of responses

In our everyday lives most of us develop a pattern of responses and assumptions for dealing with moral questions and social reality. Like seedlings, these patterns often grow unnoticed, sprouting from family, friends, church, school, and chance events in our lives. Except for philosophers and theologians, few try to discover the roots of these responses and assumptions or, for that matter, even to articulate the patterns themselves. Rather, the patterns emerge with the rest of our personality and become simply a part of who we are.

What is right conduct? What is truth? How much proof is required before something is accepted as true? How do we react to hierarchy and authority? How do we solve problems? How do we respond to people in need? What is the nature of commitment? What does it mean to stand up for something we believe in? What do we mean by equality? By fairness? How do we measure success? Even if the questions and answers are never formally conceptualized, each of us works out responses in order to thread our way through life. In their professional lives, lawyers likewise normally do not articulate these questions. But for those practicing law, unlike in everyday life, answers to these questions are expressly and formally recorded.

Right conduct is conduct in compliance with professional ethical rules. Truth is the conclusion of a judge or jury. Proof of truth must be in accord with the rules of evidence and must be achieved by a preponderance of the evidence or beyond a reasonable doubt. Hierarchy and authority are unquestioned principles of order that structure the institutions, reasoning, and interpersonal relations of the legal system. Problems are solved by logical, objective, rational thinking within a system of defined authority. How lawyers respond to people in need depends on the place of the person in the system and often on the ability of the person to pay. Clients in need are attended to very differently than opponents in need, or than those too poor to become part of the system. Even clients are generally met with a controlled, carefully defined response. Commitment is impersonal and fungible, yet vigorous and unwavering. It is for sale. When a lawyer fervently advocates a client's cause, the lawyer is supposed to suspend judgment as to the truth or justice of that cause. Despite appearances, what the attorney in fact believes in is the imperative of advocacy within the context of an adversary system. Fairness and equality are terms of art defined over decades by constitutional adjudication. Although in a given circumstance the meaning of fairness or equality may not be self-evident, court decisions, legal treatises, and reasoning by analogy usually yield clarity. If not, a lawsuit will ultimately produce truth. Success is delineated by winning, either the dramatic victory of the courtroom or the more subtle victory that emerges from negotiation.

These professional responses for dealing with moral questions and social reality have an esoteric quality that separate them from the everyday life responses formulated by most people. Personal responses and assumptions are worked out over time, and have been tested at least tentatively before an alternative professional morality is available to an individual. To the extent that patterns have begun to solidify, new patterns make us uncomfortable if they are at odds with the old – particularly when established patterns work reasonably well, as they do for most would-be lawyers. The social and intellectual success that makes a legal career a possibility usually indicates that an individual has done a relatively good job of developing workable personal responses and assumptions. Potential for strain adheres in any profession that carries with it a morality of its own. So long as the moral assumptions of a profession and associated institutions are at odds with the everyday life morality of those who practice the profession, a moral tension will exist.

The terrain between a lawyer's personal morality and the imperatives of the attorney role is the subject of this chapter. For some attorneys, the moral distance between the two is indiscernible. Dictates of personal morality so mirror the obligations of professional role that no stress is perceptible between these worlds. For others, the gap between personal and role morality is sufficiently wide to create tension and a demand for strategies to deal with the disparity. This is particularly true for those in the law whose personal responses and assumptions incline toward a morality of care. That end of the moral spectrum presents a challenge to the primacy of professional role as a guide to moral conduct. For a few, the moral distance between who they are as individuals and what they must do as attorneys is so broad as to require a redefinition or partial abandonment of professional norms.

An attorney with whom we talked describes the conflict inherent in a role that requires the player to say words and think thoughts on behalf of another, creating the danger that public posture will conflict with personal identity. For Leon Gilder, the practice of law is a profession pregnant with potential for disharmony.

I see a problem when I'm asked to do something that conflicts with my value structure or when I see a social result that conflicts with my value structure. Both of these would be problems in not being able to obtain a result that I personally am comfortable with on a value and moral level. That does happen. And also being asked to advocate a position that I'm not personally comfortable with on a moral level. The latter problem is that it is part of the system that you do that, and it is socially acceptable to advocate not your own feelings, but your client's position as best you can. . . . And one of the most difficult things about being a lawyer is being put in the position to advocate something that you personally have trouble with. . . . The dilemma is speaking something you don't believe. That is the dilemma. Speaking is a very powerful thing. Speaking something you don't believe − even though it's socially acceptable to do that − creates an internal tension. For me it creates an internal tension because I don't believe it, and it may be a defensible position, it may even be a socially acceptable position, it may even be a legal position, but it can create problems.

Calling the space between the goals of an advocate and his personal beliefs "dynamic tension," Leon generalizes his perception to others in the profession:

I believe that tension is a part of the system, and that there's no attorney [who] doesn't face it. Whether they're aware of it and think about it or not, they face it. . . . It's a difficult position to put yourself in all the time. I think it creates a lot of stress, and I suspect that being an attorney is one of the most stressful things a person can do and that that's probably one of the reasons. The tension is not just in a narrow area, but runs throughout the whole practice.

As with any moral problem, one way of dealing with the strain between personal morality and role obligation is to suppress the conflict from consciousness. Numbness or insensitivity blunts the differences and eases the tension. Speaking of moral dissonance, Susan Constans recognizes the practical efficacy of quieting personal awareness when faced with ethical issues: "I think maybe you tend, in this business, to become numb to those things a little bit. And those kind of things don't bother me about the practice. And if they did, you wouldn't be practicing, you just couldn't." According to Janice Orens, "Ethical dilemmas are so tenuous in most cases that it's like a little cobweb that you don't even notice when you're brushing it aside. It's something that you become aware of and then you brush it aside." This, of course, is a psychological solution; it does not solve the moral problem. In many instances, lawyers are not successful in brushing aside moral concerns, but rather continue to experience tension.

A spectrum of endless variations describes the encounter between an attorney's personal morality and expectations of role. As we examined the transcripts of our interviews with practicing lawyers, however, four positions along the spectrum became evident as representatives of the alternatives attorneys have for responding to demands of professional responsibility. The positions trace a range of increasing stress between personal morality and role morality, and also indicate a changing understanding of professional obligations. The four positions extend from maximum role identification, in which personal and role morality coincide, to minimal role identification, in which personal and role morality diverge widely.

In Position 1, an attorney identifies strongly with role and experiences little or no moral conflict in discharging the obligations of an advocate. Lawyers in Position 2 undergo some disharmony in responding to requirements of role, but subjugate their personal morality to professional concerns. In Position 3, the conflict is heightened, and, although attorneys continue to follow their professional obligations, they do so only with a recognition of moral cost. Lawyers respond to moral cost either by undertaking reparative action to lessen the impact of fulfilling professional role, or by internalizing the cost and thus experiencing personal discomfort. The conflict in Position 4 becomes so extreme that in certain instances lawyers abandon professional obligation in order to be faithful to self and personal morality.

This four-part model serves as a vehicle for addressing additional questions of our study. Do lawyers with a strong care orientation experience more conflict between their personal morality and the demands of professional role? If so, how does the conflict affect their understanding of role and of their relationship to the legal system? As we see in this chapter, a personal care morality most often produces conflict with demands of professional role. Lawyers with a dominant care orientation experience a stressful distance between their personal responses and assumptions and the expectations of the profession.[1]

Here we also explore the more complex question of how this tension affects lawyers' understanding of their relationship to the legal system. How does an individual who has internalized the role deal with the issue of personal responsibility? What psychological strategies do people employ when personal morality and professional role conflict? Do lawyers find ways of compensating for what they perceive as the moral costs of their professional actions?

POSITION 1: MAXIMUM ROLE IDENTIFICATION

An attorney in Position 1 completely identifies with role and feels no moral conflict in meeting professional obligations. Role expectations, the code of professional ethics, and the legal system determine appropriate moral considerations and conduct. A match of personal and role values makes it possible to stand in this position. Choices might still need to be made within the system, but without distance between personal and professional morality, the precondition of tension is absent. To reach this position, either a lawyer independently develops a vigorous rights orientation, or acculturation into the profession is sufficiently encompassing to supplant aberrational aspects of personal morality.

Such an attorney is George Willis. "I think a lot about what I personally think about right and wrong, but what I personally think about right and wrong is not incompatible with what I do for a living." The same confidence that personal morality lies well within the conventions of role is expressed by Jim Smallwood: "I have no trouble in following the law, and following the canons, and so I'm telling you I've never had a situation where I've had a conflict. I mean, I think the law and the canons and what I perceive to be my morals most times coincide." For such attorneys, instances of conflict between everyday life values and role obligations are rare because in day-to-day living they follow the same patterns found in the role morality of lawyers.

The close match of personal and institutional values which allows the unequivocal acceptance of professional morality has several implications affecting responsibility, the range of moral considerations, and justification for conduct and personal detachment. First, in common with any instance of institutionalized role, once the institution is morally responsible, the individual ceases to be. If an institution authoritatively determines right and wrong, individuals no longer feel personally responsible for their moral choices. This occurred in cases of corporate irresponsibility such as those involving Dalkon shields and exploding Ford Pinto gas tanks. Ironically, collective responsibility may in fact mean that no one is responsible. Where the institution is sufficiently powerful and comprehensive, individuals, even those at the top, may be left with little control over their own morality.

There are also positive aspects of institutionalized morality that are particularly pertinent to the legal system. Institutionalized values provide clarity and collective understanding seldom possible when morality is the province of individuals. Moral wisdom accumulates in the institution and matures over time. Community rules and expectations generate consistency in decision making. The burden of responsibility is lifted from the individual and borne by the institution.

When personal and professional values coincide, attorneys can readily accept the positive aspects of institutionalized rights morality without concern for personal responsibility. Shielded by the neutrality of the advocate, lawyer Jane Triminger talks about responsibility for undesirable results in response to the first hypothetical dilemma, involving the murderer whose confession can be excluded from evidence:

I guess I always view the legal system as, you know, it's the State's burden to prove every element of a crime beyond a reasonable doubt with the evidence they gather. So the ultimate decision of guilt or innocence is made by the jury and isn't made by you. Your job is to represent the guy in the system as well as you can. . . . It doesn't present a dilemma because it doesn't present a decision for me. It's the judge's decision and my, your role in the system would be to present for the client whatever is available, whatever rules and regulations the legal system has developed.

There is no decision for Jane, because the institutionalized legal system with which she aligns has already made the choice. Asked if she would feel responsible if the defendant went free and seriously hurt someone else, this attorney replies:

No. . . . I guess I would blame the system that says let's exclude the confession. I guess I would blame the judge who made the ruling on it rather than myself. . . . No, I just would not feel responsible. . . . I think the attorney's role is to represent his client without regard to his opinion or his judgment about his guilt or innocence.

Marsha James talked about a similar exclusion of personal moral judgments in the face of a comprehensive system of rules that control lawyer conduct. Because the rules dictate conduct, they absolve lawyers of responsibility for the consequences of complying with the rules. Speaking of an armed robbery case, she describes how she does not

let my moral judgments or society's moral judgments play a part in how I represent him. If there's a legal reason or argument to get him off, I'll use it because that's in his best interests and the law says that you can use that legal argument. So I don't think there's any moral conflict there. . . . But I don't feel bad because I get some-body who's guilty off. . . . Because no matter what he did, I think our system of law applies to him equally as it does to anyone else. And if the State doesn't follow the law in their prosecution of an individual, then they lose. And that's the way for a guilty person as well as an innocent person. You know, it's got to be equally applied or it isn't any good. So I don't feel bad about it.

Beyond the issue of responsibility, Jane Triminger and Marsha James point to a second implication of wholehearted acceptance of role as a moral guide: Professional role narrows the range of relevant moral considerations that an attorney must take into account in evaluating conduct. Because role ethics adequately answer moral questions, considerations that might engage a lay person are systematically ignored.

Ethics of role at one and the same time provide the lucidity of spectacles and the vision restriction of blinders. Lawyers in Position 1 vividly perceive moral obligations primarily in terms of responsibility to client. They leave out others who in ordinary life might be seen as having moral claims. Explaining how he might handle a victim in a rape trial, George Willis said, "I wouldn't feel bad about smearing her if I had to do that to adequately represent my client zealously within the bounds of the law, consistent with my ethical obligation to my client." The lens of responsibility focuses narrowly, and consequences of professional conduct rest with the system and not with the attorney.

Jane Triminger abandons her personal sense of fairness when she steps into the role of attorney. Rather than retaining a personal moral perspective which can test obligations of profession, she suspends personal judgment and takes the rules of professional conduct as authoritative. Without an opposing ought, Jane is free to identify fully with role. Speaking of the two hypothetical dilemmas, she says:

It's just clear to me that how I view those problems is in relation to the code of professional ethics, and so it seems like I don't have a sense of fairness anyway. (*That you don't have a sense of fairness? Or you think it is not appropriate to bring your sense of fairness to bear?*) I think it's more the latter, that I have a sense of fairness but I don't think it's appropriate to bring it to bear in the legal work I do. (*How do you feel about being placed in a situation where your own sense of fairness is irrelevant to the decisions you make?*) I think I view it that in any profession or some kinds of work you get into, your sense of fairness doesn't come into play in any event. If I were working for welfare or handing out money to poor people, my sense of what was fair would not come into play because I have the rules and regulations of that agency to deal with. So I guess that I view that whatever system you are working in, whether it's a state system or private employment, you have to go by the rules and regulations, and your own sense of what would be fairest doesn't come into play in that work.

When personal fairness is excluded, only institutional fairness is left to measure right and wrong.

A third implication of unreserved identification with role morality is that institutional convention provides not only an outline of acceptable conduct but also a justification for that conduct. Lawyers in Position 1 voice both of the justifications for maximum role identification discussed in Chapter 2: It is necessary to make the system work and it fulfills a moral commitment to the client. These lawyers easily identify with a role they perceive as critical to a legal system that guarantees our social well-being. Attorneys with whom we talked consistently associated the value of their role with a larger societal good. For instance, George Willis remarks, "I think our whole set of ordered liberties that we enjoy in our country flow from that. Our criminal justice system is . . . geared to protect the rights of the individual. . . . To me that's justice. To me that's what makes the world go around, and that's how I justify my existence to myself."

George also observes that partisan neutrality is essential "if you're going to have a system of justice in the country, and if that system's going to work." Making his involvement in that system more personal, he says: "You know, you go home at Christmas time. Your mom asks what you do. 'Gee mom, I'm representing this guy who is supposed to have brutally raped this young girl or slit somebody's throat or set somebody on fire or so on.' Somebody's got to do that, because if they don't, the system starts to break down." To justify acts that contradict everyday morality, these lawyers rely upon the greater good they accomplish. Their responsibility is to do their part well, not to second-guess the institution and its rules.

Leon Gilder remarks on fulfilling a moral obligation to the client as a second justification for commitment to role. "Attorneys must realize that their responsibility to their client has to be greater than to society at large, and there's morality in doing what your responsibility as a lawyer is, too." Just as children have higher, at times exclusive, claims on their parents, so also do clients extract special, at times exhaustive, commitment from their lawyers.

The legal system defines a scheme of moral conduct and then labels action consistent with that scheme as moral. The institution specifies both appropriate attorney conduct and the proper recipient of attorney obligation, and then proclaims the rightness of acting consistent with its requirements. By internally logical though circular reasoning, the legal system justifies an attorney's narrowed field of moral concern. It becomes a closed system of self-justification which is immune to challenge by anyone who accepts the premises of the system. The obligation to client is an overriding moral obligation because the professional code says it is.

A fourth implication of the role identification indicative of Position 1 is an attitude described earlier as stoic detachment. Without regard to the morality of the cause or the likability of the employer, an emotionally distant hired gun is available for service. Role requirements of neutrality and partisanship so imply a posture of detachment that the posture itself becomes a part of the role definition. The hired-gun metaphor and the title of professional were often used by lawyers in Position 1 to describe their understanding of self in relation to role. Larry Smith speaks of himself in this way: "My primary responsibility in the practice of law is to do the best job for my client that I can. Somebody has a dispute and they need a hired gun and I step in, keeping in mind my responsibilities to my client and to the profession, the court, things like that. I think my responsibility is to try to get the best result I can for my client."

The hired-gun metaphor brings to mind the image of the lone cowboy, seemingly without permanent loyalties, whose skills are for hire. Hidden in the metaphor is the dissociation of the personal self from the work an individual does. When part of the self is available for hire, stoic detachment is an inviting psychological device to protect oneself from the consequences of surrendering control and responsibility.

Akin to the hired gun, George Willis stresses his professionalism: "I'm a professional. I live and die by my reputation. I'm going to do a good job if I think you're an asshole, if I think you're a nice guy. I try and be as professional as possible and I try to have a thick skin." Here the term "professional" connotes a zealous loyalty of lawyer to client, and it is professionalism that allows this attorney's strong sense of personal integrity. Professional commitment is juxtaposed with a thick skin, a barrier that limits the nature of attachment and separates emotion from action. The commitment of attorney to client is not the devotion of marriage or friendship, but an objective dedication which maintains separation. Both commitment and barrier may be essential to career success and psychological peace for someone whose job it is to act as the mouthpiece of another.

The degree to which lawyers identify with role varies depending upon the situation. Different circumstances challenge in their own ways the beliefs of personal and professional morality. In interviewing attorneys, we observed that the same lawyer might have adamant role identification in response to one situation and back away from that position under other conditions.[2] Nonetheless, we found that men more often reacted from Position 1.[3] Such maximum role identification occurs most readily when care reasoning does not separate lawyers' personal morality from the values of professional role. Because professional ethics reflect a strong rights orientation, the absence of care reasoning in personal morality eliminates the stuff of which conflict is made.

As we saw in Chapter 3, female attorneys to whom we spoke are much more likely than men to use care thinking in their personal morality; not surprisingly, women are also much less prone than men to adopt without equivocation the voice of role morality which excludes care considerations. Women were much more likely to examine consequences and express concerns of personal responsibility even where dictates of role were clear. Attorneys in Position 1 seldom talked of care considerations in their perception and resolution of moral problems. When professional responsibility authoritatively dictates moral assumptions and responses, there is no need to delve into irrelevant considerations. Those lawyers who fully identify with role can depend on the accumulated wisdom and clarity of the legal system to resolve moral conflict.

POSITION 2: SUBJUGATION OF PERSONAL MORALITY

Lawyers who subjugate their personal morality to role have much in common with those in Position 1. For attorneys in both positions, commitment to client is a primary value, responsibility for consequences resides in the system, partisanship and neutrality guide action, and role morality supplies the standard of acceptable conduct. The chief difference between them is that in Position 2 a lawyer recognizes disagreement between the world of personal morality and imperatives of professional role. Resolution of conflict comes through subjugation of personal values in response to the requirements of neutrality and partisanship. As attorney Spencer Jones told us, "My personal sense of justice is completely overwhelmed by the professional area." After gaining acquittal of an admitted child molester, he again expresses a similar sentiment. "My professional job completely subverts my own feelings in cases that I'm involved with." As with those in Position 1, "It's part of my job as a lawyer" sufficiently answers why an attorney pursues a given course of conduct.

In the way they respond to the legal system and play out professional role, attorneys in Position 1 and Position 2 are largely indistinguishable. They both act according to the time-honored and internally justified expectations of an advocate within an adversary system. The critical difference between the two positions is psychological. Lawyers acting from Position 2 knowingly give up something of the self, a part of their personal awareness. Yet the value of systematic, collective, authoritative moral judgment reflected in the legal system renders subjugation of personal morality routine. That personal morality should give way to values embodied in a logically consistent system forged over time by wise people is readily accepted.

Tom Wooding described the two moral worlds that coexist for him. Because of his facility in setting aside personal values, noticeable tension is absent. Having unequivocally subordinated personal moral vision, Tom becomes indistinguishable from an attorney in Position 1 in the zeal of his advocacy.

Morality to me as a person, individual, means keeping in harmony with the universe and with the environment around me, not doing things that I perceive to hurt other people. . . . That's morality to me as a person. As an attorney, I have to be an advocate. I take on an advocate's morality. I really do. To represent someone who's killed a couple of people may involve some moral issues for some people. I'm an advocate. I can be very cold and cruel and act as an advocate. I don't consider morality. In that sense it's a double standard, because to be a great trial attorney I may not do something that's absolutely in tune with the world and the environment.

When personal morality is set aside, a whole range of ethical considerations is excluded. The two sides of himself that Tom describes hardly seem to be the same person. In the absence of "morality to me as a person," the advocate is less complete, less human, and yet exactly what the system requires. The imposition of a double standard makes possible unqualified deference to traditional imperatives of professional role, despite a personal morality of care.

This posture of professional competence at the cost of diminished self raises a question that echoes throughout our work. In the long run, how does suspension of personal morality and narrowing of moral vision affect an individual attorney, service to the client, and social utility of the legal system? What does it do to a person to be regularly called upon to subjugate personal morality, to leave aside a portion of themselves? What does it do to a system when its main practitioners are expected to subordinate their everyday morality?

An ability to mute a personal moral voice while carrying out role commands is accepted as a requirement of the profession by lawyers in Position 2. Given the already stressful job of an attorney, to allow personal and role values to compete creates complexity and tension which many attorneys find psychologically and professionally unacceptable. Spencer Jones describes how his personal morality is "some sort of an alarm system somewhere in there that would go off or jangle and say, 'wait a minute, this is really bad.'" He talks of an indecent liberties case where "representing my client is damaging to the little victim." Yet, for him this concern is "probably the minimal factor of what I make a decision on." Spencer describes how lawyers develop the ability to turn off their personal alarm system

either to protect themselves, or it's overwhelmed by other aspects of the work that you're doing as far as professional pride and feeling that you know what you're doing is important, and it's necessary to do those sorts of things. So they completely overwhelm your sense of discomfort which comes from having to be involved in whatever the particular situation is.

Spencer does not dispose of individual morality by an active personal ordering of priorities. Rather, powerful role and ominous responsibility completely overwhelm his sense of discomfort. To avoid agonizing difficulties, such as confounding the testimony of a child victim, professional requirements silence the personal moral alarm system. Repeatedly turning off the personal alarm has an erosive effect on the claims of personal morality. Over time, what is subjugated grows accustomed to its secondary status and becomes less insistent in its claims.

This notion that role itself dictates subordination of personal morality appears again in our conversation with Jennifer Hall. Despite her personal values, she impugns a witness by bringing to light past sexual conduct. Even though Jennifer "felt real strongly about women's rights," she describes how "when it came right down to it the lawyer in me just took over. I had no personal compunction about doing that." Explaining how it could occur, she says, "you sort of go on automatic pilot and that's just what happened in this case. That's what I found so amazing. There was no decision at all."

Even when conflicting values are consciously recognized, the pull of the law job is seemingly irresistible. Law school, professional success, peer approval, the importance of the legal system, a commitment to professionalism, all combine to accomplish what the bramble bush did for the blind man — implanting a new vision which for some lawyers leads to an almost automatic subordination of the old. As Jennifer said, to her own amazement, "there was no decision at all." Sounding a bit like the Nuremberg defense, another attorney acknowledges a collision of institutional and individual commands, but resolves the conflict with the observation "It's part of your job, you know, I had my orders."

Attorneys in Position 2, like those in Position 1, feel little or no personal responsibility for the consequences of their professional acts. When on automatic pilot, the system is in control. Having identified with the role, lawyers in Position 2 experience its invasive quality. The attorney does not accept personal responsibility for professional conduct, for the attorney did not create the system, but simply plays a part in it. Yet, for the lawyer who recognizes a conflict with personal morality, the question of responsibility may linger.

Janet Milgram recounts how she got "someone out of jail, and they went back two days later and did the same thing again." Describing how she "tries not to feel a sense of responsibility for it," she lists factors that offset this feeling, including minimalization of contextual considerations. "You have a job to do, you have a certain role to play, and the chain of events that happened after or before . . . were not something you had a part in." Regarding whether she should feel responsible, she contends, "I don't think you should. And I can't really say why you do, maybe because you're human."

Moving to the border between Position 2 and Position 3, Janet struggles against her own feelings of responsibility. Finally, justification for not feeling responsible comes directly from her role as an attorney. "We cannot accept that responsibility, because we have to do what we have to do." With subjugation of personal morality there comes disavowal of responsibility. Once an attorney accepts role definition as the standard for acceptable conduct, the parameters of the role rather than personal morality dictate how to feel about that conduct.

As we saw earlier, the metaphor of masks symbolizes for Tom Wooding the separation of personal and professional selves. He describes how he protects himself and disengages from clients by wearing an "advocate mask," which means that the client is "relating to the you they know. They don't realize that the you − the me − that they knew was not me." Like the hired-gun metaphor, masking of personal self at once removes that self from the arena of professional decision making and at the same time distances the client from the attorney. The mask of objectivity protects the lawyer from the vulnerability of involved concern. Detachment of role allows a lawyer to serve the client and protect the self. As Valerie Knight says, "I need to disengage myself and take a look at the situation rather than take the personal approach to something."

Masking and disengagement are ways of protecting the self from the potential trauma of subjugation. While the strength of institutionalized rules externally justify subordination of personal morality, separating personal from professional morality is a psychological device for keeping personal morality intact when professional values prevail. If the attorney role is a mask, it can be given full authority in the theater of law without concern for its effect on the morality of everyday life.

Attorneys in Position 2 most often reason with the moral orientation of rights.[4] Although more care response is present than in Position 1, the powerful dictates of the lawyer's role still submerge weaker statements of care. Because personal moral orientation generally synchronizes with demands of professional role, personal morality seldom challenges the dominance of institutional expectations.[5]

When lawyers occupy Positions 1 and 2, the principles and values of the legal system provide a clear framework for decision making. Moral judgment used in addressing conflict is overwhelmingly rights-oriented. Little need arises to reconcile conflicting beliefs and expectations. Either through maximum role identification or by subjugation of personal ethical concerns, judgments in Positions 1 and 2 focus on considerations of justice, equality, procedural fair play, and uniform application of general rules. Excluded from view are contextual evaluations of harm and harmony and the importance of human relationships. Thus, the clear parameters of legal ethics truncate the full range of moral vision. This limitation appears in the metaphors lawyers use to describe their moral vision in Positions 1 and 2: "blinders," "tunnel vision," "blurring the finer lines between right and wrong," and "moral suppression." Not until Position 3 does vision broaden. There personal morality demands a share in decision making and attorneys begin to see and accept responsibility for the wider consequences of decisions.

POSITION 3: RECOGNITION OF MORAL COST

When individual morality is not subjugated but remains in the arena of decision making, tension often results. As we saw previously, care-tinted spectacles provide an alternative vision for evaluating behavior, reasoning about moral conflicts, and understanding responsibility and relationships. Conflict occurs when a care orientation calls into question the validity of rights dictates emanating from the lawyer role. The coexistence of care reasoning and professional role ethics in the same decision-making arena often creates moral dissonance which leads to an experience of moral cost — the sacrifice of one legitimate moral end so that another might be accomplished. When personal and professional ethical commands are inconsistent, an attorney may be forced to choose and consequently experience the loss of integrity of the moral option not selected.

The presence of personal morality as a continuing touchstone for decision making differentiates Position 3 from Positions 1 and 2. Whereas the first two positions were associated with a rights orientation, in Position 3 care thinking becomes prominent. When care considerations have an increased presence and tenacity, they are less easily pushed aside by institutionally supported values of rights morality. Position 3 is the most complex and subtle of the four positions because two legitimate claimants vie for control of decision making. Position 3 maximizes tension within an individual and, at the same time, offers the possibility of access to the strength of both institutional and personal morality.

Existence of personal moral values in professional decision making has negative and positive consequences. Wider moral vision may cause an attorney to experience irreconcilable conflicts which lead to internal distress. With blinders removed, a lawyer may perceive damage to other people or to the integrity of principles that otherwise could have been ignored. On the positive side, breakdown of tunnel vision means that a richer mix of moral facilities are vital and active. The enlarged vantage point of a dual perspective increases the range of available considerations. An attorney will be able to feel more psychologically complete and see beyond immediate client demands to broader questions of social impact.

From the outside, lawyers in Position 3 may appear to occupy the attorney role in much the same way as lawyers in Positions 1 and 2. They may reach the same decisions and act in the same manner. Differences lie in the process of decision making, evaluation of the decision, and perception of and response to moral cost. Conflict between role and personal beliefs cannot be resolved without undesirable consequences to other people or compromise of moral standards. In response to perception of moral costs, attorneys may express reluctance or regret. Recognizing harm that flows from fulfilling professional responsibilities, an attorney may take concrete action to mitigate or repair destructive consequences. If the lawyer undertakes reparative action, then outer behavior may also vary from expected conduct. Importantly, recognition of moral costs alters an attorney's feeling of personal responsibility and moderates the commands of neutral partisanship.

Unlike lawyers in Position 2, those in Position 3 neither set aside their personal morality nor allow the role of lawyer to take over and put them on "automatic pilot." Personal responsibility insists upon a not necessarily peaceful coexistence with professional role. In extreme cases, personal morality feels the demands of role as abnormal and invasive. Words that denote involuntary or commercial sex reveal how deeply the intimate self of a lawyer at times feels violated by role requirements. Janice Orens: "It's like being forced into a sex relationship you didn't anticipate. It's a screw job. It feels horrible to do something that you wouldn't do normally." Diana Cartwright: "I have to contradict myself depending on what role I'm taking. . . . It's sort of professional prostitution." Ann Hollins: "Sometimes you feel almost like a pimp or something. . . . It felt sleazy to cut the truth that finely."

When requirements of professional role are incompatible with dictates of individual morality, tension is inevitable. One attorney foresees the trap in this situation: "To follow what the law says your obligation is sometimes leads to something that is very contrary to your personal morality. . . . I can't impose my morality on another person . . . because then you're representing yourself, you're not representing the client anymore and your job is to represent the client." The lawyer is faced with an either/or choice – to be a good lawyer and represent the client according to professional obligations, or to be a good person by following personal principles. Professional performance vies with individual integrity.

Good in this context is not judged by an objective, external moral measure. The good lawyer is the person who abides by lawyers' rules; the good person is the person who lives by the axioms of personal morality. In the larger scheme of things the lawyer may be judged a shyster or a Samaritan and the good person a bigot or a saint. Our concern here is with the judgments attorneys make about themselves, including judgments about professional competence.

This problem of moral distance between personal and professional self is inherent in an occupation that defines professionalism in terms of neutral partisanship and the ability to speak the words and champion the cause of another. If an attorney speaks for someone else, there is always the risk that those words will conflict with the lawyer's personal moral beliefs. How often this happens in the career of an attorney is not clear, but our discussions with lawyers convince us that it does happen among advocates who have a strong personal morality of care. Lawyers use traumatic words to describe the clash: "I feel torn to shreds." "I . . . do it with reluctance and with a heavy heart and feel badly about that." "It takes away my virtue and integrity to proceed like this." "You're denying the wholeness of the person within that context [legal practice], and does that cause conflict? Yes, that's what drives lawyers to the bars after work. . . . Yes, it's a constant questioning process. Am I being true to myself if I proceed in this respect?"

On occasion, moral stress may also arise through the conflict of a personal morality of rights and professional role morality. While these normally coincide, there are instances where a personal rights orientation quarrels with the procedural fairness of the legal system. In discussing the hypothetical moral dilemma involving a confessed but crazy murderer, William Moresby reasons from a firm rights perspective reminiscent of Aristotle's arithmetic equality in corrective justice:

You have responsibility if you're a defense attorney in a criminal case to defend. . . . We have a system of procedural justice that has no touch with . . . execution of justice in this specific case, because here procedural justice requires that you diligently protect that guy from being punished for a crime which he obviously committed. I'd have to do that, OK, because my sense of duty to the individual has to exceed my duty to society at large. . . . I would hate it, OK, but I would, if I were in a situation where I can't get out. I have to represent this guy. I have to protect his interests.

When asked why he would hate it, William says, "I would hate knowing, absolutely knowing that I was preventing actual justice from being done." For him, "actual justice" is a category of personal morality that calls for the same resolution as corrective justice in the *Nicomachean Ethics:* "One who commits the crime should be punished for his crime."

The problem for William comes from the discrepancy between "actual justice in the circumstances of the case as opposed to the justice system we have in the country, which is a procedural justice system, which has nothing to do with — it only peripherally deals with — the justice of a particular outcome." Like other lawyers in Position 3, William experiences moral cost because of this discrepancy between what the system requires and his own moral sense. The crimping of his personal idea of justice comes from fulfilling his role responsibility "to represent this guy." He protects the integrity of the system at the expense of his own moral feelings about a larger meaning of justice, and, as a result, "I would hate it."

Jennifer Hall[6] experiences a similar moral anguish, but here, in more typical fashion, the conflict stems from a persistent morality of care. Even in her description of personal morality, she acknowledges the tension she faces through complying with lawyerly obligations:

If you live a moral life, I think it means that you help people, you help other people when you can and you don't hurt them. You don't hurt other people. And obviously for a lawyer, you've got to put some refinements on that because you hurt other people all the time when you win in court. But I just hope that on balance the world is a better place when I leave because of what I did.

The balance to which Jennifer aspires is the ecological harmony of the Zapotecs and not the balance of reciprocity that comes "when you win in court." Mindful of the tension inherent for her in being a lawyer, she presents a situation that depicts the stress of feeling responsible for results that she advocates but does not condone:

I was asked by a landlord to handle an eviction matter. I needed the money and I did it, and I'd made the commitment to do it so I did the whole thing. I hated doing it. The tenants were bad tenants and I had all the law on my side, and really, they'd been really bad. It wasn't that I felt that what I was doing in this particular situation was wrong. But I decided at the end that I'd never represent another landlord again in an eviction thing, just because of regardless of right or wrong, I don't want to be responsible for putting somebody out on the street, even if they deserved it. . . . The wear and tear that it brings on me isn't compensated by whatever money I would make doing it. . . . I felt so ashamed. I mean I realized that it was me, you know, that I wasn't really doing something shameful in public. I understood that this was my problem, or my feeling, not being put on me by the public. . . . Landlords are the haves and tenants are the have nots. And I don't like to have cases against the have nots, even if I'm right.

Jennifer perceives moral costs in this situation as harm to the tenants. She responds to this cost by taking responsibility and feeling shame. Moral judgment divides between personal and professional perspective as Jennifer recognizes that, in fulfilling her role, she inflicts hurt. Personal self-evaluation leads to criticism and negative feelings; professional self-evaluation reveals a lawyer's job well done.

Sandra Tinnel also describes the no-win, either/or dichotomy between role obligations and personal imperatives — where fulfilling role violates personal morality and fulfilling personal morality requires breaking with role. Being unwilling to play the hired gun or to defer to the client's judgment regarding an acceptable outcome, she tries to avoid a dilemma by sending the client to another attorney.

> This was a case where a guy was drunk and beat up a man. And it became clear to me after I started working on the case that the guy had a tremendous alcohol problem. [The prosecutor] was recommending initially that the guy go to alcohol treatment, and I was agreeing with him. But my client wouldn't agree to it at all. His goal was for me to get him out of this charge. And I was looking at it from the standpoint of what's going to help this character. And certainly alcohol treatment would have provided an opportunity for help. Maybe ultimately it wouldn't have helped him if he didn't want it, but at least the opportunity would have been there. And that was the dilemma for me. Because I knew he wanted off the charge, and I figured it was my responsibility to get him off the charge, but I didn't think it'd do him any good. And finally I recommended that he see another attorney because I just didn't feel like I could rest with myself if I got him off or get the charge reduced . . . because he'd just be out there, still having the same problems.

When asked what she means by a good result in this case, Sandra answers, "something that would have a chance of helping somebody." This accords with her morality but conflicts with the wishes of her client. Looking at the case from a care standpoint, she describes how following her role responsibilities means that she would be facilitating the continuation of a hurtful situation. Yet, honoring her moral concerns by sending the case away leaves her feeling unfulfilled both personally and professionally. In her words, "All I'm doing is shifting responsibility." Lois Halley likewise feels the bind when professional expectation and personal values judge one another. After portraying a morality that revolves around not "hurting other people . . . how we interact with each other . . . a moral obligation of being nice to each other," she steps back and reflects, "so, do I sound much like a litigator?"

The hypothetical dilemma concerning child custody proved a rich ground for exploring the cost of imperatives in conflict. For a number of lawyers, it poses a Hobson's choice[7] between loyalty to client and welfare of children. As care concerns are elevated by the facts of this case, moral costs become increasingly difficult to ignore. For example, Phyllis Travis characterizes dealing with the custody situation as "very, very hard, because I'd be very torn between protecting those kids and screwing up the client's case, and breaching whatever confidence there was with that client. . . . I think I'd have to look into myself and decide whether or not I could really adequately represent the person." From the either/or perspective so characteristic of Position 3, she describes her professional "duty not to breach the confidentiality and the confidence of my client" on the one hand, and on the other "a duty to protect children – that's a moral duty."

Given the breadth of moral concerns incorporated by the joining of these two perspectives, personal responsibility is difficult to avoid. For Phyllis, sending the case to a new attorney "wouldn't absolve me. But what it would mean is that I would always worry about those kids, and I would probably say to the other attorney, 'you need to talk with the client. There are just some problems here that I don't really care to deal with.'" Following this course of conduct and judging herself by how attorneys are "supposed" to act, Phyllis says that she would describe herself as a "hypocrite." Yet she observes that if she did not compromise her role and alert the new attorney to an impending problem in order to protect the children, she would feel "terrible." As long as morality of care insists on being heard, the either/or dilemma seems unavoidable. She sees a choice of being either a good lawyer or a good person; given the engulfing quality of the lawyer's role, moral costs are almost inevitable.

For both Sandra Tinnel and Phyllis Travis, the either/or tension between role and moral imperatives creates a bind: Either they fail to live up to role requirements or they fail to abide by tenets of personal morality. They value both sides of the either/or. The role of lawyer is critical to the legal system, a source of livelihood and esteem, and the

generator of its own moral injunctions; personal morality is an intimate indicant of who one is and of the ideal self one might be.
Traditionally, this rigid, dichotomous construction has tended to
limit a lawyer's personal morality in the professional arena, making
it difficult for an individual attorney to integrate the two perspectives. If personal and professional morality agree, the problem is
avoided; however, with the influx of women, the legal system can no
longer safely assume such moral unity.

The good lawyer or good person dilemma engenders stress, which
provokes some attorneys to compensatory conduct. Staying within
the boundaries of role, they address personal moral concerns by
taking specific reparative actions to offset the moral costs they perceive as stemming from fulfillment of role obligations. These actions
are intended to minimize the harm resulting from adherence to legal
rules. Attorneys who follow this course hope to moderate the ei-
ther/or choice by at least partially meeting the requirements of both
personal and professional morality.

Kathryn Colby understands how the demands of personal morality and professional responsibility conspire to necessitate mitigating
action. Explaining her response to the hypothetical dilemma involving the crazy murderer, she contrasts personal accountability with
role perspective:

You would create the dilemma for yourself by saying, "I'm going to be responsible
for this man being out on the street." The [role] perspective is to say, "I am a pawn
in the game and the rules of the game say this, and this is the role that I play in the
system, and if there's something wrong with the system, then we have a process
whereby it's changed."

She goes on to explain that for her, there would be a "divergence
between what you thought and what you felt. You'd feel really badly,
I'm sure, especially if he went out and did something again. That's
what makes it so hard." Faced with a seemingly either/or choice,
Kathryn employs corrective action to allay her moral concern about
the consequences of professional acts. She tries to discharge both
personal and role responsibilities. "I would do what needed to be
done as defense counsel. I would do my best to see that the confession was excluded. I would probably try to compensate somewhere
else by either dropping the ball, or going to the prosecutor or maybe

even going to the judge. I'd probably try to find some way to help them catch him."

In the hypothetical dilemma concerned with child custody, John Crowell likewise takes mitigating action to alleviate problems resulting from moral distance between professional role and personal values. "It would be difficult for me to accept my role as responsible for putting these children in an abusive situation." When asked why he would feel responsible, John responds with a care definition of responsibility which includes an obligation to prevent harm actively. "I guess because I would have the power to change it. And if I had the opportunity to prevent something and didn't prevent it, and something terrible happened, then I would feel personally responsible for that." Confronted with this responsibility, he tries to stay in his attorney role, and yet offset the possible negative consequences of partisanship.

If I were at a stage in the case where I could withdraw without prejudice to my client, I would likely withdraw. I might even use that as leverage against my client, that I would stay in the case if my client would do certain things. And that any custody order that was entered perhaps might involve certain conditions on it, or something like that. I would feel some responsibility to the children to do that, and I would make it clear to my client that that's the position I was taking. And maybe through their wanting to have me represent them because of how they felt about me, use that as leverage to get them to do what I wanted to.

In this and other examples recounted under Position 3, we see a subtle erosion in traditional concepts of unqualified partisanship and unquestioning neutrality. Partisanship loses some of its fervor when a lawyer forgoes neutrality and uses the position "as leverage to get them to do what I wanted to." The lawyer remains an advocate but no longer acts as a mouthpiece in the traditional sense. Neutrality rather than judgment is suspended; responsibility ceases to mean restraint from interference with the rights and values of others. Whereas lawyers in Positions 1 and 2 describe themselves as "detached," as "hired guns," as "assuming a distance," lawyers who recognize moral cost portray a different way of inhabiting role. They take on a more morally responsive way of practicing law which involves active assessment of the moral stance of the client.

Once neutrality is compromised, partisanship may have to be adjusted in order to lessen moral cost. Attorneys who become judging moral agents place restrictions on the terms for which they are available for hire. Asked about his primary responsibility as an attorney, William Moresby paints a picture unlike that of the traditional advocate:

I have a responsibility to my clients to assist them in doing what is good for them. Now, that doesn't necessarily mean to assist them in doing what they walk in thinking they want to do. I have a real sense and feeling and belief, I guess, that my role as an attorney should not be just as a hit man, a hired gun to go out and get whatever your client wants. I think that lawyers can exert a certain influence on their clients, tending to push them in the direction that would be, well – I'll call it a moral choice – a more moral way to resolve a situation or dilemma.

Leon Gilder also rethinks the role to accommodate in part his care concerns. "Sometimes I see myself more as a social worker than anything else. Just in the kind of working with people, half counselor, half social worker, or half advocate." When asked to characterize the difference between his tasks as a social worker and as an advocate, he keeps traditional obligations in mind but finds room for his own moral judgment.

That's a place of constant tension . . . part of your job is to represent their position and get the best results for them that you can. And yet often to do that, you have to work with clients to rearrange their expectations. . . . And a lot of times they come in in emotional crisis and a lot of times they want to strike out, or want you to take actions, or do actions, and I end up, in my own opinion, making a judgment that's not in line with what they say they want. And I have to do that a lot. And so I see some of that as social work – you know, working people through their crises. The advocacy role is probably more clear-cut traditionally. You go in there, and you build the best case you can to get the best results for your client.

Likewise rejecting the role of a detached stoic, Phyllis Travis depicts "being a domestic relations lawyer as having the exposure to people's basic and most personal problems and dealing with that for them, and trying to help them." From her point of view, dissolutions are

the most personal and basic part of your life, and I'm just not interested in doing somebody's taxes, but I am interested in the emotions and all the other things that go along with the children and who's going to take care of them. . . . And so I wanted to be part of that so I could be in there saying, you know, "Now are the kids OK?" and "Do they need this?" "Do they need that?" – kind of watching out for it.

In our conversations with lawyers, this kind of contextual caring for the wholeness of a human situation is not reserved for domestic relations law. Business lawyer Robert Whitfield was intimately concerned with restoration of relationships and the impact of enmity between father- and son-in-law on the next generation. Similarly, Jane Milton, a criminal defense attorney, talks of her job as trying "to get the whole picture, put it together, and figure out how to move from this point that has them in a whole lot of trouble to some place that's going to be better for them. And that carries over into your own life, and that's beneficial and important." For these lawyers in Position 3, an involved concern for clients and a willingness to engage with their problems replaces the detachment often considered central to an advocate's role.

Lawyers in Position 3, with its broader moral vistas and higher moral stress, express significantly more care thinking than those in Positions 1 and 2. In accordance with our finding that women carry a disproportionate share of a care orientation among the lawyers we interviewed, they also appear in this position in a substantial majority.[8] From our interviews, we would predict that women will most often experience tension between personal and professional moralities in practicing law. In Position 3's tempering of partisanship, neutrality, and detachment, we see the seeds for rethinking the lawyer's role in a way that preserves the virtues of institutional ethics while infusing the critical concerns of care morality.

POSITION 4: MINIMUM ROLE IDENTIFICATION

For some attorneys with whom we talked, role recedes in prominence, and personal morality at times becomes determinative of moral thinking. Attorneys who normally follow role directives may find themselves in a particular situation where the profession requires action unacceptable to individual values. Unable or unwilling to compromise personal morality, a lawyer selectively abandons professional obligations or modifies them to accord with personal beliefs. Because lawyers in Position 4 have not so thoroughly internalized the role, they retain the capacity and willingness to define themselves in action independently of professional norms. For this personal moral freedom, both the legal system and the lawyer potentially pay a price. Functioning of the legal system presupposes the lawyer role, and if enough lawyers were to fail in their role, the system, together with all of its social value, would flounder.

Likewise, an attorney runs substantial professional risks. An advocate cannot continuously sustain a position that contradicts the requirements of role and still maintain a law practice. Nevertheless, several attorneys described to us examples where distance between personal and professional values so expands, tension so heightens, that the moral cost of role compliance is unacceptable. In special situations of moral conflict, these lawyers modify or avoid the rules. Such circumstances are marked by a failure of neutrality to shield the attorney from feelings of personal responsibility for consequences of professional acts. Once neutrality falters, it becomes difficult to ignore personal imperatives that compete with role obligations. Almost invariably, prevention of harm to others plays a leading role in these situations where individual moral concern prevails over professional duty.

Of the lawyers we talked to, none occupied Position 4 lightly. Those who assume this risky posture understand the obligations of role and acknowledge the importance of the advocate's job in the legal system. They accept responsibility for diminished commitment to client, suspension of neutrality, and lessening of partisanship. A vast majority of the time, these lawyers meet role expectations and act as uncompromised counselors and advocates. Stance in Position 4 is taken only in extreme moral conflict. Under these circumstances, attorneys are willing to take the professional consequences of compromising role and personal responsibility for the implications of their actions.[9]

Constance McElroy describes a situation from her practice where consequences and personal morality push her to break with role. In a criminal case a battered wife refused to testify regarding repeated abuse because "she was too terrified." Faced with the possibility of the "prosecution going down the drain," Constance recounts how

sometimes we'll go for a deferred prosecution, stipulating family counseling and alcohol counseling and this and that and the other thing. I'm not supposed to do it. Now, I guess that's a moral issue because I'm technically, I suppose– am I subverting the law? The law says you can't do it. Judges say you can't do it. . . . (*Why do you choose that course?*) Because it's better than leaving people unprotected if it falls apart.

Constance goes on to reveal the type of care considerations that influence her decision not to follow the letter of the law. Contextual analysis of harm to specific people moves her beyond the narrow confines of role as she searches for a result that will benefit the individuals involved.

Let's say he's come home, and he's promised her he's never going to drink, and he hasn't been drinking, and she desperately needs the paycheck. She's got three little ones and no education herself – all those factors are very, very real. They just don't fit in a law book that says, "I'm sorry, you can't do it to prevent a different abuse." And if I can make him go to counseling and make him go to AA or the hospital for the alcohol problem, . . . or I'm going to put him in jail– I figure the kids are better off, and she's better off, that someday some insight might strike. It also means that if it does cave in in a week or two and she gets her face beat in again and goes to the shelter, that now I've got two prosecutions and she may be more likely to hold on next time.

This lawyer's actions are governed by the intent of the law, as filtered through a perspective of care which emphasizes not protection of rights but prevention of harm. From her care perspective, Constance identifies the long-term consequences of the situation: "The ramifications are so great in a situation like that. It's not just them getting beaten up, because then the children grow up and beat each other and then they – you know – you've got to do what you can." Because, for her, aggression signifies the "fracture of human connection,"[10] Constance responds to provide corrective help which keeps open the possibility of future healing. Rather than take refuge in her role to limit her involvement, she moves beyond professional obligation to make relationships safer for these people, and for their children.

When the interviewer starts to move to another question after she has described this incident, Constance interrupts to add:

One thing before I forget: I think the moral issue there comes in quitting too soon. I mean, that's where I would feel the moral crunch. I would have questioned whether I gave up too soon if I dismissed it. (*Why would that raise a moral issue?*) Because I would keep wondering if there was something that I could do to fix it. I feel like I should do it; and if I don't do it, then I'm wrong. That's where I think the moral thing is. (*What do you mean, to fix it?*) To assist people in dealing with those problems. By not giving up . . . doing what you can.

The moral "should" for this attorney is a responsibility to exert herself in order to protect others from harm, a moral obligation for continuing involvement until she has done all that is possible to help. This position contrasts with that of the person who subjugates personal morality and looks for role to define and limit responsibility.

One of the advantages of role perspective is that it greatly simplifies the moral universe of the attorney. As we see in the battering situation, once Constance moves beyond the moral considerations appropriate to the world of an advocate, circumstances become more complex and her own choices less clear. The security of institutional rules is sacrificed for the freedom to make an individual moral choice.

Marlene Rivers describes another situation in which moral complexity springs from broadening of perspective. Her client wanted child custody under circumstances in which Marlene foresaw harm to the child and little chance of success for the client. Marlene felt

torn between my obligation to represent my client, and to do things according to her wishes, and my feeling of responsibility to the child who really– The child is not my client. I could have possibly gone to court and forced the father to get an attorney on the other side and fight it out. Then I could say [to the client], "Gee, I'm sorry, but you lost."

Instead, she talked her client into another course of action, and in so doing, she sensed "betraying my client to a certain extent." Her commitment to client comes from the "code of professional responsibility" and the "obligation to do the best you can with your expertise." Her obligation to the child "comes from my innate feelings of responsibility to a higher order, I suppose you'd call it." Asked what she means by a higher order, Marlene elaborates:

Well, that the child didn't have anybody basically representing him. At least in this case the child didn't, and there was not enough money around to enable us to get lawyers for everybody including the child. So where did it come from? I just felt that it was necessary to protect the child because the child didn't have anybody to protect him.

While Marlene did not bend legal rules in order to follow personal morality, she did reshape the advocate role to accommodate her concern for the child. Partisanship and neutrality yielded to her own moral judgment that the best solution is the one that enables all parties to continue to relate with the least bitterness.

In our conversations, Position 4 emerges most often when the children in the second hypothetical dilemma were placed in danger of serious physical harm.[11] Faced with unacceptable consequences to especially vulnerable people, some lawyers declare that they would break confidentiality, even when told that the situation hypothesized would not allow this under the Rules of Professional Conduct. One attorney bluntly states that she would reveal the damaging client letter because "the right of my client to have the confidence respected only goes to the point where I know that those confidences will not harm someone else. . . . At that point my duty to the children would override my ethical duty to my client." Kathryn Colby is also adamant about her obligation to depart from role duties. "I'd probably manage to get fired, whereupon I'd be free to go to the guardian *ad litem* and tell them why I got off the case. If they asked me to testify to that effect, I would." If she could not get fired, she "would probably express my concern to the guardian *ad litem* indirectly and, yes, it would be a breach of confidentiality."

Tom Wooding, who throughout the rest of the interview was in Positions 1 and 2, likewise moves to a Position 4 when the possibility of physical harm to children conflicts with his role obligation. "If I deem that they are in serious jeopardy, I'd report them," even at the risk of "being sued and the whole works, yes. . . . Not only that, I'd take a copy of the letter to make sure I had it." This is the same attorney who earlier talked of wearing an "advocate mask." The efficacy of the mask changes dramatically when personal morality is put to an extreme test, when "I'm the only one who knows and the danger of damage is very, very high. The only one who can do something about it is me. So it's very different. At that point the mask that I've had on disintegrates, at some point when I realize the real danger and I'm the only one who can stop it." He contrasts this situation with a criminal case where the system "is set up with the police and protections and the prosecutor. We have a lot of people involved in the system. . . . They all know. There are a hundred people who know. . . . The FBI knows." In the custody case he is the only one with knowledge of possible harm, and that knowledge brings special responsibility, special enough to destroy his usual mask of neutrality and distance.

Mel Moore responds to the hypothesized danger to children not by a temporary departure from role but by abandoning career: "You're poking around in all the very areas that made me not want to lawyer any more, among other things." Faced with harm to the children and an inability to withdraw from the case, he says, "I'd quit. I'd quit practicing law. I would. I would. I mean I would just say to the judge, 'I'm not going to do this, your Honor. I mean, if you want to bring disciplinary action against me for that, let'er rip.'" This is not a flippant statement by this lawyer, for in fact he recently quit practicing law because "the whole system is directed to the wrong goals. I had a deep philosophical problem with the whole concept of lawyering in that sense."

Attorneys who forsake the requirements of role in order to honor competing moral claims discuss relationships with clients in terms similar to those of lawyers in Position 3: active, involved concern; a tendency to see clients as whole human beings; the willingness to

deal with clients as people rather than as legal problems. I don't think you can dichotomize people like that when they're emoting right in front of you. You can't say, "Listen, I don't want to hear about that; take it to a counselor; let's just stick to the legal problems." Half the time they don't even know what the legal problems are and they're all intertwined with the emotional problems. It's up to me to sift those things out.

In our discussions, attorneys who occupy Position 4 demonstrate a very high degree of care reasoning,[12] which provides the alternative perspective necessary to overcome the persuasiveness of the lawyer's role. Perhaps more confident in discarding neutrality, lawyers in Position 4 claim the freedom to act independently of role and in accord with what they perceive as higher dictates. Such unbounded individuality allows the attorney to be true to self, with all of the private and public benefits of such a posture: personal integrity, psychological wholeness, resolution of moral tension, and broadened value considerations in the public arena, including the possibility of challenging the public ethical order. There are also losses: damage to career, isolation, becoming unmoored from historical and community wisdom, masking immorality as renegade morality, injury to a legal system on which depends much that is valuable in our society. As we show in the two concluding chapters, we believe the extremes of Position 4 can be avoided without either giving up its benefits or running the risks that it entails.

The four positions: responsibility and relationship to society

Our interviews reveal a telling relationship among the four positions and the amount of care reasoning used by the attorneys with whom we spoke. Strong role identification and little or no moral tension characterize Positions 1 and 2. Attorneys in these positions have a relatively low degree of care reasoning and a high utilization of rights thinking. In Positions 3 and 4, strength of role identity diminishes and moral tension rises. The percentage of care responses correspondingly increases. A graph relating the four positions to degree of care response shows a linear rise in care thinking as the number of the position rises.[13]

We conclude from this that lawyers identify more easily with role when they have a strong rights orientation. This is not surprising, since, as we noted in Chapter 1, the premises of the legal system closely parallel those of the morality of rights. Both share concern for fairness, equality, procedural regularity, integrity of rules, and the duty to prevent interference with autonomous others. Like a hand in a glove, rights-oriented lawyers fit snugly into professional role. Moral tension is absent because personal and professional values are in synchrony. Since the dictates of role and personal morality are mutually reinforcing, such an attorney does not frequently encounter thoughts of moral cost or role modification.

Conversely, a care-oriented lawyer fails to experience the same reinforcement from professional role. As the gap between personal and role moralities widens, identity with role becomes less comfortable and compensating strategies develop. When care increases, so does tension. Lawyers with a dominant morality of care feel more conflict with professional role, a conflict causing them to reassess the nature and scope of their responsibility as practicing attorneys. It remains to be seen whether this conflict can be generalized beyond the individual situation to a reassessment of elements of the legal system itself.

Lawyers in Positions 3 and 4 keep their personal morality as a vital force in decision making and maintain an expansive ethical vision. Although they regularly act as committed advocates, in certain situations they are able to make a broader perspective available to clients and to society. In doing this they infuse the cardinal virtues of care morality into the rights-oriented legal system so that avoidance of harm and preservation of relationships are given a place in legal thinking. Because legal decision making is often also moral decision making, this seems appropriate, given that care values are paramount in the moral lives of many people in our society.

The four positions we have described represent a spectrum rather than a set of discrete boxes. Lawyers' understanding of the relationship of role and personal morality leads to a distribution of attorneys along the spectrum. The range of positions can be summarized by tracing the changing meanings of responsibility it encapsulates. For an attorney with maximum role identification, responsibility means fulfilling professional commitments in order to protect the rights of others. The lawyer assumes a social model of autonomous individuals, and exercises caution not to interfere with their rights and independence. The prohibition against "playing God" restrains conduct. A characteristic response to questions about personal responsibility is "I didn't make the rules that you play by. The government did." Since the advocate is just a player following somebody else's rules, "I've never had any qualms about defending and getting off a person who is guilty." Because these lawyers relate to clients from a professional distance, and speak the words of another rather than their own, they readily shed responsibility for professional acts. To lawyers in Position 1, moral ought is defined by parameters of role. The client is considered a legal problem.

For a lawyer who subjugates personal morality, responsibility differs only in degree from Position 1. Responsibility still lodges in the system rather than in the individual practitioner. The hallmark of responsibility is self-restraint, the avoidance of acts that interfere with the rights of others. But for an attorney in Position 2, there may be the beginnings of a struggle not to feel responsible.

In Position 3, responsibility widens from fulfillment of role to include responsiveness to other people. Self-restraint is replaced by the imperative to extend the self to administer to what the lawyer believes are the needs of others who share the social matrix. The feeling of responsibility is personal and may include experiencing moral costs. Relationship to clients is active and involved; they are whole persons with a variety of problems, legal and emotional.

A lawyer in Position 4 departs from strictures of role under compelling conditions. Responsibility for professional acts resides within the self rather than within the system. In certain circumstances, these attorneys "play God," infusing their own values into the attorney-client relationship. Neither the system nor the client is the final arbiter of what is right. Responsibility is active, personal, and involving.

Moral developmental psychology generates another way to understand these four role identity positions. Lawrence Kohlberg formulates three levels of moral thinking distinguished by differing perceptions of the relation between the self and the rules of society: (1) preconventional, in which a person does not feel like a member of society but accepts social rules as externally imposed; (2) conventional, in which a person experiences the self as a member of society and accepts its rules as mutually agreed upon and inherently valuable; and (3) postconventional, in which an individual assumes a more universal perspective and makes moral judgments considering, but independent of, group norms.[14] This schema is helpful, since we are exploring just such a relationship of individual attorneys to a system of rules defined by professional role.

Attorneys in Position 1, of maximum role identification, speak with a conventional voice fully accepting the tenets of professional role.[15] They see themselves as part of a social system and comply with its conventions. Being a good member of society is synonymous with being a good attorney; both entail fulfilling obligations of role and complying with rules of the system. These attorneys speak frequently of the rules of the game, which they must observe for the legal system to function smoothly and for them to discharge their primary responsibility of client representation. The rules are rooted in a social contract. To attain equal treatment and fair play, the rules must be followed without regard to personal moral considerations.

Lawyers meet role expectations because they agree that this is the best way to facilitate accepted moral ends.

Positions 2 and 3 are characterized by tension that results in subjugation of personal morality and perhaps in moral cost. These are transitional positions between conventional and postconventional thinking. A perspective outside of social convention questions the rules of the game, but the powerful social expectation inherent in the attorney role still prevails. Attorneys in these positions use both societal and universal perspectives, both conventional and postconventional stances. Personal moral standards compete with institutional and professional values. In the end, behavior yields to the convention of social judgment, but tension persists as long as conduct is questioned from the perspective of personal morality. While deference to role comes more quickly in Position 2, postconventional thinking remains available to lawyers in Position 3, as a source of both tension and enhanced moral perspective.

In the minimum role identification of Position 4, postconventional attorneys stand beyond the social contract and make independent judgments about morally correct conduct. Rules of the legal system and standards of professional conduct are weighed but no longer provide a final answer to what is morally right. This risky enterprise lacks the support of institutionalized social sanction. Although attorneys in this position may carefully evaluate the implications for themselves, the legal system, and their clients, they nonetheless act with independent judgment and control. Having passed the bar examination is not a sufficient credential to become a philosopher king, and it is doubtful whether society should or would give someone the power that goes with a license to practice law without imposing at least some of the restrictions of defined professional role.[16] The goal is to provide an attorney with both boundaries and freedom, to alter present structures so that tension is less when a lawyer has access to both care morality and the accumulated wisdom of the legal system.

How do care-oriented lawyers, particularly women, adjust to the practice of law amid structures and attitudes long the province of male, rights-oriented thinkers? Here our concern is not with response to a given legal task or moral quandary but, rather, to the whole set of mores, forms, and assumptions that underlie the legal apparatus. Moving from individual instances, the problem here is reconciling systems of perceiving, valuing, and responding.

The rules of the game: preparation of the players

When lawyers talk about their work, they commonly liken it to a game. People in other professions – physicians, teachers, therapists, ministers, scientists – seldom use the term "game" to describe what they do. For attorneys, the metaphor is apt, in part, because law can be understood as a contest with rules, winners, and losers. An attitude of emotional detachment reinforces the idea that law is a game to be played for its own sake; the adversary nature of law makes it easy to maintain personal distance.[1] From an attorney's point of view, moral neutrality is easily reinterpreted to mean "it's just a game," even though the stakes are often high and lawyers get deeply invested in the contest. When taking part in a game, it is hard not to become preoccupied with winning, by whatever the prescribed rules. And it is difficult to examine the premises behind the rules when they provide the parameters for play. If we take the game metaphor seriously, what does it tell us about the nature of the contest, about qualifications to play, about training of the players and about who owns the game?

In 1932, Swiss psychologist Jean Piaget observed that childhood games offer a window for understanding the moral development of children. He noted marked gender differences, especially regarding how children relate to game rules. Boys stick to the rules, resorting only to "legal elaborations," whereas girls emphasize harmony and continually invent new rules to suit their play. Of girls' attitudes toward rules, Piaget wrote, "A rule is good so long as the game repays it."[2] When faced with an argument over the rules, girls end the game, starting over or finding something else to do; boys argue their way through the dispute with continual references to the rules of the game. Girls seek to preserve the relationships of the players, while the boys maintain the rules. Taking boys as the standard, Piaget judged girls as lacking: "The most superficial observation is sufficient to show that in the main, the legal sense is far less developed in little girls than in boys."[3] By preferring boys as the norm, Piaget mirrored a common cultural practice of valuing one moral orientation at the expense of the other, whether the games be childhood play or law.

Recent work on children's play confirms that at an early age girls and boys interact differently.[4] Girls choose smaller play groups, often consisting of two or three "best friends" whose interactions are based on shared confidences. By comparison, boys' groups are larger and tend to center on some competitive, goal-directed activity with clear rules and with winners and losers. Boys learn to "depersonalize the attack," to enter adversary relationships with friends and cooperate with people they dislike. Whereas team games teach boys emotional discipline and self-control, traditional girls' games reinforce nurturant skills, expression of personal feelings, and cooperation rather than competition. In summary, girls play more than boys; boys "game" more than girls.[5]

From early childhood, then, our culture prepares females and males for different roles. For boys, prelaw training begins almost from birth – in the home, on playing fields, in relation to peers. For girls, these same influences instill different values, different ways of assimilating and responding to life's experiences. Each gender receives its own gifts, its own limitations, and its own ways of making sense of life. Experiences of most boys prepare them for a world of advocacy, stoic detachment, autonomy, and suspension of judgment.

Girls' experiences usually instruct them for roles requiring sensitivity to others' feelings, cooperation, involvement, and contextual understanding.

Parents and coaches regularly tell boys that sports build character, teach respect for rules, engender a healthy sense of competition, and generally prepare them for life in a depersonalized, adversary society. Mentors might also add that competitive sports supply the first stage of prelaw training. Until recently, relatively few girls got this same message or childhood practice for skills useful in the lawyer game. Though these generalizations about early acculturation for gender role admit of many exceptions, they nonetheless describe patterns deeply rooted in the history of our culture.

It's a man's game: pressure to conform

Women entering the practice of law find that mores of that game bear the imprint of boys' play rather than that of girls. Simply put, in subtleties of custom, structure, and decorum, law is still a man's game. In its Summary of Hearings, the American Bar Association Commission on Women in the Profession (1988) stated:

> While several witnesses emphasized the great strides women have made in entering and succeeding in the profession, most participants at the hearings expressed frustration and disillusionment that barriers are still great and that progress has been far slower than expected. Witnesses cautioned that we must not be lulled into complacency about the status of women in the profession simply because the numbers of women entering the profession continues to increase.
>
> The barriers women face consist of overt discriminatory behavior, subtle attitudes and institutional structures. Although several witnesses indicated that many blatant forms of discrimination have been eradicated, other individuals presented a significant amount of testimony about instances of overt discrimination. . . .
>
> The bottom line, according to the witnesses, is that progress has been made but obstacles remain. The issues that should be addressed by the Commission are not legal, but structural and attitudinal.[6]

Not only must care-oriented lawyers face the puzzle of integrating their moral perspective into a rights-oriented system, but women attorneys have the additional task of accomplishing this in an atmosphere of discriminatory attitudes and structures. Beginning in law school, women learn that feminine ways of participating are not always welcome. Given that qualities learned by women at home and in play make them vulnerable in a predominantly male profession, one solution women have attempted is to eradicate "feminine" characteristics. For example, a female partner in a large firm advises, "Don't think of yourself, or allow anyone to think of you, as anything but a hard-driving, capable lawyer."[7] The safest way to success is emulation of males, even to the extent of learning to "speak louder and lower," and "actively becoming an intimidator."[8] Even clothes, a worldwide symbol of gender difference, are to be homogenized to the male mode. "Dress and talk in a conservative and professional style. Avoid wrap-around skirts, casual shoes or hair color changes. Dress like a lawyer, in a conservative suit. Don't chew gum."[9]

A general social devaluation of femininity prepares women entering law to separate from the disliked characteristics of their sex and to align with the culture against feminine attributes within themselves. Particularly in the legal profession, which prides itself on objectivity, professionalism, and combativeness, traditional feminine traits are unacceptable. For many women, this results in an internal tension of "me/not me" when they define themselves as feminine yet try to negate within themselves the stereotypes that discount them in the legal world.

The law as a jealous mistress not only demands that women rid themselves of feminine characteristics but also demands a commitment to work that may be incompatible with the place of relationships in the lives of care-thinking attorneys. As law firms are more and more operated as is any other business for profit, and beginning lawyers can command up to $75,000 starting pay, there is little room for divided loyalties, especially when an attorney enters with already suspect characteristics. That women may place relationships over professional success threatens both the old paradigm of law as a profession and the emerging perception of law as a business.[10] The American Bar Association Commission on Women in the Profession (1988) reports:

Several witnesses emphasized that the problems facing lawyers of both sexes, but especially women, in trying to combine professional demands with important human relationships and children, involve questioning the values and ethics of the profession. The concern is that, at a time when the pressures are growing for law firms to be successful businesses and for lawyers to produce even greater numbers of billable hours, lawyers are becoming dehumanized, unable to relate to clients and family members.[11]

In a similar vein, a woman lawyer, who advocates following the traditional male path to success, writes:

While most male lawyers are assumed to be serious and to be embarking on a lifelong career, females still are viewed as question marks who may quit and stay home to raise children. Each woman, therefore, must establish herself as a committed and competent professional and convince each judge and opposing counsel that she means business and is in the profession to stay.

Top quality, hard work will do this. Work longer and harder on tough assignments. Don't shirk late hours or weekend projects. Don't go home to cook dinner – or if you do, don't tell anyone. Get the work done on time, and in the best possible manner.[12]

Old stereotypes that women are less rational and more emotional undoubtedly contribute to the requirement that they have to play longer and harder to earn the right to compete on equal terms.[13] Family roles must be kept invisible, so as not to intrude on professional life. For women in law, rejecting a one-sided emphasis on professionalism in order to affirm interrelatedness, cooperation, and involved concern carries the liability of being dismissed as a "question mark" within the profession.

Yet for a woman to play the law game as a man does violates sex role norms, a transgression that is negatively judged by others and that can create anxiety in the transgressor.[14] To fit the stereotypical image of an advocate means being argumentative and aggressive, characteristics that are traditionally condemned in women. If a woman chooses to reject the usual lawyer image and follow a less combative form of participation, she may be labeled too feminine, and others may doubt her fiber as a tough lawyer. Speaking of the double bind female lawyers face in playing a man's game while held to standards of feminine behavior, a male attorney testified to the New Jersey Supreme Court Task Force on Women in the Courts:

A woman attorney must walk the fine line between being feminine and being assertive. She is held to a different standard than a man. If she is too feminine she is accused of trying to use it to her advantage and is therefore resented, but if she is equally assertive to her male counterpart, she is accused of being too aggressive. To their credit, most of the women attorneys with whom I have had dealings have been able to walk that fine line, but it is usually with much more pressure than is experienced by a man.[15]

This "damned if you do, damned if you don't" walking-the-line metaphor was also used by the ABA Commission on Women in the Profession (1988): "Individuals . . . testified that women walk a fine line between being regarded as too feminine (and thus not tough, lawyer-like or smart) or too tough (and thus unfeminine or not the kind of woman male colleagues feel comfortable relating to)."[16]

Saundra Douglas, a lawyer in our study, is aware of demands for walking the line and of the costs of erring on either side:

I picture myself as a pretty low-key person, in the sense that I don't think of myself as terribly strident or aggressive. In fact, that's one of the issues women as lawyers have to face, trying to be human and also letting people know they can't walk on you. If I have more trouble with one than the other, I think it's being afraid that people will walk on me. There are a couple of women who are lawyers who I think kind of deliberately made the choice that they'd be as aggressive as all get out in order not to face the stereotype of women not being able to stand up to combat. In this community I think people were just sort of waiting for other women to fulfill that stereotype.

As women experience a clash between their values and those of the legal game, they are beginning to express discomfort with what it takes to be a successful lawyer.[17] The conflict surfaced at Yale Law School in 1984 when a number of female and minority law students documented their "dissatisfaction and alienation" in an open letter to the law school community.[18] As our interviews might have predicted, they identified alienation as the opposite of feeling "connectedness, belonging, engagement." Noting their success as law students, the women asserted that "for many this success comes at a price – a price, paid gradually and often silently, of alienation and disillusionment." The students cited the "combative, monopolizing and self-promoting style of discussion" encouraged in the classroom as a source of alienation.

The voice that troubles us is the monolithic, confident voice of "insiders" who see themselves as the norm and who have (often unconsciously) little tolerance for our interest in diversity and difference. This voice, tone, style is often defended as "the way lawyers speak." . . . To the extent that this *is* the way lawyers speak, *we* must conclude that we cannot be lawyers – or that we cannot be ourselves.[19]

These students bring a perspective to the law that generates a compelling dilemma: Forsake the law or forsake the self. Because the

adversary structure of legal discourse precludes the voice of cooperation and interdependence, women and men with such an orientation
risk alienation. They are the outsiders, and theirs is the different
voice. These women recognize that law school offers only one alternative of how to lawyer. If they want to practice law in different
ways, they must invent those for themselves. With insight perhaps
most feasible before law school has fully done its work, the Yale
women are saying that legal education has an obligation to help
invent alternatives to an adversarial style and not simply to excom-
municate those with a different perspective.[20]

Both we and the Yale law students identify a set of problems that
fall disproportionately on women. In our study, female attorneys
most often experience the gap between personal morality and the
role they are supposed to play. What price do women pay for following the male and, at present, the only officially sanctioned version of
the lawyer role? Are there other alternatives compatible with remain-
ing in the profession? Can care-oriented women reshape the role to
make it acceptable to their personal values? Is it possible to protect
both relationships and rules, to be caring advocates?

Women we interviewed describe differing patterns of adjustment
to the practice of law. For the most part, all play by the rules of the
game, but at the same time they acknowledge conflict and the need to
modify professional expectations. The incompatible demands of personal and professional imperatives led most of the female attorneys
with whom we talked to choose the stressful challenge of trying
simultaneously to meet divergent standards – the rights orientation
of the legal system and the responsiveness orientation of female development. A central problem for all care-oriented women is what to
do with their personal morality when they enter the practice of law.
The official solution, tried by some women, is to adapt to the lawyer
role: talk like a (male) lawyer, think like a (male) lawyer, act like a
(male) lawyer. This solution contrasts with other adjustments wom-
en describe – shaping the role to fit their own values and trying to
live up to the standards of both professional role and personal morality. The latter two adjustments are attempts to maintain a care orientation while taking on the characteristics of role. Because care remains, women pursuing either of these courses must decide how the

responsiveness and concerns of care fit into the life of a practicing lawyer.[21]

Emulating the male model: denial of the relational self

We begin with the story of Kathryn Colby, a woman who tried to deny a part of herself in order to be a lawyer by men's rules. As much as any woman we interviewed, she accepted the male model and tried to mold herself to fit its dictates. She did this well and was rewarded with professional success. We use her story to illustrate both the pressures women face in trying to copy the traditional model of law practice and the personal costs of doing so. Changing the self to conform with what the system demands produces an archetypal, successful lawyer.

At age thirty-six, Kathryn Colby had practiced law in a small, well-established firm for six years. Hers was a diverse practice, including personal injury, criminal, business, and domestic relations law. The legal community evidenced its respect by electing her president of the local bar association. Kathryn was a role model of today's successful, self-made woman. "I have women who have called me almost on a daily basis, just to have contact with someone who is out in the world and surviving." Emphasizing how the law "makes me feel important," she says that she derives a lot of satisfaction from her work, "more than I thought possible."

Kathryn portrays herself as a dedicated, hardworking professional who subjugates personal concerns to role demands. She describes how "criminal attorneys have a real tight spot . . . characterized by whether you would represent the guilty person . . . who's atrocious and his crime's atrocious, and he's psychotic on top of that." Though she recognizes the difficulty that defending such a person presents for some attorneys,

it does not pose a problem for me. Of course you do. That's your job. You're an advocate. It's not your decision whether they're guilty; that's not the way it works. The jury over there makes that decision. It's your job to present the case and make sure that the person — if they have a defense — has an opportunity to present it. That's your job. You're not that person. There's no reason for you to feel badly about it.

Kathryn maintains distance by seeing herself as part of the legal system, and by following the rules. Turning to an actual case in which she defended a man accused of raping and murdering an elderly woman, Kathryn shows herself as a neutral partisan:

The standard that I had in my own mind was, if the defendant was my brother, what would I be doing. Would I be doing more or would I be doing less, and that was the kind of standard. If it were me or if it were someone that I truly, truly cared about that was in his position, what would I be doing? . . . Within the budget I had, how much work would I be doing? And I did it just like that. I shut down my private practice and did the case for several months. And that's what I would have done if it had been my brother sitting there. So that was sort of the standard. I would have done the same job if that person had been my own brother.

To describe the intensity of commitment to client, Kathryn compares it with the loyalty of family relationships. It is as though Antigone's devotion to her brother became the standard for the lawyer's commitment to duty.

How did Kathryn become this ardent advocate? She describes law school as a turning point, as the replacement of one way of seeing with another:

I felt it happening in law school. I honestly felt it happening. I know people thought I was crazy, but I can remember first-year law school — I have this feeling when I am being forced to change my set and I can feel it. It's hard to describe but I felt it. And I remember saying to my friends, "They're fucking with your brain; can't you feel it?" I could feel them changing my perspective on situations, and yet I honestly think that happens. I don't think you ever look at situations the same after you go through three years of legal training. I'm not saying it's bad or anything like that. It's probably in many respects better.

Kathryn's response confirms that her previous ways of seeing and interpreting the world were not tolerated by her new environment. To opt for the norms of the legal system, she had to deny her culturally formed feminine ways of knowing and relating to the world.[22]

This adjustment to law by suppressing a part of herself establishes a central motif in her practice — the subordination of personal to professional life. To fulfill the role of the dedicated advocate, Kathryn describes how "there's a whole side of me that stays at home," which is her "affectionate side." In fact, professional life so overshadowed everything else that the affectionate side became nearly dormant. "I just denied everything in my life except work." The affectionate, feeling side is incompatible with "conducting myself in a professional manner," which she finds is essential for women in the practice of law.

Kathryn explores the roots of her decision to become a lawyer when she describes her desire to differentiate herself from a mother whom she saw as devalued:

Coming from my background, I was climbing, I was scratching, I was trying to get out of what I saw was going to be my destiny in terms of married with children, and a husband that got up and went to work every day, where cleaning the house was it. I was afraid of that. I made a decision at a young age: I did not want a life like my mother's. . . . I can remember thinking, I don't want to live like my mother. My father, he goes places, he does things, he meets people, he goes to the office, he's an important person there, and I couldn't figure out what my mother was doing.

Choosing law, she rejected the dependence and unimportance she saw in her mother's life in favor of the self-reliance and excitement she perceived in her father's world. Kathryn adopted the culture's negative attitude toward her mother and turned that attitude toward what she identifies as the feminine aspects of herself. She associates femininity with an orientation to relationships, and relationships with vulnerability and dependence. "I joined the National Organization [for] Women in 1971 – that was my senior year in college – and I was definitely getting the impression that if you married and stayed home you were settling for less." Kathryn's denial of traditional feminine attributes fits perfectly with her decision to enter a profession that likewise negates femininity and that makes demands experienced as incompatible with intimate relationships.[23]

In addition to a childhood that taught her to devalue her mother, a second influence leading this woman to subordinate relationships to work was a marriage that ended in divorce while she was in law school. In her mind, the divorce confirmed her belief that close relationships and career are incompatible. "I took full responsibility for the divorce. I thought it was definitely my fault, and I'd obviously chosen a career over marriage and family; therefore, I was not entitled to marriage and family." She thought that her husband could not "handle it, because I was succeeding at this, and therefore he wanted out." After the divorce, Kathryn denied her own healthy needs for relatedness and intimacy: "Particularly after I went through my own divorce, I had decided for myself for various reasons that I did not need anything or anyone and I had never said 'I need you' to anyone in my life, because I would not allow myself to need. I would not acknowledge dependency, because I had to be in control."

This inner psychological stance of self-protection against the vulnerability of loving was reinforced by a professional environment that demands unwavering commitment to career. Kathryn's belief that the divorce was her fault mirrors the social norm that women are responsible for the success or failure of their intimate relationships. The convergence of outer factors and inner beliefs influenced her decision to suppress her relational self and to pursue independence, autonomy, and career success.

Saying that she feels "OK" about elevating her professional life at the expense of her affectionate self, Kathryn notes that "if I had children it would become increasingly difficult to break out of that segment of myself, or to have enough time." Her decision against having children was not made simply on the basis of her own desires and needs but involved a choice between conflicting demands from seemingly incompatible worlds. Assessing the requirements of fulfilling the lawyer role made the practical realities of simultaneously raising children seem impossible.

Equating marriage and children with settling for less, she reiterates her decision not to have children unless she could have what men have, a "wife-servant" to take care of them.

How would you feel if you had a partner who was going to take this extended leave of absence to have children or who was working part days because of their obligation for children, or would have to cancel appointments because their child was sick. I don't have a wife to take care of those things. Those guys go down with their little brown bag and have lunch in the lunchroom. I don't have a wife to pack my lunch in the morning. I mean they have this servant. I don't have that, and it would be very difficult to maintain the level that I'm maintaining with children.

Kathryn recognizes that women in law are forced to accommodate their private lives to the public sphere, just as men have had to do. Yet, traditionally, men have had wives to take care of the private sphere, the world of children and family. She designates the private sphere as the appropriate domain of a servant, clearly less valuable than the job of a lawyer. While Kathryn describes the decision not to have children as very difficult, she speculates that her solace in old age will come not from relationships with family but from feelings of "having helped somebody" in her lawyer role: "I figure, when I'm an old lady sitting in a rest home and people are looking at pictures of their kids, I'll get out my folder of thank-you notes. I have saved every thank-you note that I have ever gotten. The first one I got was from a little old lady. It was a handmade note, had glue, sprinkle stuff on it; I mean, it was just incredible." In this vision of the future, she ends up alone, finding her continuing connection to others through memories of her contributions to their lives as a lawyer.

To flourish as an attorney, Kathryn subordinates relationships to achievement, love to work, femininity to professionalism. In her words, she feels she "was sort of sacrificed in terms of creating options for women." Giving up a part of herself in the interest of career, Kathryn paves the way for others. She opts for a new feminine standard of achievement rather than the standards of subservience, self-sacrifice, and dullness which she sees exemplified in her mother's life.

Although the conflict between her relational needs and her professional goals was evident, Kathryn manifested no outward ambivalence about being an attorney. It appeared that she had successfully resolved the tension by leaving her relational needs out, by becoming the model of the successful lawyer. A year and a half after the first interview, however, we were surprised to hear that she was "taking an extended leave to develop the personal side of my life, which means separation for a time from the demands of practice." We reinterviewed her and discovered why her adjustment to law had not worked: "I am making room in my life for priorities other than work. Giving priorities to a relationship is something that I had never done; and so, when I say my thinking has come full circle, it means coming back around to that. Because at some point in my life – earlier on, I think – I did in fact give relationships priority." As in the movement of a pendulum, a one-sided emphasis on profession is balanced by a corrective swing back toward a personal life that includes relationships. Kathryn appears to be picking up the pieces of a shattered "home world" – a prior self cast aside in the socialization of law school and legal practice.

Talking about her unsatisfactory adaptation to the rules of the game, Kathryn describes how repressed relational needs haunted her with two images. One was

this cartoon image that really bothered me; and what it was, was a woman who is about thirty-five years old, unmarried, without children, getting out of her BMW, complete with little tie, briefcase, with money, going into a shrink's office and saying, "I don't know why I am unhappy." You know, it is just so classic. I have accomplished these things, and I don't know why I am unhappy.

The other picture was "of myself on the [judicial] bench, unmarried, without children, as a dried-up prune." These images of herself, with all the outward manifestations of success, depict isolation and sadness rather than the culturally promised satisfaction of achievement. From these visions, she sees "the things that are missing, of course, are any kind of love and what we call a meaningful relationship, a growth situation with another individual, totally missing."

In her second interview, Kathryn comments on her earlier adjustment to the role through denial of relational needs:

It appears to me that the law is a real bastion of male dominance, and so you adopt all those trappings. You see, my goal in life up until a year and a half ago— my goal in life was to be respected by my peers, and the goal that motivated me through law school was I wanted to be taken seriously. My mother was someone who was never taken seriously. You assume education will achieve that for you, so you pursue that route. You get into a profession, and for me I just denied everything in my life except work. I was a classic workaholic, and it was just denial not of just feminine realities or needs, but of human needs. Because of the age that I was in, my confusion was that I thought it was feminine and I thought that's what I was denying, and then I would achieve success and pursue things, just as a male. All I had to do was deny the feminine, OK? Well, as I come along, I've decided that what I'm denying is not necessarily male or female but is human, and to be a whole person, you don't walk around denying need and love and nurturing and those kinds of relationship things. I just denied all that because I was intent on succeeding. That's what I did, and it took a couple of major traumas for me to step back and look at it.

Kathryn perceives that traditional roles have relegated women to dependence and nonachievement in a market economy. Femininity loomed as an obstacle to success in law. As she begins to examine what it means to be a whole person, she reclaims the formerly denied aspects of herself, renaming them as human rather than feminine needs. Her goal of success also comes under the scrutiny of a broadened vision that reveals her prior notion of succeeding as limited and constricting to her development.

When Kathryn decided to take a leave from the law, she had become a member of the first and only all-woman firm in the town where she practiced. Simultaneously with Kathryn's decision to get married, the second of three partners announced that she was pregnant and would likewise temporarily withdraw from private practice.[24] Kathryn recounts: "So here's this woman law firm, and we're disbanding after two years because of these life changes, and I'm going, 'Oh, my God, everything I have tried to strive for in terms of women being accepted into this profession I am just flushing down the toilet by doing this.' " After remarking to the third partner, "Can you imagine the butt of the jokes we are going to be?" she put things into perspective:

My partner pointed out that firms disband all the time. They fall apart because of their disagreements, their pay, their disregard for each other. I mean, there are terrible reasons for law firms to disband. She says, marriage and childbirth are not bad reasons. So I got to thinking about that, and I thought more about it, and I thought, you know, that's true.

Kathryn's solution to dealing with the rules of the game is not every woman's solution. In her reexamination of how she fulfills the lawyer role, Kathryn replaces emulation of the societal model for lawyer success with self-awareness and reflective choice as the basis for her decision making. Her struggle to define herself is not simplified by this change, but the solution of her conflict becomes inner-directed and authentic rather than dictated by external standards.

As Kathryn's experience indicates, society presents people with competing alternatives for adulthood, either achievement or relationships. Traditionally this problem was solved by division of responsibility within a marriage. While men achieved, women knit together the fabric of social relationships. Each gender was denied the rewards and benefits of the other's world. With changing social mores, this arrangement has broken down. Because feminine roles and characteristics are still socially devalued, there is relatively little pressure on men to assume responsibilities in the private sphere or to take on feminine attributes. On the other hand, the traditionally masculine domain of competitive achievement is increasingly seen as desirable to men and women alike. The result is that women are told that to achieve adult social worth they must be professional and homemaker, competitive and nurturing. Rather than seeing the public and private as interdependent and continuous, society teaches women and men alike to accommodate their private lives to the demands of professional role. For women, this often translates into the experience of impossible demands from each sphere.

Kathryn's conflict raises a central question for women in the professions: How is it possible to have both love and work? The social context presents women with choices that seem mutually exclusive and so limits the framework for thinking about alternatives. Dichotomous thinking fails to apprehend a reality of paradox, contradiction, and change. Not only are both sides of the choice between relationships and career valued, but increasingly for women, neither alone is sufficient for satisfaction or self-esteem. The students at Yale Law School and many of the women with whom we spoke seek social support and approval for new arrangements that will address the dilemma. Kathryn chose career, but was haunted by a need for relationships. She sees no way to be a lawyer without forfeiting relationships, and no way to have relationships without jeopardizing her career. For Kathryn, an integration of personal self and professional self may come from her plans to marry, take a leave, and then reenter practice with a new equilibrium of work and relationships.

Rather than conclude that there is something wrong with Kathryn's decision to quit the practice of law, we should try to understand how the role of lawyer as currently defined pushed her into an untenable position. She made this choice not only because of conflicting values but also because of the failure of the legal profession, like most of the rest of society, to respond to women entering the work force with the kind of imaginative, flexible structures needed to facilitate a merger of public and private obligations.

Splitting the self: a problem of background, foreground, and unity

Unlike Kathryn Colby, who, for a time, emulated the male model with all of its exclusivity, most of the women with whom we spoke try to combine care priorities and law. One strategy for both being a lawyer and preserving the values of the female world requires dividing the self into two parts – the attorney self and the personal self. At work, the attorney self dominates the foreground and the personal self remains subdued. Outside the office, positions are reversed. This allows the appropriate self to respond to situations suitable to its training and values. When the self is split in two, each part should have the opportunity to develop and remain proficient. Thus, the two parts of the self, each in its own compartment, should remain healthy and on call. At least this is the plan.

In fact, female attorneys told us of two related problems. First, at the office the relational, care-oriented self did not readily remain boxed in the background; rather, as the first learned morality of these women, it insisted on a more prominent role. The second problem was that of disunity. While conceptually neat, division of the self can lead to tension instead of mental peace. For these lawyers, compartmentalizing the personality and keeping care in the background are both stressful and often unsuccessful. Without integration, the results of a divided self are conflict and self-condemnation. At the same time, giving a care perspective full reign at work causes pain and threatens professionalism. Jennifer Hall, a lawyer in private practice, sums up the situation: "You feel like emotions are a luxury that you can't afford. But sometimes you want to afford them."

Describing her most difficult adjustment in practicing law, Jennifer talks of the necessity and the loss involved in dividing the self:

People are mean to you a lot. I hate it. . . . A lot of times I'll have a bad day, with a number of different people calling up and yelling at me about various things. And I try to put on a persona that makes it appear to them that it's water off a duck's back. And as I grow in the profession, my skin gets thicker, and it increasingly is water off a duck's back. In terms of doing the job and surviving emotionally, it's essential. I remember, when I was first starting out after law school, it was my first phone call, . . . and a secretary was really mean to me, and I got off the phone and cried because she'd been mean to me – you know, very calmly walked to the door of my office, closed the door, sat down and cried, wiped my eyes, and kept going. You can't do that every time somebody's mean to you. You know, you need to develop defenses so that those things go away. But as you do, that carries over to the part of me that's not a lawyer. That defense mechanism carries over into the part of me that's not a lawyer. . . . Recently some of my partners' wives worked in the office, and I was really struck by the difference between them and me. . . . I was always rushed. They had time to talk about how they felt; I never did. That was really an experience for me because I realized that here we were, women who'd had similar backgrounds and yet, because of our experiences, had taken off in real different directions, and I really was the hard-bitten career woman. At times it made me feel impatient with them because I had a job to do, damn it, and why were they so busy caring about how they felt? It made me envious of them too.

Jennifer lays out a series of contradictions between her private and public lives. To survive emotionally, she must develop a thick skin; yet the thick skin negatively affects her personal life. "Being a lawyer makes you real good at things like arguing and cross-examining, which are not especially positive elements to bring into a relationship."

Jennifer values the qualities associated with both being a lawyer and being a woman. Whereas the detached lawyer requires lack of emotional responsiveness, a kind of character defense against feeling, opposite qualities are required for interpersonal sensitivity. Jennifer describes how the solution of compartmentalization is not tidy. Qualities of lawyering spill over into personal relationships, sensitivity to relationships spill over into lawyering – with the result that she feels discordant in each sphere.[25]

In a like manner, Janice Orens attempts to reconcile a care orientation with the legal system by splitting her intuitive, personal self from her rational, objective lawyer self. She describes two different ways of knowing, one of which the law values and the other of which it devalues. Her most difficult adjustment in practicing law is

being rational and intellectual a lot of the time. I mean, this has nothing to do with what's hard about being a lawyer; this is what's hard *for me* about being a lawyer. . . . I'm just different now; my thought has– The emphasis on the intellectual and analytical has really changed me. I'm different, but I'm not lost to that. It's just harder to reach back for it.

Aware of the difficulty of reaching back for her feeling, intuitive self, Janice voices concern about ever being able to express that side within the law: "The legal system demands that you divorce emotion from reason in order to convince the reasoners, men, the judges, that you have a case. . . . The vast majority – and I'm proud to be among them – choose to use analysis solely and leave emotion out, because you're unsure whether that will work or turn off the person listening to you." Janice recognizes who owns the game and in whose language she must speak. Uncertain of its effect on those who may negatively judge it, she relegates her own voice to the background.

To rediscover personal unity, Janice requires retreat from the law's one-sided emphasis on rationality.

After law school and the bar exam, I took myself up into the mountains for a week, and I couldn't feel; I couldn't feel. And I'd always gone to the mountains backpacking to— It would take a couple of days, but I would get the feeling of being— of a unit, a part of a unity. And I couldn't feel that at all. All I could see was this sort of poster picture of beautiful scenery, and that wasn't must satisfaction. I couldn't feel. It took a long time, a week of sitting around, then being at a girlfriend's place on a lake, and sitting under the rocks and swimming all day and watching the sun go down, talking to the herons – you know, just dealing with nothing but physical sensations and animals. . . . I had darkened out my brain somehow – I'm serious. It felt silly, but it was that much of a number I did to myself. I had overextended – had just overemphasized the intellectual.

Analytic thinking in law requires objectivity, skepticism, and impersonal reasoning, which effectively separate the knower from what is known. This impersonal way of knowing temporarily alienated Janice's ability to feel. It also eroded her sense of identity as part of a larger context, part of the ecological web of life.

In a similar vein, Jane Milton expresses the problem of bringing her whole self, including her compassion and empathy, into her practice. She experiences the hurt of the world and her own inability to prevent it.

God, there was a day last week when just so much was happening – I mean, the full moon or something like that. There was just so much stuff and grief and misery and bizarre stuff that was happening. At the end of the day it was like, ohhh, stomach in a knot, you know, just wrought apart by it. I don't think you're thinking as clearly then and doing as good a job. I think I even told my last client of the day, "Well, we'll reschedule because I just can't hear any more."

Trying to reduce the pain, she "disassociates the emotional, intuitive self from the analytical, professional. I have a certain job to do here for my clients that has very little to do with who I am as a person." Yet the consequences of splitting herself in order to deal with conflict between the demands of role and personal orientation are risky.

To be a full person you don't want to lose the emotional side of yourself. You would hope to be able to have in your personal life that emotional response that you aren't necessarily allowed in your practice. And you hope that your analytical, critical self just doesn't eat all that up, because then you're left with a void. That's something I fight against, you know, and almost all the other women I know fight against also.

Jane recognizes a danger that her analytical, critical self might gain ascendancy and make emotional capacity a void. She struggles to maintain a vital, feeling response while the lawyer role continually emphasizes professionalism, detachment, and neutrality. "That is the struggle for me. I think some other people would say their biggest struggle is time — finding enough hours in the day to do all the things they can't do at the office. But I'd say my number one problem is maintaining myself as a full person, including emotions and such."

Aware of the danger of banishing feeling to the background, Jane tries to compensate for leaving "who I am as a person" out of legal work: "I have in my life tried to keep myself a full person so that outside of the office I have other things besides the law to do. I try to maintain real strong relationships so that I can keep developing myself as a person as well." For Jane, growth as a person takes place through relationships, whereas her development as a lawyer depends on splitting off what she calls her "emotional, intuitive self." She continually experiences stress from carrying out role demands that conflict with her personal orientation, and from her inability to respond to the human pain she witnesses as a lawyer. In part, this stress is born of living with competing world views.

Like Jane, all people develop structures of knowing which allow them to make meaning of events and to commit themselves to certain courses of action. Meaning making involves one's whole being and includes an "existential process of generating a new vision"[26] to which one can commit oneself. When the new vision taught in law school is partially blocked by old ways of seeing, the new vision may not root deeply enough to become a structure of knowing, a new way of making sense. If this happens, lawyers may effectively use the new vision as a tool, but it may not reach deeply enough into who they are to give meaning to their lives.

Jane Milton and Janice Orens effectively use lawyerly vision but are uncertain about their commitment to a profession that excludes their familiar way of making meaning, which forces them to separate off a valued part of themselves. Janice daydreams about how she can express an aspect of herself that the law excludes:

I spend a lot of time daydreaming now about what I want to do instead, and about whether I want to do this [law] and how I want to do it differently if I do law at all. And I write a lot of poetry. I'm going to send some of it out for publication, because I want to balance it, you know, and bring that part of myself into more focus and more power.

Similarly, Jane despairs about the costs of playing the lawyer game:

It's a constant questioning process, you know. Am I being true to myself if I proceed in this respect? If you cannot be true to yourself and proceed in that respect, maybe you should quit the game. Most of the whole lawyers I know are trying to quit. I think maybe I should quit too. I can't take this anymore, the conflict over yourself as a person and yourself as a lawyer; and at the point that one outweighs the other, it's time to leave.

She arrives at the same dilemma as the women at Yale Law School: Forsake the self or forsake the law. Because the choice is unfair and destructive to individuals, and because society risks losing an enrichment it can ill afford to do without, the legal system must push beyond the dilemma to find what new structures and attitudes will invite integration of the fairness of rights and the responsiveness of care.

Reshaping the role: changing ownership of the game

Several strongly care-oriented women discuss another strategy for adjusting to the lawyer role. Rather than emulate the stereotype of the successful lawyer or split the personal self from the lawyer self, these women try to shape the role to conform with their personal morality. Despite devaluation of feminine traits in the law, they assert themselves as women and infuse their care orientation into legal practice. Integration of care transforms the way the job is conceived and the meaning of a lawyer's responsibility. But again there are risks. This posture, like the one before, could expose an empathetic practitioner to an array of client demands and misery which at times may become unbearable. The stress of being a caring advocate is heightened, for unlike with the divided self, care does not slip in the back door of the office but is manifest as part of how the job is done. This points to a second danger. An openly caring attorney may be seen as unprofessional and perhaps incompetent. As long as the rules of the game remain unchanged, care will appear marginal to the profession.

Phyllis Travis designed a domestic relations practice in which her whole self is included. By intention, her work allows "exposure to people's basic and most personal problems . . . and trying to help them." Identifying her "feminist perspective," she describes herself as "interested in what women go through in their lives . . . and in helping them through a period of time . . . giving them some insight into maybe why they are where they are economically, or why they're responding a certain way to something." She has structured her practice to conform to her values. "We sat down and talked about our philosophies and the kind of firm we wanted to have" – informed clients, nonhierarchical office relationships, responsiveness to clients in need.

To deal with tension between the demands of role and her morality, Phyllis limits the types of cases she will take. "What I've tried to do is just be honest with myself about what I feel comfortable doing within my own set of values, and I've excluded certain things because of that set of values. Therefore, I don't have to deal with them, and I do the kind of work that I feel comfortable doing." This self-consciously constructed integrity of her practice protects her from much of the moral distance traditionally associated with law.

Setting aside detachment and neutrality, as Phyllis says, "to be there for the client when they need you," an attorney often still is unable to prevent harm, to give as much as the client needs. This is a serious problem for women who bring their care orientation into the attorney role: how to deal with the stress of caring in the context of the profession. While all lawyers describe the press of meeting deadlines, attending to details, and billing and collecting fees, those who maintain a strong care orientation identify an anguish that comes from empathetic perception of unmet human needs. Susan Constans tells how involvement exposes an attorney to the client's hurt:

I have never done a custody battle yet that I haven't gotten totally involved in. When I lose them, I'm totally bummed out . . . because I obviously believe in those cases, that my client really loves those children, is the better parent for those children. . . . When you lose, it's just as devastating for the attorney, for me, as it is for the client. And then I'm left– It's like they're so consumed with their own devastation that I'm always left in an empty courtroom with my devastation, by myself.

This emotional vulnerability is one reason lawyers erect barriers of detachment and objectivity. The price of involved concern and the anxiety attached to caring may be more than they are able or willing to bear.

Women most persistently high in care statements experience the greatest tension due to their inability to meet clients' needs. Their language of personal cost is graphic: "I bleed for clients; I really do." "I wanted to be there for the client all the time, but it was making me crazy." "You've got to be much more than an attorney – you've got to be a psychologist, you've got to be a mother, you're playing multiple roles. You're giving a lot of energy out – it's really emotionally draining." These attorneys stand in the emotional as well as the legal shoes of their clients. They take personal responsibility for the consequences of professional relationships. Because such courtroom lawyers see a parade of human problems daily, reaching out to each in turn can be overwhelming.

By its very nature, to limit care is, in part, to be uncaring. Bringing care to the office while restricting its reach is not easy. Lawyers who try this solution vary in their success at finding workable boundaries. For example, Constance McElroy takes on considerable responsibility to fix situations of broken relationships and personal hurt with which she deals in her role as a prosecuting attorney. She condemns herself when her attempts fail, even though intellectually she recognizes she did the best job she could. Describing a case of child beating which occurred after she agreed, with conditions, to return the child home, Constance says, "I felt very responsible at that point, and I felt that I had done something very, very wrong by agreeing to the conditions. But I know, when you look at it logically, I wasn't wrong. I didn't do anything wrong, but I felt that way. You know, I felt that I should have been able to save this kid." From the perspective of her role, Constance knows that she did nothing wrong, but her moral imperatives tell her she failed to prevent harm. To the extent that attorneys integrate care into the profession and do not change conventional understandings of feminine goodness, they inevitably fall short of unreachable personal standards.

In responding to such pressure, female attorneys who reshape roles must also change their sense of responsibility and care. Rather than compartmentalize care or suppress it in their lives, they comprehend the limits of their ability to give and to take on the problems of others. After eight years in practice, Phyllis Travis describes the major sources of tension in her work and the need to protect herself from her own demand to give:

It's very hard to sit and listen to someone whose child has been kidnapped. I mean, that's stressful; it's horrible. You go home at night and you worry: Where's this child? and how's my client? and is she going to kill herself? and, you know, that is very hard. I eventually last year had my number unlisted because I had so many people calling me at home because they were hysterical, and I feel guilty about it because I– I wanted to be there for the client all the time, but it was making me crazy. I would come to work the next day, and I wouldn't have slept, or I'd still be upset from talking to people all night on the phone, . . . and I can't give that much; it's too much.

Phyllis encounters the limits of her own selflessness, and reassesses what it means for her to be responsible as a lawyer:

It used to be my attitude that somehow I was responsible for that client's troubles. The minute the client came in to see me, I became responsible for everything that happened – in an abstract way, but yet responsible. And it did not matter how hard my efforts, the child being kidnapped occurred anyway. That particular incident was so stressful for me because of that factor, because of taking on the responsibility. And I realized with a couple of cases that I really didn't have the control over every client I would like to have, to make sure that they did everything they should do so their case worked out OK. Once I admitted that to myself, I realized that if I didn't have the control, I also didn't have the responsibility, because if the person isn't going to listen to me, I can't do anything about that. I started kind of letting go a little bit and realizing that as long as I did everything I could do, as long as I communicated, and as long as I felt for that person and tried to solve that person's problem, and if I knew honestly that I had done every single step that I could do, that it was the best I could do, and if they still turned around and gave their kids back to their ex-husband because they were upset that night, that's not my fault.

Recognizing her lack of power to control what happens to other people, Phyllis places boundaries around her feelings of personal responsibility. Her limitation of responsibility allows her to feel care without guilt and pain each time a negative result occurs.

Hillary Johnson also finds unbounded responsibility exhausting. A lawyer for people with physical disabilities, she was "approaching burnout in terms of my practice" because she heeded inner imperatives learned from socialization to the female role. The already demanding norms of the "good woman" become impossible when taken into a law office.

I think I had to deal with an upbringing which I think a lot of women have, which is it's my job to take care of people, and it's my job to make everything OK. I had to go through a process of realizing there's no way that I can make everything OK or take care of people and that the people had done some incredible things to get their lives to the point that they were at, and that I could not undertake that as my job to fix it, or to do it. I had to go through a real conscious process of trying to free myself of that expectation.

Modifying her expectations of herself, Hillary limits the reach of her responsibility. Like Phyllis, she does not withdraw from clients but changes her understanding of responsibility so as to allow herself to relate to them in an empathetic but realistic manner.

I think, almost ironically, I have maybe a more caring relationship with clients now because I don't feel the burden of responsibility. I feel that I can acknowledge that there is a lot of pain, or can acknowledge that is a terrible situation – "you are in a real mess, and we'll see if we can start breaking it down into small pieces and working on sorting that out" – and I guess acknowledging that. I think that I do end up having a pretty personal relationship with most of my clients.

The change in her understanding of responsibility allows her to "deal with the expressed concern but not take it on as your own," which means that she need no longer "find myself going home at night and agonizing over cases for the most part." She is able to respond empathetically to problems rather than to feel responsible for them.

For these women who integrate care into their law practice, shifts in the meaning of responsibility coincide with changes in their understandings of morality. They recognize that always putting other people's needs ahead of their own leads to self-sacrifice and hurt: "It will kill you." "It will eat you up as a person." When considering human need, the demand always exceeds the ability to respond. Faced with realistic limits on how much they can give, these women assert the right to respect for their own needs. They reorder their understanding of care to include themselves as recipients of the care they extend to others.[27]

Despite the ideal of feminine unselfishness, these lawyers realize that they cannot hold themselves ultimately accountable for the happiness and well-being of others, just as they cannot hold others accountable for their own sense of satisfaction and professional competence. Hillary Johnson says:

Part of the process, I think, had to come from realizing that a client's response to the case isn't necessarily a measure of the quality of the work that was done, or how much I had helped them. . . . Learning to give myself my own feedback, and setting up my own standards in terms of what constitutes a good job for me in doing that, and realizing my own limitations began to replace looking to the client for the measure of my worth as a lawyer.

By separating their care orientation from conventions of stereotypically good women, Hillary and Phyllis maintain involved concern and also attenuate the stress of caring within their attorney role.

Both of these attorneys – one a feminist domestic relations lawyer and the other a specialist in representing the physically disabled – reshaped their roles and in so doing gained the respect of the legal community and a sense of personal satisfaction. We believe that their openly caring style can be employed in other areas not so obviously adaptable to a morality of care. Domestic relations law, like all law, is part of the public sphere. When domestic issues of marital break-up, child abuse, and child custody are brought into the legal arena, they become social policy questions; moral response to such issues has rights and care components, just as does moral reflection on property transactions, contracts, and criminal law. As was illustrated by the business case of Robert Whitfield in Chapter 3, each involves elements of relationships and harm, obligation and responsibility, rights and rules; and thus each of these areas of law is a proper domain for the influence of care as well as rights thinking.[28]

The care-oriented women discussed in this chapter all face a common problem of how to enter a system alien in many ways to their most fundamental values. They show three ways of entry and adjustment to practice of law. All three ways are possible, but none without risk. Under the current rules of the game, care-oriented lawyers suffer difficulty because the rules are not theirs. They pay a psychological price not extracted from most rights-oriented lawyers. Sacrificing the caring self, compartmentalizing it, or integrating it into an unreceptive system is psychologically costly and robs both the individual and the profession.

Given our history, there is also the understandable fear that a higher incidence of care thinking among women lawyers will be used to emphasize the differences between men and women and to direct women into a restricted number of positions supposedly suited to their abilities. To do so would be not only to regress toward inequality offensive to a morality of rights but also to miss a significant opportunity for constructive social change. As the lawyers we interviewed demonstrate, traits associated with care and rights thinking are not mutually exclusive or gender-specific. A person can be empathetic, intuitive, and understanding while also being rational, competent, and quick-witted. The challenge remains to nurture this integration in individual lawyers and to generalize it to legal institutions.

A small step in this direction has been taken by the women who appear in this chapter. The perspective of these attorneys and the paths they follow challenge conventional definitions of the lawyer role and raise new possibilities for a synthesis of equal rights and human caring. While changes in structure and attitude are needed to support their efforts, these lawyers are already doing what was called for before the ABA Commission on Women in the Profession (1988):

Witnesses believe that lawyers will lose their sense of perspective and ethics under the weight of pressure to produce billable hours and the stress of cutting back on family involvement. These witnesses suggest that women, by raising the crucial issues of family and workplace, can take the lead in helping to restore sanity, balance, and respect to the profession.[29]

What is a reasonable response to the fact that many people entering law find basic incompatibilities with the advocate role? One attorney suggests, "If you can't stand the heat, get out of the kitchen." A thoughtful reply would be to ask what is wrong with the kitchen that there is so much heat? Why do so many bright, competent people find it difficult to work there? What happens if people work all day in a kitchen that is too hot? If we carefully examine the sources of stress particular to care-oriented lawyers and their strategies of adjustment, what do we learn about the legal system and about possible changes that need to be made? If all parts of the law are to benefit from the attributes of care morality, the individual initiative of imaginative, energetic lawyers will not be enough to overcome the inertia of a system so set in its ways. Institutional redefinition and a shift in mores will be required. Given the social value of care morality, changes necessary to make the legal system more compatible with care values would be of great benefit, so long as basic tenets of rights morality retain strength in their appropriate place.

6   Toward a more morally responsive advocate

In 1927, Felix Frankfurter, then a professor at Harvard Law School and later a justice of the United States Supreme Court, wrote to a Mr. Rosenwald regarding lawyers, law schools, and American society.[1] For reasons not made clear, Frankfurter sought to counter Rosenwald's "skepticism as to the usefulness of legal research and legal education in furthering [the] purposes of a healthy and good American society." Hoping to enlist Rosenwald's support for Harvard Law School and for the peace, justice, and prosperity that he associated with Harvard-trained lawyers, Frankfurter began his syllogistic response with: "The great, big fact about American national life which differentiates it from that of all Western countries (and of course, also, Eastern countries) is the part played in our affairs by lawyers. . . . ours is a *legal* society." And what kind of lawyers do we need to meet the lofty and diverse challenges that Frankfurter assigns to them? "We must have law and lawyers . . . that are sensitive to the feelings and needs of the various ingredients that make the sum total of the American Nation, lawyers that are hard-headed without being hard, lawyers that are wise rather than smart." Given the centrality of law and lawyers, how do we get these people "who have a wide outlook and an intimate familiarity with the conditions of modern life"? Frankfurter answers his own question: "In the last analysis, the law is what the lawyers are. And the law and lawyers are what the law schools make them."

When Frankfurter wrote this, the place of law schools in initiating young would-be lawyers was as yet unresolved. Again today the proper role of law schools is being questioned, and new issues have surfaced regarding the qualities and habits of minds that law schools should nourish. Is there an important moral vision that law schools and the legal system have systematically denied? Are there large num-

156

bers of people bringing into the profession a new voice which must be heard? In the classroom and in the courtroom, what is to be done with their demand for legitimacy? Although no one doubts the need for critical, analytical thinking and legal knowledge, are other crucial values being slighted, values essential to a fully mature moral understanding? Does the law school eulogy "to think like a lawyer" say as much about the gender bias of our system as about skills inherent in doing the attorney's job? While it would be neither wise nor possible to abandon our liberal, rights-based tradition of individualism, can we at the same time recognize that we are interconnected parts of a community and that individual freedom and community conflict only at their extremes? How can we implement an integrated morality of care and of rights in law schools, in the legal system, and in the professional lives of individual attorneys? To a large extent each of two groups carries a part of this full moral vision; one group was outside but has now been admitted. How can the parts be shared and the vision made whole?

Our work validates these questions and remedies any claim that they might be merely academic or esoteric. Lawyers we interviewed find different avenues for representing clients. One branch of the road is marked by maximum role identification or subjugation of personal morality, and leads to a narrowing of moral considerations and little or no moral stress. Central to professional success and to efficient functioning of the legal system, this conventional course is followed in the routine, daily work of everyone with whom we spoke. The alternative branch is characterized by moral cost and in extreme cases subordination of professional role to personal values. This way keeps a broad moral vision intact, but creates continuing stress. Nevertheless, under proper conditions, nearly every lawyer was tempted by the less conventional road at some point in the interview. The extent to which a divergent route was kept available and was actually followed by a number of attorneys in extreme situations is a hopeful, and unanticipated, sign that a more morally responsive advocate may be a real possibility. If so, attorneys with a strong moral orientation of care will have the primary responsibility for instituting change.

That women have traditionally been the chief exponents of care morality is a cultural and psychological fact but not a statement that this is the way it should be or the only way it can be. Rights considerations are by no means foreign to moral decision making for most women, and many men rely on care concerns in assessing moral conflicts. Neither rights nor care thinking imprisons either gender. That women have symbolized care values in the past does not mean they alone must embody them in the future. What is critical is that they have nurtured those values and assumptions in the private sphere to which they were culturally relegated and that they now make those values available in the public sphere, particularly the public sphere of law. While the two moralities coexist in society by a division of turf, law does not lend itself to separation into public and private spheres. Law is part of the public sphere. Absent the alternative of a division of spheres, the two moralities can exist together there only by integration and balance — both in the institution of law and in the women and men who ply the legal trade.

Several contemporary writers on legal ethics call for a fresh conception of the lawyer's role that makes fuller use of mature, integrated moral sensibilities. This new idea of professional role occupies a middle ground between the rigid rules of Creon and the uncompromising compassion of Antigone. Gerald Postema's vision of the new role allows attorneys to serve important functions of the legal system while integrating personal moral responsibility:

It is far more desirable to recognize at the outset that the lawyer as well as the client bears at least some responsibility for the harms done by both "institutional" and "personal" actions. The question, then, is whether in particular cases there is a moral justification for the harm done. Whether there is or not will be determined by the substantive moral considerations relevant in the case, and it is these substantive moral considerations that the responsible lawyer must take into account in making his decision.[2]

Lawyers with a strong care orientation are more likely to reflect contextually on the prospect of harm resulting from professional actions; those with a strong rights perspective more often identify with the partisan neutrality of role. Because psychological orientations are important determinants of social structure, care thinking holds the potential for a corrective shift from unbridled zealous advocacy which has little regard for the social and individual consequences of professional acts.

In a vein similar to Postema's, Deborah Rhode argues for a conception of the lawyer's role much more consonant with a morality of care than with traditional conceptions of partisanship and neutrality:

To argue for individual assumption of responsibility, however, only begins analysis. The more difficult issue, which remains a highly contextual determination, is what that responsibility entails. Relevant factors include not only the magnitude and likelihood of potential harm and the attorney's capacity to affect it, but also the personal and social costs that corrective action would impose. Among those costs, the possible loss of client or collegial trust is entitled to weight. In some instances, an individual's dependency, or a lawyer's limited leverage and access to information, may make suspension of judgment the only practicable course.[3]

Nevertheless, Rhode makes clear that there are compelling situations where suspension of judgment is not the only feasible alternative. In these instances, the lawyer must move beyond neutrality to a position of personal responsibility.

That clients may have a "legal right" to engage in certain conduct or to invoke a particular procedure is conclusive neither of their moral right, nor of the appropriateness of counsel's aide. Lawyers cannot simply retreat to role in the face of larger normative questions. To cite only the most obvious example, attorneys who delay safety standards they would privately endorse, or who knowingly assist the distribution of products with significant undisclosed risks, are implicated in the human suffering that may result. . . . In effect, the attorney can no longer avoid responsibility for allowing client interests to trump all competing concerns.[4]

Central to the problem of integrating care and rights concerns and bringing a broader moral vision to bear in the practice of law is the concept of neutral partisanship. As we saw earlier, the two terms sustain an uneasy marriage, requiring both mental and psychological gymnastics. Neutrality enables partisanship. If no judgment of right or wrong is made, it is easy to see client representation as a game. The rules tell partisanship to gallop ahead, and neutrality removes any obstacle that might cause it to balk. Marsha James describes the thoughtful, neutral counsel which might be appropriate in some situations, but which lawyers traditionally provide without distinction to all clients:

No. It's not a moral question. I'm not the moral judge of what people do. That's not my job; I don't view it as such. My job is to represent the client, explain to him the law and how it applies to his case, go over with him the alternatives, his options, how much room he's got to move within the societal structure, and what's going to happen to him in my estimation. So it's not moral. I don't make moral judgments about what my clients do. That's not my job.

Stoic neutrality occurs only when thinking and feeling defer to external standards, to rule and role. Tom Wooding depicts the threat to himself of such deference:

There are rules. So morality, as long as I stay within the bounds of the law, I don't even think about how I feel about it — except to the point I say my own personal feelings don't have anything to do with me being an advocate for this person. (*I realize you act that way, but do you also feel that way?*) I feel that way, yeah. I think sometimes I'm sick because I feel that way. Like *The Stranger*. You ever read Camus? He didn't cry in court about his mother's death. I might not cry about my mother's death. It doesn't mean I'm not sad. It means I'll have to wait and see.

The inhibition of feelings required by detachment of role makes this attorney think sometimes he is sick in his ability not to feel. This assessment of himself indicates that he has not totally put personal morality to rest; yet he has accomplished what the role asks — neutrality with regard to judgment and feeling.

In contrast, Lois Halley tells of an instance in which she refused the call of neutrality, and thus preserved her own integrity. She withdrew from representation because her moral commitment to environmental protection overrode her allegiance to client. Because of her values, she was unable to continue representing a land developer. In her presentation of the elements of her dilemma, career and financial considerations weigh against social concerns:

We were strapped, and I was trying to decide how far can I go, being basically democratic and environmentalistic and all this, at heart, in representing this guy. And he wanted me to just go in and move all the zoning ordinances. And I really thought about it because, on the one hand, it would have been a great learning case. Then I decided to just let it go, and I wouldn't do it, because I felt I would be too uncomfortable over the long haul, and there was too much chance that he wouldn't be getting what he wanted either. As a client, I couldn't really do the best for him because he wanted someone who was just very gung-ho development anywhere. . . . I felt there was enough of contention in our philosophies that he would be happier and better served by someone else. So that was the dilemma at first, my career and advancement in gaining this juicy client versus this other belief.

When asked about the nature of the belief that caused her to leave the client, she responds with the utilitarian formula: "What's the greater harm versus the greater good."

The issue is not whether Lois's calculus of the good is more persuasive than that of the developer. What is revealing about this example is that, despite her role as a lawyer, Lois makes the calculus at all. In doing so, she attests that her personal morality matters and needs an avenue for integration into the legal system.

At least in part, conflict between personal morality and professional role stems from the unqualified way in which the profession defines the obligations of partisanship and neutrality. Even in the face of the near-absolute dictates of role obligations, a few attorneys integrate their care orientation into the role, much as Postema and Rhode suggest. John Crowell provides a clear statement of how to bring together personal and professional morality:

I think one of the problems with being an attorney is that attorneys often see that as a license not to develop their own conscience. Not only do they not have to, but they are required not to. I think just the reverse is probably true. If you're an attorney, you're in a position of power and authority that requires you, more than the average person, to develop your own conscience and then to exercise it. And that doesn't mean that you'll represent all people in all cases, but that's not a bad result. You don't have to represent all people in all cases, but somebody might come to you with a case that offended, or might ask you to do something that offended your conscience or your sense of morality. But because they come to you, you might have the chance to help them see that a different conclusion would be better for them, might be a better result than what they originally wanted. The person who wanted to be acquitted or to have the charges dismissed might be thankful to you sometime later if they received mental treatment that changed their life and saved them from later harm or later misery. And whether it's a religious world view, I don't know, but I guess I'm comfortable with the idea that we're where we are because of the possibility that we might be able to do some good and we have a responsibility to do that.

If such integrated activity were more institutionally encouraged and accepted as lawyerlike, attorneys might find it easier to include their moral sensitivities in professional conduct. This occurs only when neutrality is compromised and partisanship is moderated by the value judgments that ensue. If neutrality is maintained as required by the traditional conception of an advocate, a lawyer's personal morality is excluded at the expense of a full moral vision. As we have suggested, this eclipse of possibility may be a psychological loss to the attorney and a moral loss to the client and society.

Lawyers are not more moral than other people and have no special right to have their views heard. It is, however, beyond dispute that law schools historically have laid claim to some of the brightest minds in the country. Can a culture afford to place people with the ability, skills, training, experience, and authority of many lawyers in a central decision-making arena and then neutralize their moral concern and judgment as they operate there?

Lawyers need not go far afield to find authority for diluting neutrality and taking active responsibility for the moral quality of their actions. The Rules of Professional Conduct adopted by the American Bar Association in 1983 provide that "a lawyer may withdraw from representing a client . . . if . . . a client insists upon pursuing an objective that the lawyer considers repugnant or imprudent" (RPC 1.16[b]). To exercise the discretion permitted under this rule, of course, requires relinquishment of neutrality and the assertion of moral judgment.

This theme of independent attorney judgment recurs in Rule 2.1: "In representing a client, a lawyer shall exercise independent professional judgment and render candid advice. In rendering advice, a lawyer may refer not only to law but to other considerations such as moral, economic, social and political factors, that may be relevant to the client's situation." A comment explaining this rule recognizes the limitations of a strictly rights orientation:

Advice couched in narrowly legal terms may be [of] little value to a client, especially where practical considerations, such as cost or effects on other people, are predominant. Purely technical legal advice, therefore, can sometimes be inadequate. It is proper for a lawyer to refer to relevant moral and ethical considerations in giving advice. Although a lawyer is not a moral advisor as such, moral and ethical considerations impinge upon most legal questions and may decisively influence how the law will be applied.

These rules indicate clear authority for attorneys, as John Crowell urged, "to develop your own conscience and then to exercise it."

Tracing the current code to its origins provides a more detailed portrait of the attorney as an independent moral agent. In 1854, George Sharwood, Philadelphia lawyer, law professor, and chief justice of the Pennsylvania Supreme Court, composed an essay that in 1907 became the basis for the first professional code of ethics adopted by the American Bar Association.[5] Sharwood began his discussion of "fidelity to client" with a question that encapsulates our inquiry:

But what are the limits of his duty when the legal demands or interests of his client conflict with his own sense of what is just and right? This is a problem by no means of easy solution.6

After acknowledging the "delicate and dangerous ground" this question lays bare, Sharwood set forth "a few propositions, however, which appear to me to be sound in themselves, and calculated to solve this problem practically in the majority of cases."7

His first proposition makes distinctions in a lawyer's obligation to a client, depending on the type of case and the position of the client. Sharwood differentiates among prosecution and defense in criminal cases and plaintiff and defendant in civil cases. Attorneys in each of these situations have different obligations of neutrality. A criminal defense attorney has the most urgent claim on unlimited advocacy and the most solemn duty of neutrality. At the other extreme, attorneys for civil plaintiffs, according to Sharwood,

have an undoubted right, and are in duty bound, to refuse to be concerned for a plaintiff in the legal pursuit of a demand, which offends his sense of what is just and right. The courts are open to the party in person to prosecute his own claim, and plead his own cause; and although he ought to examine and be well satisfied before he refuses to a suitor the benefit of his professional skill and learning, yet it would be on his part an immoral act to afford that assistance, when his conscience told him that the client was aiming to perpetuate a wrong through the means of some advantage the law may have afforded him.8

More important than the particulars of Sharwood's first proposition is the general suggestion that the lawyer's job be seen not as one but as many, as a spectrum of obligations that vary with circumstances.9 As it now stands, a future public defender, a future child custody lawyer, a future corporate counsel, and a future plaintiff's personal injury lawyer are all taught the same rules of client relations and are all trained to play the same professional role. Sharwood suggests, however, that attorneys should exercise personal moral judgment to varying degrees, depending on the nature of client representation. Although the murder suspect in the first hypothetical dilemma justly claims the allegiance of a devoted advocate, the potential child abuser in the second dilemma commands less neutrality.

Following Sharwood's lead, the legal profession needs to reassess the appropriateness of the adversary model for the total spectrum of the lawyer's job and to develop new rules for those situations where fully neutral partisanship is not appropriate. These rules should invite contextual concern for individual need and continuity of relationship.

Certainly there is a danger if lawyers assert too much of their own moral views into the legal system. This could mean that some people would not get representation and thus would be denied access to the essential mode of dispute resolution in our society. Also, who is ready to claim that lawyers' values are superior to those of other people? Why should the values of lawyers be the only ones heard in the legal forum? These are legitimate concerns, but not ones against which it would be difficult to safeguard. There is much room for lawyers to bring personal morality to bear short of total domination.

Sharwood's second proposition is related to the first and again invites tempering of zealous advocacy and enhancing of moral reflection.

Another proposition which may be advanced upon this subject is, that there may and ought to be a difference made in the mode of conducting a defense against what is believed to be a righteous, and what is believed to be an unrighteous claim. . . . Counsel, however, may and even ought to refuse to act under instructions from a client to defeat what he believes to be an honest and just claim, by insisting upon the slips of the opposite party, by sharp practice, or special pleading – in short, by any other means than a fair trial on the merits in open court. There is no professional duty, no virtual engagement with the client, which compels an advocate to resort to such measures, to secure success in any cause, just or unjust; and when so instructed, if he believes it to be intended to gain an unrighteous object, he ought to throw up the cause, and retire from all connection with it, rather than thus be a participator in other men's sins.[10]

Here Sharwood asserts not only the moral agency of an attorney but the moral responsibility as well. Unlike the curriculum of law schools, Sharwood recognizes, as did the attorneys we interviewed, that advocacy is a matter of degree and that, as moral reflection replaces neutrality, the zeal of advocacy is dampened. This suggests that advocates should not regard lawyering as a monolithic task but, rather, should engage some of the power to make subtle distinctions and fine judgments which is the lawyer's trademark.

In his third proposition, Sharwood directly addresses the relationship between personal morality and advocacy. Concerning counsel who lends weight to an unjust cause, Sharwood notes that "some sound and judicious observations have been made by Mr. Whewell in a recent work on the Elements of Moral and Political Science, which deserve to be quoted at some length":

Every man when he advocates a case in which morality is concerned, has an influence upon his hearers, which arises from the belief that he shares the moral sentiments of all mankind. This influence of his supposed morality is one of his possessions, which, like all his possessions, he is bound to use for moral ends. If he mix[es] up his character as an advocate with his character as a moral agent, using his moral influence for the advocate's purpose, he acts immorally. He makes the moral rule subordinate to the professional rule. He sells to his client not only his skill and learning, but himself. He makes it the supreme object of his life to be not a good man, but a successful lawyer.[11]

Sharwood judges harshly the advocate who does not keep a keen eye on his own personal morality. The lawyer who subordinates personal morality not only sells his skill and learning but prostitutes himself. If there is an either/or choice between being a good lawyer and being a good person, there is no doubt where Sharwood sides, although he later makes clear that no such choice is required, for it is to the "candid and honest" lawyer "that the best clients resort; they have the most important and interesting lawsuits, and enjoy by far the most lucrative practice."[12]

From George Sharwood to the present Rules of Professional Conduct, there is support, though largely ignored, for a controlled but pointed assertion of personal morality in the practice of law. If Holmes is correct that "the life of law has not been logic; it has been experience," what can be done to make the legal system better reflect the full panorama of human experience – the morality of care as well as the morality of rights? How can we legitimize feeling bad about beating the widow on behalf of the insurance company, even while recognizing the importance of doing it? Where do we start to train lawyers to be actively responsible for the consequences of their professional conduct? Where do we begin in teaching lawyers to be engaged moral agents? How do we elevate the virtues of the morality of care while protecting individual rights and social equality? By what changes can we balance both the scales of justice and the ecology of relationships?

The answers to these questions are a lengthy agenda which far outstrips our enterprise. Although our work does not lead directly to specific suggestions of reform in either law school or the profession, it does affirm that care-oriented lawyers face the choice of either stressful, perhaps painful, conformity or the risk and challenge of innovation. Furthermore, the work indicates the direction that reform must take if law schools and the legal system are to receive and to legitimize the concerns of a care morality. From what we have learned through our conversations with attorneys, we can suggest some points for beginning.

Historically law schools have been crucibles of change in the legal profession, and we expect that movement toward a more morally responsive advocate will likewise begin there. A good place to start is with teaching methods. Law schools model what they teach, an adversary system. They must modify or supplement traditional combative teaching techniques with the inclusion of more cooperative, less alienating forms of instruction. The so-called Socratic method may be effective in breaking down the old "home world" but does little to encourage open inquiry, to incorporate divergent points of view, or to foster cooperative learning.

Second, law schools must create an atmosphere that both affirms the morality of care concerns and challenges suppositions traditionally rewarded in the law school context. Male and female attorneys must be made to feel free to express values that go beyond rights, rules, and duties and ask about harm, consequences, and community. These concerns will have to be not only tolerated by faculty but shared by them. Ultimately, this agenda may require the development of a new jurisprudence.[13]

Third, law schools must modify their curricula to include new questions. For instance, what is the impact of merely filing lawsuits on people psychologically, financially, on their businesses, on their positions in the community? How do different kinds of dispute resolutions alter people's attitudes and abilities to relate to those with whom they have disagreed? What is the effect of various types of contract provisions and business arrangements on attitudes and the long-term quality of relationships? Where do you draw the line in pressing client interests at the expense of other individuals, the community, the environment? When should the attorney suspend neutrality and become a moral agent? How can this be done without compromising or offending a client? What is the relationship between assumptions and structures of our legal system and feelings of alienation and loss of community?

Fourth, in teaching legal ethics, law schools should explore the role of personal moral judgment as a counterbalance to neutrality. Provisions of the Rules of Professional Conduct that encourage attorneys to exercise moral responsibility should be given higher visibility and made understandable in relation to other code sections such as that requiring client confidentiality. Law schools must begin the difficult task of learning how to teach the development of judgment and moral sensitivity, from both perspectives. Together, law schools and the legal profession should begin to work out new rules for understanding the lawyer-client relationship as a continuum with differing obligations depending on the nature of the circumstances. Systemic structures should be developed to encourage both lawyers and judges to exercise care values, including problem assessment and resolution that take full account of broad contextual considerations.[14] Law schools might set up special topical seminars to deal with such questions and to explore substantive alterations in the law that challenge a rights-oriented jurisprudence.

What substantive changes might be kindled by infusion of care thinking into the moral world of law is difficult to predict. A provocative example appears in a recent recommendation to the Canadian government in a document titled *A Feminist Review of Criminal Law*. The report asserts that the human need for shelter, food, and clothing is more important than property rights and calls for "explicit recognition of this hierarchy of values." A recommendation elevates concern for human well-being over traditional ideas of rights and redefines rules of justice in accord with the morality of care: "There should be a statutory defense of necessity insuring a right to interfere with the property rights of others in order to feed, clothe, shelter oneself and one's children."[15]

This example concerning property rights is particularly interesting because no area of the law has been more bound by application of rules, claims of right and duty, and Aristotelian notions of mathematical equality. The proposal is radical in that it goes to the heart of the legal system and says that claims of need are superior to claims of right. The relevant moral and legal question shifts from whether rights have been violated to whether critical needs have been met. Sacrificing certainty for ambiguity, absolute rules give way to contextual analysis of hunger and hurt. The responsibility to act so as to avoid harm supplants the basic property right to be free from interference by others. Such a revision of priorities may be the ultimate challenge that care-oriented attorneys present to the legal system.[16]

Changes are needed not only so that care thinking will be better accommodated in law school and in practice but also to give more scope to the moral development of all lawyers, to bring a broader moral vision to bear on legal problems, and to make the legal world better reflect the morality of our whole society. To live with half a vision is to limit what is possible under the law and to sell short our individual and societal potential. The loss of one eye is the loss of perception in depth. The danger of having partial vision for a long time is that we cease to see that we cannot see. G. K. Chesterton notes:

The horrible thing about all legal officials, even the best, about all judges, magistrates, barristers, detectives, and policemen, is not that they are wicked (some of them are good), not that they are stupid (several of them are quite intelligent), it is simply that they have got used to it. Strictly they do not see the prisoner in the dock; all they see is the usual man in the usual place. They do not see the awful court of judgment; they only see their own workshop.[17]

Now that we are beginning to understand the morality of care and its relationship to gender and law practice, it is up to law schools and the legal system to make use of the bramble bush to create full vision in the legal profession.

As the lawyers in our study present various solutions to the interface of role and personal morality, we see differing risks to the lawyer's sense of integrity, to the development of full moral capacity, and to the wider social community affected by lawyers. The extremes of each position – the inflexibility of adherence to rules and the vulnerability of responsiveness to need – bring us back to Creon and

Antigone. Creon demonstrates the dangers of noncontextual reasoning, which can lead to an insensitivity to human need and ultimately to the destruction of others. For Creon it does not matter that his daughter-in-law and son are pleading for flexibility, for attention to the relationships at stake in the situation. He ignores their need, focusing instead on the importance of rule.

In the face of the state's power, Antigone is vulnerable. To enact her perspective, she must be heard and acknowledged by the institutional authority within which she operates. Defiance of rules can, indeed, lead to problems, particularly when power is unbalanced and defiance threatens social order. The extremes of Creon and Antigone point to the importance of a middle ground, a position that recognizes the value of equal application of law as a guard against anarchy and oppression but that also responds to the specific needs of the people and community it seeks to serve.

When we move across the positions on the spectrum that describes how lawyers relate to their role, we encounter irony. An increase in possibility for greater individual responsiveness inevitably entails an enlarged opportunity for personal irresponsibility. The more a person departs from conventional wisdom, the greater the potential for creative, perhaps heroic, thought; but there is also the risk of error and tyranny. The line is thin and uncertain, and often a person walking it is too close to the action to be a reliable judge. Only history tells whether the heretic was a fool or a saint. Just as Plato despaired of finding those qualified to be philosopher kings, there is no reason to believe that law schools will provide adequate training for the job.

Nonetheless, two factors make it possible to bring care thinking into law without risking legal anarchy or demagoguery. First, the rights morality of law is well established and will not yield easily; at most, care concerns will integrate and provide a balance. The moorings of conventional wisdom remain a check against arbitrariness and arrogance. Second, morality of care is not simply the personal predilection of individuals. It is itself a conventional wisdom, one shared by a large part of our society, and one well tempered in its own province. By definition, the rules are not clear because the thinking is not rule-bound, but underlying principles and assumptions are well understood. Thus, ultimately we are talking not about blending institutional and idiosyncratic moralities but about combining two moral viewpoints, each of which has a well-established social tradition.

The relationship of these two moralities is affected by the structure in which they operate. Dichotomous, exclusionary structures which push toward either/or thinking tend to accentuate differences and tensions between them. A more encompassing, synthesizing structure, which moves toward inclusionary thought, emphasizes the way in which the moralities complement and support one another. This interactive quality was remarked upon by Patricia Wald, chief judge of the U.S. Court of Appeals, D.C. Circuit, in accepting the Medal of Merit from Yale Law School: "We must consider the results of our rulings, not merely their conceptual consistency. Principled decision making does not require that we be blind to how our decisions play out in the real world." Noting that law is a "system for resolving human disputes," she states, "The human component could not be left out of it; just as the law must have some stability, so must it have adaptability too."[18]

In our culture, we all seek the freedom to carve out our separate identities and to achieve according to our individual abilities. We also find identity through membership in community, and we are linked in our fate with those around us. Social reality is both individual autonomy and the linkage of interdependence. Our individualism enriches and diversifies community while community gives context and succor to our separate selves. Society and every person need autonomous space and the possibility of individual fulfillment protected by a jurisprudence of rights. At the same time we must have caring protection, a sense of belonging and attention to basic human needs.

Competition promotes initiative, achievement, self-expression, and vision, but a society preoccupied with competition loses equity, compassion, and identity. Community addresses these losses but, if unchecked, can squelch creativity and impose a deadening conformity. Human dignity resides both in realization of our separate selves and in responsiveness of our interdependent selves. Moralities of care and rights together safeguard the right to compete and the need not to be wantonly hurt by the competition. Like two parts of a whole, they tell us that fairness and equality both of the race and of the outcome matter.

Both care and rights speak to a quality of justice. From the perspective of our culture, a society in which people are not free to speak, interact, form alliances, strive for achievement, and guard against governmental intrusion is not a just society. Likewise, a society of plenty where some people lack basic necessities of food, shelter, and health care, where fellow humans do not respond to unjustifiable harm, is not a just society. Both the approach of rights and the approach of care aim at a just society, and each checks the faults of excess in the other. Both have something vital to offer, and human welfare is not complete without the contribution of each.

Appendix I: Coding Manual

Section A of this coding manual uses conceptualizations by Carol Gilligan and colleagues to identify rights and care reasoning (Brown et al., "Reading for Self and Moral Voice;" "Coding Manual," Gender, Education, and Human Development Study Center; Lyons, "Two Perspectives"). Throughout the manual we are mindful that the "distinction between justice and care cuts across the familiar divisions between thinking and feeling, egoism and altruism, and theoretical and practical reasoning by reconstructing the meaning of these terms" (Brown et al., "Reading for Self and Moral Voice," 4). After the Coding Manual was developed, it was sent to Carol Gilligan, Jane Attanucci, and Kay Johnston from whom we received helpful comments.

What is being measured in the Coding Manual is not discrete *words* but a point of view, a way of seeing moral problems. Often words like "justice," "truth," "obligation," and "fairness" are employed by attorneys with either orientation. These words may mean different things to the individual, depending on the underlying orientation that organizes moral perceptions. Even though the "lawyer talk" of rights and justice frequently appears in all the interviews, these words mean different things to different people. (See particularly Chapter 3 for examples.)

After having been trained to understand and identify rights and care orientations in narratives, coders relied on the following manual in order to code the interviews.

Section A: identifying elements of care and rights morality in the hypothetical and real life dilemmas

1. HOW IS THE PROBLEM PERCEIVED?

172

Care orientation

> Problem perceived contextually, as a situation where
> people may be hurt (or are being hurt).

Moral problems are perceived as a part of particular situations, as
arising out of specific contexts that reveal the threat of hurt to someone. The threat of hurt to someone may include the possibility of
physical harm, or the perception that a relationship is in jeopardy,
one person is going to hurt another, someone fails to care, or someone fails to recognize their interdependence (Langdale and Gilligan,
"The Contribution of Women's Thought," 57). A morality of care
responds to the person/situation in context (in particular) rather than
focusing on a problem in general (an issue, as with conflicting principles, standards, obligations). The person expresses a concern not just
for people's rights, but for people themselves, as they are seen in
relationship to one another (*Ibid.*, 61). The intent to exercise care not
to hurt others underlies the thought of the care orientation. The wish
to avoid or minimize harm is central.

Code care morality in perception of problem as *Care A (1-5):*

> Problem seen contextually, as a situation where people
> may be hurt (or are being hurt).
>
> 0 = not present
> 1 = mentioned, but not prominent
> 2 = dominant and detailed, including a contextual description of the
>   situation, and/or a description of the hurt to be avoided

NCareA(1-5). Total number of times a situation where people may
be hurt is described.

Rights orientation

> Problem perceived in terms of conflict or violation of
> rights, duties, or abstract principles of right and wrong, or
> standards of role.

The perception of moral problems does not arise out of considering
others in their own contexts. Rather, the person focuses on conflict-

ing principles, claims, duties, or rights. Moral problems emerge as an issue of how to uphold one's values or standards or "right" and "wrong," of how to maintain one's rights and respect the rights of others in a system of rules, roles, and laws. Moral oughts may stem from the duties, obligations, and commitments that flow from roles (Lyons, "Two Perspectives"), or may stem from a commitment to certain absolute standards. The person faces "the problem" rather than facing specific people who have problems.

Code justice morality in perception of problem as *Just A (1-5)*:

> Problem perceived in terms of conflict or violation of rights, duties, or abstract principles of right and wrong.
>
> 0 = not present
> 1 = conflict or violation of rights, duties or principles mentioned once
> 2 = conflict or violation of rights, duties or principles is dominant, and detailed

NJustA(1-5). Number of times a conflict or violation of rights, duties, or principles mentioned (as above).

2. THE GOAL OF MORAL ACTION: WHAT IS THE GOOD TO BE SERVED?

Care orientation: To avoid harm, to maintain and/or to restore relationships, to protect others from hurt

In the care orientation, the person wishes to ensure that others are not hurt through the self's action, and/or wishes to protect others from hurt. One acts in order to prevent hurt, and to maintain or restore relationships, out of the recognition of interdependence (Lyons, "Two Perspectives"). The goal is the avoidance of harm, hurt, violence, and the restoration of positive relatedness to others, including harmony and dialogue.

Variable name: Care B (1-5)

> 0 = not present
> 1 = the wish to "help," or "not to hurt others" is expressed, but not detailed or dominant
> 2 = concern for others dominant and detailed

NCareB(1-5). Number of times the goal of avoiding harm, of maintaining and/or restoring relationships, and/or protecting others from hurt is mentioned.

> *Rights orientation: Goal of moral action — the good to be served*
>
> Achieving fairness, justice, equality, and/or the maintenance of standards of rightness and wrongness (includes maintaining the rules of the legal system).

In the rights orientation, the goal of moral action is symbolized by the scales of justice and a blindness to those who bring the claims. The focus is on fairness, equilibrium, on achieving a balance. The goal is to be fair, or to follow the rules and roles which have been provided by society (or the legal system), to maintain fairness and reciprocity. Relationships to others are mediated through rules and roles which maintain fairness and reciprocity. Fairness includes the goal of making sure that everyone has an equal chance; not impinging on the rights of others. Reciprocity means how one would like to be treated if in another's place, not considering their specific context or their difference.

Variable name: Just B (1-5)

    0 = not mentioned
    1 = goal of fairness, justice, equality, and/or the maintenance of stan-
          dards mentioned, but not prominent
    2 = goal of fairness, justice, equality, and/or the maintenance of stan-
          dards is prominent and detailed

NJustB(1-5). Number of times the goal of fairness, justice, equality, and/or the maintenance of standards mentioned.

3. WHAT IS THE PROCESS OF DECISION MAKING? HOW DOES THE PERSON DECIDE WHAT TO DO?

Care orientation

Assesses the relative harm given the context and the vulnerabilities of those involved.

In deciding what to do, the person considers the context/situation of the people involved, including their vulnerabilities. The subject recognizes the inapplicability of general rules applied to all people, and instead tailors an individualized response to particular people in a particular situation, guided by the wish to prevent harm. The person weighs the relative costs, the relative harm which will result from action or inaction, and the person's task is to understand what response will cause the least harm to those most needing protection (who is most vulnerable?).

Variable name: Care C (1-5)

> 0 = not mentioned
> 1 = brief mention of relative cost or harm stemming from action or inaction
> 2 = considerations of relative harm given context and vulnerabilities of those involved is prominent and detailed

NCareC(1-5). Number of considerations of relative harm or cost stemming from action or inaction, taking into account the context and vulnerabilities of those involved.

Rights orientation

> Application of rules or standards, or considerations of role obligations in order to arrive at clear, absolute answers.

In the rights orientation, the person decides what to do (how to intervene) by application of rules or standards, or by consideration of role obligations — or by reference to others (what do they think?) or to the system. Standards or rules allow the individual to reason logically and deductively, applying general standards to particular situations in order to be fair. The person reasons by generalizing — using rules or standards that s/he would be willing to apply to all people in all situations. The subject's task is to perceive the higher value, standard, or claim so as to apply the right one in order to arrive at a solution.

Variable name: Just C (1-5)

NJustC(1-5). Number of times the person considers role, rules, what others think, or the system in order to arrive at the decision of what to do.

4. HOW IS THE DECISION OR ACT EVALUATED?

Care orientation

What are the consequences of action: have I minimized harm?

The person evaluates the goodness or rightness of the action or decision in terms of its consequences to others. In the given situation, have I minimized harm? Have I done enough?
   Variable name: Care D (1-5)

   0 = not mentioned
   1 = consequences to others in terms of avoiding harm mentioned, but not prominent
   2 = consequences to others in terms of avoiding harm prominent and detailed

NCareD(1-5). Number of times person considers consequences to others in terms of avoiding harm in evaluating the decision.

Rights orientation

Protection or restoration of the principle (fairness), rule, or role standards.

The person evaluates the rightness of what to do in terms of the protection or restoration of the principle, rule, or role standards. The person asks, have the rules been maintained, have I done my duty, have I made a proper determination of the highest moral obligation in this instance?
   Variable name: Just D (1-5)

   0 = not mentioned
   1 = brief consideration of above questions and issues, not prominent
   2 = detailed and prominent considerations of the above questions and issues

NJustD(1-5). Number of times person evaluates decision or choice in terms of the protection or restoration of the principle, rule, or role standard.

Section B, Coding for Relation between Personal Morality and the

Lawyer Role, designed to operationalize and measure our under-standing of how lawyers relate their personal moralities to profes-sional role. Coders were not aware of the hypothesized relation be-tween personal morality and "position," and the coding for rights and care was done separately and independently from coding for lawyer position (Section B).

Section B: coding for relation between personal morality and the lawyer role

As described earlier, please code the hypothetical dilemmas for the following positions:

1. MAXIMUM ROLE IDENTIFICATION

a) Variable name: Role A (1-4)

Duty to fulfill lawyer's role

The attorney refers to the legal system or the attorney role as deter-mining his/her conduct. The person considers that his/her profes-sional (and therefore, possibly) moral obligation is to fulfill the duties and ideals of the role.

0 = not mentioned
1 = mentioned in passing, not prominent
2 = prominent in subject's explanation of why dilemma presents no significant conflict, or how it should be resolved

NRoleA(1-4). Number of times the lawyer refers to his/her duty to fulfill lawyer's role in the reasoning out of the dilemma. A count of the number of times this element is mentioned in each hypothetical.

b) Variable name: Role B (1-4)

Partisanship as a central element of role

By "partisanship" is meant client advocacy, the obligation to zeal-ously represent the client's interests to the best of the attorney's ability. This ideal of role means that the client's interests and con-cerns should come before the lawyer's personal values and feelings.

0 = not mentioned
1 = mentioned in passing, not prominent
2 = prominent in subject's explanation of why dilemma presents no
    significant conflict, or how it should be resolved

NRoleB(1-4). Number of times the lawyer refers to partisanship in the reasoning out of the dilemma, etc., above.

c) Variable name: Role C (1-4)

Denial of personal responsibility for professional acts

The attorney sees the self as a part of a larger system, of which s/he has only one small role to play, with the rules clearly spelled out as to obligations and duties. The attorney does not feel personal responsibility for professional acts. The attorney may refer to the fact that s/he did not make the rules and thus is not responsible for what s/he does – or it may be simply implied by reference to the predetermined part s/he has to play in the system.

0 = not mentioned
1 = mentioned in passing, not prominent
2 = used to explain why dilemma presents no significant conflict

NRoleC(1-4). Number of times system referred to, and/or denial of responsibility mentioned as above (count each).

d) Variable name: Role D (1-4)

Code of ethics determines response

Lawyer says there is no dilemma, or resolves dilemma, by referring to the code of ethics which s/he uses to tell him/her what course of action to follow.

0 = not mentioned
1 = reference to ethical rules or code
2 = code of ethics used as the way of saying there is no dilemma, or
    code of ethics is prominent in resolving the dilemma

NRoleD(1-4). Number of times code of ethics mentioned, as above.

e) Variable name: Role E (1-4)

Denial of conflict

No conflict is apparent in the narrative between role duties and the attorney's personal morality. The attorney may also mention that s/he has no concern or conflict about the consequences of professional acts, when the acts are done according to the canon of ethics.

    0 = not mentioned
    1 = says have no conflict with personal feelings/values
    2 = says doesn't feel bad about consequences of professional acts

NRoleE(1-4). Number of times denial of conflict mentioned, as above.

NOTE TO CODERS:

Code with the subscripts in all cases as follows:

    1 = Hypothetical one, initial response
    2 = Hypothetical one, final response
    3 = Hypothetical two, initial response
    4 = Hypothetical two, final response
    5 = Real life moral dilemma

2. SUBJUGATION OF PERSONAL MORALITY TO ROLE
MORALITY

a) Variable name: Subjug A (1-4)

Conflict perceived between personal values and role requirements, but personal values subordinated to role requirements

The attorney accepts the lawyer role, recognizes a conflict with personal values, and subordinates his/her personal morality. The lawyer may or may not say s/he recognizes a dilemma, but if s/he does, the dilemma is resolved by describing the subjugation of personal values/principles/beliefs. The conflict does not appear to "bother" the lawyer: there appears to be no struggle with the conflict, even though the conflict is recognized.

> 0 = not mentioned
> 1 = subjugation of personal values mentioned, not prominent
> 2 = lawyer spells out personal values which conflict, but says they come second to professional responsibilities, or the duties of role

NSubjuA(1-4). Number of times subjugation of personal values mentioned, as above.

b) Variable name: Subjug B (1-4)

Lawyer spells out reason for subordination of personal morality by referring to the demands and requirements of role

The lawyer makes clear that the reason s/he subordinates personal morality when it conflicts with professional obligations is because it is a requirement of role: "It's part of my job as a lawyer."

> 0 = not mentioned
> 1 = demands and requirements of role mentioned in solving dilemma
> 2 = the demands and requirements of role are spelled out in detail

NSubjuB(1-4). Number of times the lawyer mentions the demands and requirements of role, as above.

c) Variable name: Subjug C (1-4)

Lawyer justifies subordinating personal morality by appeal to the system

The lawyer gives as a reason for setting aside personal morality the importance of the overall smooth functioning of the legal system, of which the lawyer's actions and duties are only one aspect.

> 0 = not mentioned
> 1 = brief reference to the legal system in response to the hypothetical
> 2 = the operation of the legal system and/or the lawyer's part in its functioning are spelled out as a justification for setting aside personal values/beliefs

NSubjuC(1-4). Number of times the lawyer refers to the legal system when reasoning out how to act (or resolve dilemma), as above.

d) Variable name: Subjug D (1-4)

Restricting self in order to protect autonomy and rights of client is considered to be an ethical act

The attorney describes holding in abeyance his/her own values/beliefs in order to represent someone else's (the client's) concerns and interests as ethical in and of itself.

0 = not mentioned
1 = mentioned in passing
2 = spelled out in detail, and specific reference to the importance of protecting the rights of others is given

NSubjuD(1-4). Number of times the lawyer mentions above.

e) Variable name: Subjug E (1-4)

No personal responsibility for professional acts

The attorney does not accept personal responsibility for professional acts. Rather, the lawyer's responsibility is to the client, and the lawyer's job is to represent the client to the best of his/her ability and not to make value judgments regarding the client.

0 = not mentioned
1 = mentioned in passing
2 = mentioned more than once, and in detail

NSubjuE(1-4). Number of times the lawyer denies personal responsibility for professional acts, as above.

3. RECOGNITION OF MORAL COST

a) Variable name: M/cost A (1-4)

Person expresses significant conflict between personal morality and role obligations

The attorney clearly states the competing claims for moral behavior: professional and personal. This position (the recognition of moral costs) differs from #2 not in terms of the decision which is reached (the person may, in fact, reach the same decision as to what to do as #2), but differs in the process of coming to the decision. This person accepts the importance and validity of the lawyer role and the demands for impartiality and client advocacy which accompany it, but his/her personal values/beliefs compete with the demands of role to cause significant conflict. The lawyer explicates how carrying out the demands of role at times goes against personal values/beliefs, which causes significant personal conflict. Personal morality is subjugated to the demands of role, but with apparent conflict. Code for this position if on the basis of such conflict, lawyer withdraws from the case.

0 = not mentioned
1 = brief reference to competing personal and professional claims
2 = one statement regarding the competing personal and professional claims for resolution of the conflict: "I have a duty to my client on the one hand, and a caring for the children on the other hand"

NM/cosA(1-4). Number of times subject refers to conflict between personal morality and role obligations, as above.

b) Variable name: M/cost B (1-4)

Conflict between professional and personal values cannot be resolved without moral costs, either internal or external

Lawyer describes the moral costs of carrying out the demands of role (see Postema handout for elaboration of moral cost). Moral cost may be perceived externally – in terms of the consequences of professional acts to others – or may be perceived internally – in terms of internal stress resulting from the tension between personal and professional values. The recognition of external moral costs may include the expression of reluctance to bring about injury, or a sense of the accompanying loss or sacrifice. Moral costs experienced internally may be expressed as a tension (stress) or internal conflict with personal costs to the self. Competing personal values and professional obligations exact some emotional costs in resolving dilemmas, or in carrying out the duties of the role.

0 = not mentioned
1 = general reference to the personal (moral) costs of carrying out the demands of role
2 = moral cost of carrying out role expressed as tension (stress) or

internal conflict, with mention of personal costs to the self ("I'm always left in an empty courtroom with my devastation, by myself") or the moral cost of carrying out role perceived externally, in terms of consequences to others. Here the focus is on consequences to others instead of consequences to the self

NM/cosB(1-4). Number of times lawyer refers to moral costs, including both costs/consequences to self and other, as above.

c) Variable name: M/cost C (1-4)

Lawyer describes concrete action or reparation for the harm done after enacting the role in order to try to mitigate the perceived moral costs

The attorney enacts the lawyer role, and in so doing acts against his/her moral values. The person recognizes the moral costs of enacting the role. The recognition of possible negative consequences to others which may stem from enacting the duties of role lead the lawyer to describe concrete acts or reparation which s/he would attempt in order to deal with the possible harm done.

0 = no mention
1 = attorney describes the wish to make up for possible negative consequences which may arise from carrying out duties of role
2 = attorney describes concrete acts or reparation for the harm done through carrying out role duties. ("I would do what needed to be done as defense counsel. I would probably try to compensate somewhere else . . . dropping the ball or going to the prosecutor or maybe even going to the judge." etc. See example in handout.)

NM/cosC(1-4). Number of times subject describes wish to make up for consequences, and/or describes concrete acts or reparation for the harm done, as above.

d) Variable name: M/cost D (1-4)

Attorney takes personal responsibility for professional acts and their consequences – either to others or to the self

The extension of self to try to deal with the consequences of professional acts indicates taking a degree of personal responsibility for professional acts. The lawyer describes a sense of responsibility not limited to the client (partisanship) or to simply fulfilling the duties of role, but responsibility extends beyond those parameters, to the self and its integrity, or to the wider social community.

> 0 = responsibility not mentioned
> 1 = lawyer indicates feeling responsible to self's values and actions (personal integrity)
> 2 = lawyer indicates feeling a responsibility to the wider social community in terms of the consequences of professional acts, or to specific others who may be affected by professional actions

N/McosD(1-4). Number of times lawyer describes feeling personally responsible, as above. Count each description of feeling responsible for consequences, and/or to self's values and actions.

4. MINIMUM ROLE IDENTIFICATION

(In situations of moral conflict, the prominence of the attorney role imperatives recedes, and personal morality becomes the determinant in resolution of the dilemma.)

a) Variable name: PerDom A (1-4)

> *Moral costs or moral concerns become so strong that role demands/obligations are subordinated to personal morality*

The lawyer cannot subjugate his/her personal values/concerns to the demands or obligations of role, and refuses to enact the role. Or the attorney will not "play by the rules," but carries out his/her professional obligations by "changing the rules" so that s/he can proceed in accord with personal values in a particular situation of moral conflict. This is not an action lightly taken, and the attorney describes the intensity of personal moral values and/or personal conflict and/or concern for others which leads to this kind of resolution. It is clear that the individual claims the freedom to define the self in action independently of his/her attorney role, and in accord with what the person considers to be a higher value or belief.

> 0 = not mentioned
> 1 = lawyer refuses to enact the role ("they'd have to fire me")

2 = lawyer carries out professional obligations by "changing the rules" so that s/he can proceed in accord with personal values in a particular situation of moral conflict

NPerdmA(1-4). Number of times subject describes refusal to enact the role and/or describes carrying out professional obligations by changing the rules, as above.

b) Variable name: PerDom B (1-4)

Lawyer feels responsible for actions – whether or not they stem from professional obligations or personal convictions

The attorney accepts personal responsibility for professional acts, and thus is unable to ignore personal imperatives regarding how to act in situations which strongly conflict with personal values. The attorney does not subjugate personal morality to role obligations, but keeps moral sensitivity while enacting the role, which may force him/her to act in accord with personal moral demands in certain situations.

0 = personal responsibility not mentioned
1 = personal responsibility mentioned, but not dominant
2 = attorney explains how s/he feels a sense of responsibility for his/her actions (while enacting the imperatives of role); the neutrality of the role does not enable the person to avoid feeling personally responsible for his/her acts and their consequences

NPerdmB(1-4). Number of times personal responsibility mentioned, as above.

c) Variable name: PerDom C (1-4)

Willingness to take the consequences of not fulfilling the duties of role if following a stronger personal value

The lawyer expresses a willingness to take the consequences of not fulfilling the duties of role, or of not "playing by the rules" – "They can disbar me." Because of the greater importance the attorney attaches to certain moral values or principles, the person is willing to accept the consequences which enacting those principles may entail.

0 = no mention of consequences which might come from not following the rules
1 = lawyer mentions willingness to accept consequences of following personal imperatives over role imperatives in response to the dilemma
2 = lawyer spells out what some negative consequences might be of following personal imperatives over role obligations, and expresses willingness to accept consequences – "They'd have to disbar me."

NPerdmC(1-4). Number of times lawyer mentions willingness to accept consequences of following personal imperatives over role imperatives, including spelling out of the consequences as (1), see above (count 1 and 2 each).

Procedures for coding

Four coders, students from Fairhaven College/Western Washington University, were trained by Dana Jack and Rand Jack to identify rights and care orientations. Coders learned to use the Coding Manual by applying it to one extremely rights-oriented interview and a strongly care-oriented interview. Coders were blind to the gender and age of the subjects.

The two major ideas – moral orientation and lawyer position – are independently conceived and scored. (See the Coding Manual.)

Coders achieved high levels of intercoder reliability (a range of 0.54% to 100%, and a mean of 0.93) across samples of randomly selected cases on the thirty-eight key variables.

Appendix II: Figures and tables

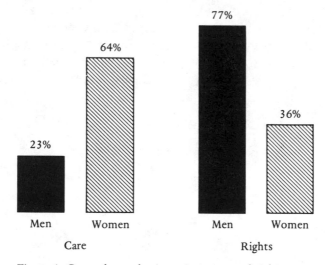

Figure 1. General moral orientation: care and rights response by gender. T-test on difference between care-orientation means reveals this difference is statistically significant: t (34) = -5.76, $p < .00005$.

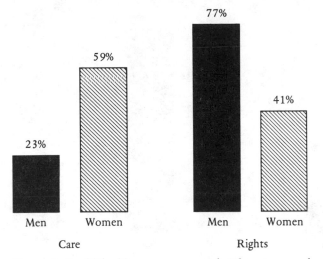

Figure 2. Real-life dilemmas: care and rights response by gender. If the lawyer described one moral dilemma, the question was asked again to see if other conflicts came to mind. The first two dilemmas in each interview were scored. Difference between men's and women's care-orientation means is statistically significant. For the first real-life dilemma, t (28) = $-2.22, p < .03$. For the second real-life dilemma, t (15) = $-2.85, p < .01$.

Table 1. *Care and rights considerations for all lawyers*

	Care state-ments (%)	Rights state-ments (%)
General moral orientation	43	57
Real-life dilemmas	42	58
2nd hypothetical dilemma (child custody)	37	63
1st hypothetical dilemma (murder confession)	22	78

Note: Percentages are means of individual scores and reflect amount of care or rights statements out of total moral orientation statements.

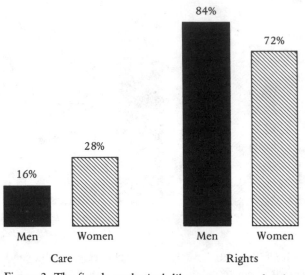

Figure 3. The first hypothetical dilemma: care and rights response by gender. Although women show more care orientation than men in this hypothetical dilemma, the difference is not statistically significant.

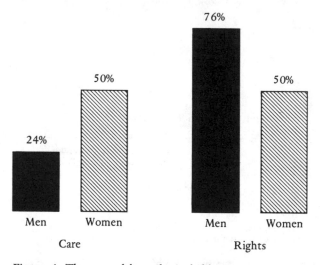

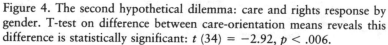

Figure 4. The second hypothetical dilemma: care and rights response by gender. T-test on difference between care-orientation means reveals this difference is statistically significant: t (34) = -2.92, $p < .006$.

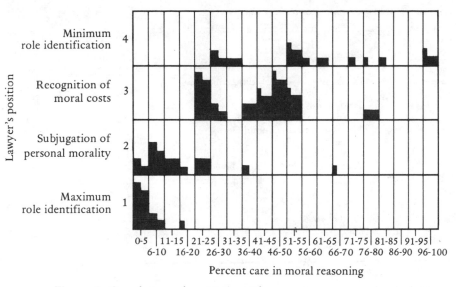

Figure 5. Correlation of positions with percent care reasoning in interviews.

Table 2. *Care considerations for women and men*

	Women's care statements (%)	Men's care statements (%)
General moral orientation	64	23
Real-life dilemmas	59	23
2nd hypothetical dilemma (child custody)	50	24
1st hypothetical dilemma (murder confession)	28	16

Note: Percentages are means of individual scores and reflect amount of care or rights statements out of total moral orientation statements.

Table 3. *Content of real-life dilemmas*

Category	Number of dilemmas
Partisanship and neutrality, conflicting with lawyer's values	24
Truth and honesty	15
Harm inflicted by application of law	12
Money (primarily around fees)	4
Fairness	4
Client confidentiality	3
Unethical conduct of other lawyers	1

Table 4. *Care-rights focus in general moral orientation*

Moral orientation	Male	Female
Rights focus	14	1
Care-rights	4	12
Care focus	0	1
Care only	0	4

Note: $X^2(3, N = 36) = 20.27, p < .0001$. Because cell counts are below five for this and the following tables, the chi-square values should be taken only as indicators of tendencies in the data.

Table 5. *Care-rights focus in first real-life dilemma*

Moral orientation	Male	Female
Rights only	8	3
Rights focus	2	1
Care-rights	3	7
Care focus	2	3
Care only	0	1

Note: $X^2(4, N = 15) = 5.41$, n.s.

Table 6. *Care-rights focus in second real-life dilemma*

Moral orientation	Male	Female
Rights only	2	0
Rights focus	3	1
Care-rights	1	2
Care only	1	7

Note: $X^2(3, N = 17) = 7.54, p < .056$ (n.s.).

Table 7. *Care-rights focus in first hypothetical dilemma*

Moral orientation	Male	Female
Rights only	12	5
Rights focus	1	7
Care-rights	4	3
Care focus	1	3

Note: $X^2(3, N = 36) = 8.53, p < .04$.

Table 8. *Care-rights focus in second hypothetical dilemma*

Moral orientation	Male	Female
Rights only	4	1
Rights focus	6	4
Care-rights	7	9
Care focus	0	4
Care only	1	0

Note: $X^2(4, N = 36) = 7.45$, n.s.

Table 9. *Maximum role identification: % of care responses from the attorneys who occupy Position 1*

	% Care[a] (number of men)	% Care[a] (number of women)
General part of interview	20 (2)	(0)
1st real-life dilemma	0 (1)	0 (1)
2nd real-life dilemma	17 (1)	(0)
1st hypothetical dilemma (initial)	0 (7)	0 (1)
1st hypothetical dilemma (final)	0 (7)	0 (1)
2nd hypothetical dilemma (initial)	7 (6)	(0)
2nd hypothetical dilemma (final)	1 (4)	(0)

[a]A mean of individual scores. The percentage indicates the amount of care reasoning present relative to rights reasoning.

Table 10. *Subjugation of personal morality: % of care responses from attorneys who occupy Position 2*

	% Care[a] (number of men)	% Care[a] (number of women)
General part of interview	19 (5)	50 (2)
1st real-life dilemma	11 (3)	16 (2)
2nd real-life dilemma	13 (2)	38 (2)
1st hypothetical dilemma (initial)	0 (2)	8 (7)
1st hypothetical dilemma (final)	0 (4)	7 (7)
2nd hypothetical dilemma (initial)	23 (5)	21 (3)
2nd hypothetical dilemma (final)	13 (3)	67 (1)

[a]A mean of individual scores. The percentage indicates the amount of care reasoning present relative to rights reasoning.

Table 11. *Recognition of moral costs: % of care responses from attorneys who occupy Position 3*

	% Care[a] (number of men)	% Care[a] (number of women)
General part of interview	24 (9)	63 (14)
1st real-life dilemma	25 (10)	51 (10)
2nd real-life dilemma	50 (1)	77 (4)
1st hypothetical dilemma (initial)	25 (8)	46 (10)
1st hypothetical dilemma (final)	24 (4)	37 (8)
2nd hypothetical dilemma (initial)	28 (6)	55 (13)
2nd hypothetical dilemma (final)	41 (5)	42 (8)

[a]A mean of individual scores. The percentage indicates the amount of care reasoning present relative to rights reasoning.

Table 12. *Minimum role identification: % of care responses from attorneys who occupy Position 4*

	% Care[a] (number of men)	% Care[a] (number of women)
General part of interview	33 (2)	83 (2)
1st real-life dilemma	33 (1)	74 (2)
2nd real-life dilemma	33 (3)	100 (4)
1st hypothetical dilemma (initial)	80 (1)	(0)
1st hypothetical dilemma (final)	62 (3)	83 (2)
2nd hypothetical dilemma (initial)	100 (1)	58 (2)
2nd hypothetical dilemma (final)	29 (6)	55 (9)

[a]A mean of individual scores. The percentage indicates the amount of care reasoning present relative to rights reasoning.

Notes

Chapter 1. Care and rights

1 See Bellah et al., *Habits of the Heart.*
2 Sophocles, *Antigone,* in *The Great Books Foundation,* 8.
3 Ibid., 2.
4 Ibid., 3–4.
5 Ibid., 33.
6 Ibid., 8.
7 Ibid., 26.
8 Ibid.
9 Ibid.
10 Ibid., 18.
11 Ibid., 17.
12 Ibid., 18.
13 Ibid., 33–4.
14 Freud, "Some Psychical Consequences," 257–8.
15 Kohlberg, *The Philosophy of Moral Development;* Kohlberg, "Stage and Sequence"; Kohlberg and Kramer, "Continuities and Discontinuities." Gilligan, *In a Different Voice,* refers to the Kohlberg schema as the morality of justice. We have elected to use the term morality of rights instead because of the place of justice in the legal system.
16 Were it not for the awkwardness of the phrase, we would have replaced morality of care with morality of responsiveness, which seems more descriptive of the orientation.
17 A huge body of literature on both Kohlberg's and Gilligan's work exists, including critiques, countercritiques, and reviews. See notes 25 and 26. Some other relevant work includes: Baumrind, "Sex Differences in Moral Reasoning"; Gibbs et al., "Sex Differences"; Kerber et al., "On *In a Different Voice*"; Lyons, "Two Perspectives"; Tronto, "Beyond Gender Difference"; Vasudev and Hummel, "Moral Stage Sequence"; Walker, "Sex Differences in the Development of Moral Reasoning."
18 Chodorow, *The Reproduction of Mothering;* Dinnerstein, *The Mermaid and the Minotaur;* Miller, "The Development of a Feminine Sense of Self"; Miller, *Toward a New Psychology of Women;* Noddings, *Caring;* Ruddick, "Maternal Thinking"; Surrey, "Self-in-Relation."

19 Chodorow, *The Reproduction of Mothering*, 44.
20 Belenky et al., *Women's Ways of Knowing*; Ruddick, "Maternal Thinking."
21 Gilligan, *In a Different Voice*.
22 See Chodorow, *The Reproduction of Mothering*; Gilligan, *In a Different Voice*; Miller, *Toward a New Psychology of Women*; Surrey, "Self-in-Relation."
23 See Hardin, "The Tragedy of the Commons."
24 Gilligan, *In a Different Voice*, 1.
25 Auerbach et al., "On Gilligan's *In a Different Voice*"; Kerber et al., "On *In a Different Voice*"; Lloyd, "Reason, Gender, and Morality"; Nicholson, "Women, Morality, and History"; Rhode, "The 'Woman's Point of View' "; Scales, "The Emergence of Feminist Jurisprudence."
26 Gilligan's work has stimulated attempts by legal scholars to go beyond a jurisprudence of rights and to consider how a care orientation affects different aspects of law. See, for instance, DuBois et al., "Feminist Discourse, Moral Values and the Law"; Karst, "Women's Constitution"; Law, "Rethinking Sex and the Constitution"; Menkel-Meadow, "Women as Law Teachers"; Rhode, "The 'Woman's Point of View' "; Scales, "The Emergence of Feminist Jurisprudence"; Schneider, "The Dialectic of Rights and Politics"; Sherry, "Civic Virtue and the Feminine Voice in Constitutional Adjudication."
27 Melville, *Billy Budd*.
28 Ibid., 68.
29 Ibid., 69.
30 Plato, *Statesman*, 1063, 1072.
31 Ibid., 1064, 1067.
32 Ibid., 1063.
33 Ibid., 1070.
34 Ibid., 1063.
35 Aristotle, *Nicomachean Ethics*, 5.4, in Hutchins, *Great Books of the Western World*, 379–80.
36 Ibid., 379.
37 Nader, "Styles of Court Procedure: To Make the Balance," in Nader, *Law in Culture and Society*, 69–91.
38 Ibid., 73.
39 Ibid., 85–6.
40 Gluckman, *The Judicial Process Among the Barotse of Northern Rhodesia*, 20–21.
41 Hoebel, "Three Studies in African Law," 440.
42 See Deloria, *American Indian, American Justice*.
43 Nader, "Forums for Justice," 152.
44 *Lyng v. Northwest Indian Cemetery Protective Association*, 485 U.S. __ (1988).
45 *Bradwell v. Illinois*, 83 U.S. (16 Wall), 130, 141–2 (1893).
46 American Bar Association, "A *Review of Legal Education in the United States, Fall 1986*."

Chapter 2. The lawyer's role

1 *Byrn v. New York City Health and Hospitals Corporation,* 286 N.E. 2d 887, 889 (1972).
2 *Shapero v. Kentucky Bar Association,* 100 L.Ed. 2d 475, 495 (1988) (O'Conner dissenting).
3 Sartre, *Existentialism and Humanism;* Postema, "Moral Responsibility in Professional Ethics," 74.
4 Curtis, "Ethics of Advocacy," 13.
5 Ibid., 9.
6 Frank, *Courts on Trial,* 82–3.
7 Auerbach, *Unequal Justice,* 12.
8 Fried, "Lawyer as Friend," 1066. The justification based on the morality of client representation is advanced most strenuously by Charles Fried and Monroe Freedman ("Personal Responsibility in a Professional System"). Deborah Rhode has questioned the general application of such an extreme notion of adversarial partisanship. The criminal defense system presents a compelling need for an uncompromised advocate, but given the small number who actually ply that trade, she doubts the appropriateness of the adversarial partisanship paradigm for all legal practice ("Ethical Perspectives on Legal Practice," 605).
9 Wasserstrom, "Lawyers as Professionals," 3–8; Postema, "Moral Responsibility in Professional Ethics," 73–4. We wish to acknowledge a special debt to Wasserstrom and Postema for their influence on our thinking.
10 Our descriptive analysis would have to be modified if we were dealing with lawyers as business counselors rather than front-line advocates.
11 Quoted in Frankel, "Search for Truth," 1036.
12 Quoted in Freedman, *Lawyers' Ethics in an Adversary System,* 51.
13 Curtis, "Ethics of Advocacy," 16.
14 Wasserstrom, "Lawyers as Professionals," 3.
15 Ibid., 8–9.
16 Postema, "Moral Responsibility in Professional Ethics," 65.
17 Stout, *In the Best of Families,* 199, quoted in Simon, "Ideology of Advocacy," 30.
18 Simon, "Ideology of Advocacy," 36.
19 *United States v. Wade,* 388 U.S. 218, 257–8 (1967).
20 Frank, *Courts on Trial,* 82–3.
21 Simon, "Ideology of Advocacy," 30. In an article on advocacy, Monroe Freedman kindled a debate when he defended conduct that would be most questionable in a nonprofessional setting – discrediting an adverse witness whom the lawyer knows to be telling the truth, putting a witness on the stand knowing that he will commit perjury, and advising a client in a manner likely to tempt commission of perjury ("Professional Responsibility of the Criminal Defense Lawyer"). Although John Noonan set out to challenge Freedman's conclusion ("The Purpose of Advocacy and the Limits of Confidentiality"), William Simon argues

persuasively that both Freedman and Noonan agree to the basic tenets of what Simon calls the ideology of advocacy. Both would endorse certain actions that a lay person might find questionable, such as the exclusion of accurate evidence where the rules permit, concealment of evidence learned from the client even though relevant, pleading a guilty client innocent, and pleading the statute of limitations to defeat an otherwise valid civil claim.

22 Rhode, "Ethical Perspectives on Legal Practice," 612.
23 *People v. Belge,* 41 N.Y. 2d 60 (1976).
24 Curtis, "Ethics of Advocacy," 9.
25 Ibid., 6.
26 Ibid., 19.
27 Postema, "Moral Responsibility in Professional Ethics," 78.
28 Rhode, "Ethical Perspectives on Legal Practice," 643.
29 A number of solutions have been suggested for the dilemma posed by role identification for the attorney. William Simon proposes what he calls nonprofessional advocacy. Under this concept, role morality yields to personal ethics so that the attorney makes moral decisions without restrictions of role and assumes responsibility for the consequences of those decisions. The lawyer–client relationship depends upon the advocate and the client justifying themselves to each other ("Ideology of Advocacy," 130). Richard Wasserstrom calls for a similar deprofessionalization of the attorney's role, which would significantly elevate the importance of personal morality in decision making ("Lawyers as Professionals," 19). Gerald Postema rejects Wasserstrom's position as failing to appreciate sufficiently the social value of the attorney role in the legal system. Favoring a middle ground between maximum and minimal role identification, he seeks a new conception of the lawyer role that would make fuller use of personal moral sensibilities. This conception of role allows the attorney to serve important functions of the legal system while integrating a personal sense of moral responsibility ("Moral Responsibility in Professional Ethics," 82).
30 Postema, "Moral Responsibility in Professional Ethics," 70.
31 Ibid., 69.
32 Ibid.
33 Wasserstrom, "Lawyers as Professionals," 5.
34 Bonsignore, "Law School: Caught in the Paradigmatic Squeeze," in Bonsignore et al., *Before the Law,* 257–61. Bonsignore relies on Erving Goffman's classic work, *Asylums,* in developing his explanation.
35 Ibid., 258–60.
36 Turow, *One L,* 90.
37 Ibid., 92.
38 Ibid., 92–3.
39 Ibid., 93.
40 27 *American Jurisprudence* 2d 518, quoting Aristotle, *Nicomachean Ethics,* 5.10.
41 Blackstone, *Commentaries on the Laws of England,* 1: 61–2.

42 *United States v. Dougherty* 473 F. 2d 1113, 1132 (1972).
43 Ibid., 1133.
44 Pound, *Philosophy of Law,* 58.
45 Ibid., 70.
46 Nader and Todd, *The Disputing Process – Law in Ten Societies,* 40.

Chapter 3. Personal morality

1 See Table 1 in Appendix II.
2 Analysis of variance indicates that percentages of care were influenced by gender, F $(1,136)$ = 12.06, $p < .000$; and by the different sections of the interview, F $(3,134)$ = 3.93, $p < .01$. There was no significant interaction effect between gender and interview part (data were pooled across the four sections of the interview to allow this analysis).

Table 2 in Appendix II indicates a close proximity of percentage of care response for women in general moral orientation and in real-life dilemmas, which previews a phenomenon discussed in detail in the next chapter. The care perspective often conflicts with the prevalent rights orientation of the legal system, thus giving rise to the moral tension of which real-life dilemmas are made. The higher percentage of care an attorney expresses in the general moral orientation, the more likely that the attorney will describe more than one real life moral dilemma [F $(1,34)$ = 4.40, $p < .04$]. Because primarily care-oriented lawyers identified real-life dilemmas in their practice, the care scores for general orientation and real-life dilemmas match closely despite the pull of real-life dilemmas toward a role perspective.

3 In reading this and the following chapters, it should be noted that we do not rely simply on specific words attorneys use in order to determine whether they reason with a moral orientation of rights or care. Often words like "justice," "truth," "obligation," and "fairness" are employed by attorneys with either orientation. These words may mean different things to the individual, depending on the underlying orientation that organizes moral perceptions. Although the words used may give some indication of moral perspective, we rely primarily on the structure and substance of the lawyer's thought. All lawyers are trained in the language of rights; all know the schema of the separate, autonomous individual whose rights are protected from interference by others through procedures and rules. Even though the "lawyer talk" of rights and justice frequently appears in all the interviews, underlying assumptions, patterns of thought, and focal points generally reveal the moral perspective of the speaker. See the Coding Manual in Appendix I.

4 See Figure 1 in Appendix II.

5 Of the 63 real life dilemmas raised by attorneys, 36 came from female lawyers.

6 See Figure 2 in Appendix II.

7 Table 3 in Appendix II shows the content of the real-life dilemmas, grouped by broad categories.

8 Bok, *Lying*, 170.
9 *Time*, July 21, 1986, 58.
10 *Nix v. Whiteside*, 475 U.S. 157, 166 (1976).
11 Compare Justice Burger's position with that expressed by Justice White in *United States v. Wade*, quoted in our discussion of the first hypothetical dilemma which follows; also see Chapter 2.
12 *Nix v. Whiteside*, 174.
13 Ibid., 171.
14 *Gideon v. Wainwright*, 372 U.S. 335, 344 (1963).
15 *Miranda v. Arizona*, 384 U.S. 436, 460 (1966).
16 *United States v. Wade*, 388 U.S. 218, 256–8 (1967).
17 *Miranda v. Arizona*, 480–1.
18 American Bar Association Model Rules of Professional Conduct, Rule 3.1, quotation from Model Code Comparison following Comment. Throughout our discussion we rely on the Model Rules of Professional Conduct as a standard of ethical responsibility of attorneys. This code was adopted by the American Bar Association in 1983 and subsequently was accepted with various modifications by a number of states. Other states still rely on the older ABA Model Code of Professional Responsibility. Regulation of attorney conduct is primarily a matter of state authority, with states free to adopt and modify ABA models as they choose.
19 See Figure 3 in Appendix II. Also note that neither this nor the second hypothetical dilemma specifies the gender of the client. Nevertheless, most attorneys projected a gender, usually describing the murderer and the errant parent as male.
20 These questions were adapted from Carol Gilligan's interview format for eliciting and assessing moral conflicts. See Langdale and Gilligan, "The Contribution of Women's Thought" and "Coding Manual," Gender, Education, and Human Development Study Center.
21 See Figure 4 in Appendix II. Of the lawyers interviewed, 70 percent felt that the second hypothetical dilemma was the more difficult dilemma, with another 15 percent seeing them as approximately equal.
22 Gilligan and Attanucci, "Two Moral Orientations," 224–5.
23 To get a picture of the relative amounts of care or rights reasoning *within* individuals in the study, we analyzed data in the following way. Within each section of the interview, responses consisting of only care or rights considerations are labeled *care only* or *rights only*. Responses consisting of 75 percent of more care or rights considerations are labeled *care focus* or *rights focus*, and responses in which less than 75 percent of the total number of considerations are care or rights are placed in the *care–rights* category. (These categories follow Brown et al., "Reading for Self and Moral Voice"; "Coding Manual," Gender, Education, and Human Development Study Center; and Gilligan and Attanucci, "Two Moral Orientations.") See Tables 4–8 in Appendix II.

Chapter 4. Personal morality and attorney role

1 The amount of care reasoning correlates with the amount of tension experienced in the role (Pearson correlation coefficient = .35, $p < .03$). Statistical analysis (multiple regression with dummy variables for length and type of practice) showed that the length and type of practice did not explain a significant amount of the variance in care and rights reasoning, or in position.

2 We scored each interview for role-identification position across the various segments of the interview: general orientation, real-life dilemmas, and first and second hypothetical moral dilemmas. In responding to the hypothetical dilemmas, some attorneys changed their positions as they reasoned through the dilemma or when, in the second hypothetical dilemma, hypothetical facts were altered. This led us to score for an "initial position" and a "final position" for each hypothetical dilemma, reflecting that tension and response may change as different moral concerns arise, or as personal morality is more heavily assaulted by differing role obligations.

3 Table 9 in Appendix II shows that compared with women, many men fit into Position 1 of maximum role identification. The table also indicates that people in this position have relatively few care considerations in their perception and resolution of moral problems. To interpret this and the similar tables for the other four positions some guidance may be useful. Every attorney interviewed was scored for position in each of seven parts of the interview. Thus, a lawyer might be in Position 1 for the first real-life dilemma and Position 3 for the second hypothetical dilemma. An attorney's statements for a given part of the interview were separately analyzed for moral orientation and for position. The Position 1 table shows that, for example, with regard to the second hypothetical dilemma (initial) part of the interview, six male attorneys (number in parenthesis) were in Position 1 and they had an average of 7 percent care in their responses. No women were in Position 1 for this same part of the interview. Because the total role identification of Position 1 precludes conflict between professional and personal morality, we did not expect to find real-life dilemmas meeting the criteria of Position 1. But as Table 9 indicates, lawyers in the study discuss three such real-life dilemmas. Two of these involved conflict between role and personal self-interest and the third a dilemma over the proper professional course of action. In all three situations the lawyer identified with the role and felt no challenge to that position by tenets of personal morality.

4 See Table 10 in Appendix II.

5 In our interviews, the instances of women in Position 2 equaled that of men despite the limited evidence of care orientation in that position. This is accounted for by several factors. First, strongly rights-oriented men gravitated to Position 1, leaving the ranks of men in Position 2 relatively depleted. Second, portions of the interview that strongly commanded role adherence attracted women to a Position 2 resolution. Third, some women with a moderate care orientation found Position 2 an acceptable accommodation in the face of professional strictures.

6 Note that Jennifer Hall also appears under Position 2. It was not uncommon for

attorneys to appear in one position in one part of the interview and another position in a different part of the interview due to the perceived difference of moral demands in varying circumstances.

7 English liveryman Thomas Hobson (1544–1631) required that customers either take the horse nearest the stable door or none at all.

8 See Table 11 in Appendix II. In Position 3, women demonstrate a better than 50 percent care orientation across the interview except for the first hypothetical dilemma and the final position in the second dilemma. The strong constitutional demands for role compliance explain the drop in care response to the first hypothetical dilemma. The fall off in care statements between initial and final response to the second dilemma is more surprising because the factual shift to increased harm to the children was expected to elicit more concern for their welfare. This apparent anomaly is explained by the drop from 13 women making an initial Position 3 response to 8 women making a final Position 3 response. Of the high-care women, 5 moved from Position 3 to Position 4 as they shifted from initial to final response, thus removing their high care percentages from the second hypothetical final response tabulation.

9 Because breaking with the omnipresent role of attorney represents such an extreme course of conduct, we rely initially on real-life situations to illustrate Position 4. Although the custody hypothetical dilemma produced the largest number of lawyers in this position, we share with other researchers a concern about the relationship between moral thought exhibited in response to hypothetical situations and moral action in a real situation of moral conflict. Certainly responses to hypothetical dilemmas tell us something about people's moral posture, but because of the sensitivity of issues implicit in a Position 4 response, we attempt to be as realistic as possible in depicting the context and conflicts in which attorneys depart from role expectations. Thus we rely on attorneys' descriptions of actual conflicts in which they followed their own moral values instead of role dictates. The real-life dilemmas classified under Position 4 include several domestic relations cases, two criminal law issues, and a scattering of general civil matters.

10 Gilligan, *In a Different Voice*, 43.

11 As one might expect, criminal law cases figure most often in Position 1 and Position 2 statements, and situations where vulnerable people are exposed to harm frequently give rise to Position 3 and especially Position 4. In the criminal law context the imperatives of advocacy are most compelling, whereas in domestic cases the rules are often less demanding and the pull of care values most evident. The weighting of our sample toward domestic law may have produced an abnormal number of attorneys in Positions 3 and 4, although a second bias in the sample toward criminal practice should provide a correction toward Positions 1 and 2. Because the sample matched women and men for type of practice, the tendency of area of practice to push toward one end of the scale or the other should not affect gender distribution across the spectrum. Also, all attorneys had the opportunity to express a full range of moral orientation across the entire interview. See Figure 5 in Appendix II and n. 13.

12 See Table 12 in Appendix II.
13 Figure 5 in Appendix II shows the relationship between Positions 1 through 4 and the percentage of care response by attorneys across the interview. Since each attorney was scored for position in seven possible places in the interview, the graph reflects a total 252 positions, which are distributed across the graph. Position and personal morality were defined separately and were coded independently. The procedure was to read through the interview to first score the personal morality, then to reread the interview in order to score the lawyers' positions. Coders were blind to the hypothesized relation of personal morality to role as they scored interviews. Thus the association between tension and care morality does not arise because of scoring overlap or because these are defined similarly.
14 Kohlberg, "The Claim to Moral Adequacy"; Kohlberg, "Stage and Sequence"; Kohlberg and Kramer, "Continuities and Discontinuities."
15 None of the attorneys whom we interviewed reasoned from a preconventional perspective. That orientation is more often associated with children and adolescents, or with members of society who feel themselves to be on its fringes.
16 See *Shapero v. Kentucky Bar Association*, 100 L.Ed. 2d 475, 495 (1988) (O'Conner dissenting): "Special ethical standards for lawyers are properly understood as an appropriate means of restraining lawyers in the exercise of the unique power that they inevitably wield in a political system like ours."

Chapter 5. Women lawyers

1 Fox, "Good-bye to Gameplaying," 37–42.
2 Piaget, *The Rules of the Game*, 76.
3 Ibid., 69.
4 See reviews by Belle, "Gender Differences in Children's Social Networks," in Belle, *Children's Social Networks;* Dickens and Perlman, "Friendship over the Life Cycle," in Duck and Gilmour, *Personal Relationships;* Hess, "Friendship and Gender Roles," in Stein, *Single Life;* Maccoby, "Social Groupings in Childhood," in Olwens et al., *Development of Antisocial and Prosocial Behavior.*
5 Lever, "Games Children Play," 482.
6 American Bar Association, "Summary of Hearings," 3. These conclusions are reiterated by task-force findings on women in the courts. See "Report of New York Task Force," 1–198, "First Year Report of New Jersey," 129–77; "Women Lawyers Get Less Pay Than Men and Less Respect," *Wall Street Journal* (February 12, 1988). Such task forces have been formed in eighteen states to document the degree of gender bias that exists against women lawyers within the profession and against women litigants (Lynn H. Schafran, Director, National Judicial Education Program, letter to the authors, August 1988).
7 Strachan, "A Map for Women," 94.
8 Gelernter, "Speak Louder, Lower, Women Lawyers Told," *Seattle Times* (October 18, 1980); Gilligan and Luchsinger, "Intimidated? Or Intimidator?" 22.
9 Strachan, "A Map for Women," 94.

10 See Auerbach, *Unequal Justice.*

11 American Bar Association, "Summary of Hearings," 9.

12 Strachan, "A Map for Women," 94.

13 This concern is shared by the "Summary of Hearings," ABA Commission on Women in the Profession (1988): "Witnesses expressed the belief that women must still work harder and be better than men in order to be recognized and succeed," 3. Likewise, Winter, "Women Lawyers Work Harder," 1387, describes a 1983 ABA Survey and reports that women lawyers assessed their own greatest strengths in this order: "being harder working or more dedicated and conscientious; being more humane and sensitive to clients and their needs; showing greater attention to detail; and being better prepared." Men agreed with these assessments. For a summary of findings on credibility and gender in the courtroom, see "Report of New York Task Force," 113–23, 125, 139–46.

14 Miller, *Toward a New Psychology of Women,* 17–19, 32–3.

15 "First Year Report of New Jersey," 142.

16 American Bar Association, "Summary of Hearings," 3–4.

17 Klemesrud, "Women in the Law: Many Are Getting Out," *New York Times* (August 9, 1985).

18 "Open Letter to the Law School Community," Minorities and Women at Yale Law School, 1984.

19 Ibid.

20 Yale Law School responded by securing a Rockefeller Foundation Grant for a study on "Gender and Professional Socialization: Issues in Law and Legal Education." The goal is "To study whether, and if so how, the style, motivating values and content of legal education and the legal profession place insufficient emphasis on the perspectives and values of women, thus leading to alienation and professional dissatisfaction on the part of women law students and lawyers." The study is not complete.

21 Although our examples are drawn from interviews with female attorneys, the problem is similar for men with a care orientation.

22 See Belenky et al., *Women's Ways of Knowing.*

23 Other professional women in business also replicate this pattern. See especially McBroom, *The Third Sex.*

24 Winter, "Women Lawyers Work Harder," 1384, states, "87 percent of women lawyers who took a leave of absence to have a baby returned to work within six months." The survey was of a random sample of 605 lawyers, two-thirds of them women.

25 Marcia Westkott, describing Karen Horney's theory of the feminine type, writes: "Fantasies of triumph in romantic and professional spheres compete because the requirements for success in each are opposed: how can a woman be both lovable and ambitious if the former requires being deferential to others and the latter necessitates triumphing over them?" See *The Feminist Legacy of Karen Horney,* 177.

26 Kegan, *The Evolving Self,* 11, quoting Fingarette, *The Self in Transformation,* 62–8.

27 Gilligan, *In a Different Voice,* 136–50, makes these points.
28 For an excellent discussion of the interrelatedness of rights arguments and contextual considerations, see Schneider, "The Dialectic of Rights and Politics," 589–652.
29 ABA, "Summary of Hearings," 9.

Chapter 6. Toward a more morally responsive advocate

1 Frankfurter to Rosenwald, May 13, 1927.
2 Postema, "Moral Responsibility in Professional Ethics," 89.
3 Rhode, "Ethical Perspectives on Legal Practice," 645.
4 Ibid., 644–5.
5 Sharwood, *Essay on Professional Ethics,* reprinted in *Reports of American Bar Association* 32 (1907).
6 Ibid., 81.
7 Ibid., 90.
8 Ibid., 96.
9 See Heymann and Liebman, *The Social Responsibility of Lawyers.*
10 Sharwood, *Essay on Professional Ethics,* 98–9.
11 Quoted in ibid., 101.
12 Ibid., 108–9.
13 See Karst, "Women's Constitution"; Law, "Rethinking Sex and the Constitution"; MacKinnon, "Feminism, Marxism, Method, and the State: Toward Feminist Jurisprudence"; Scales, "Emergence of Feminist Jurisprudence"; Sherry, "Civic Virtue and the Feminine Voice in Constitutional Adjudication."
14 See Schneider, "The Dialectic of Rights and Politics."
15 Boyle, *A Feminist Review of Criminal Law,* 47.
16 The Supreme Court case *De Shaney v. Winnebago County Department of Social Services* provides another example of moral assumptions' affecting substantive results. Is a state agency constitutionally obligated to protect a child it knows to be in danger of physical abuse? Blackmun's dissent recognizes that precedents go either way, "depending upon how one chooses to read them." Rehnquist's majority opinion is implicitly grounded in morality of rights assumptions – autonomous individuals discharge responsibility by restraint from interference: "The most that can be said of the state functionaries in this case is that they stood by and did nothing when suspicious circumstances dictated a more active role for them." Care assumptions of interdependence and active responsibility lead to a different result. As Brennan recognizes in dissent, "Inaction can be every bit as abusive as action."
17 Chesterton, "The Twelve Men," in *Tremendous Trifles,* 57–8.
18 Wald, "Yale Was There," 79.

Bibliography

Books and articles

American Bar Association. "A Review of Legal Education in the United States, Fall 1986. Law Schools and Bar Admission Requirements." Chicago: American Bar Association, 1987.

"Summary of Hearings." Chicago: ABA Commission on Women in the Profession. 1988.

American Jurisprudence. 2d ed., vol. 27. Rochester, N.Y.: The Lawyers Cooperative Publishing Company, 1966.

Aristotle. *Nicomachean Ethics.* Translated by W. D. Ross. In *Great Books of the Western World,* vol. 9, edited by Robert Maynard Hutchins. Chicago: Encyclopaedia Britannica, 1952.

Auerbach, Jerald S. *Unequal Justice.* New York: Oxford University Press, 1976.

Auerbach, Judy, Linda Blum, Vicki Smith, and Christine Williams. "On Gilligan's *In a Different Voice.*" *Feminist Studies* 11 (Spring 1985): 149–61.

Baumrind, D. "Sex Differences in Moral Reasoning: Response to Walker's (1984) Conclusion that There Are None." *Child Development* 57 (1986): 511–21.

Belenky, Mary F., Blythe M. Clinchy, Nancy R. Goldberger, and Jill M. Tarule. *Women's Ways of Knowing.* New York: Basic Books, 1986.

Bellah, Robert, Richard Madsen, William M. Sullivan, Ann Swidler, and Steven M. Tipton. *Habits of the Heart.* Berkeley: University of California Press, 1985.

Belle, Deborah. "Gender Differences in Children's Social Networks and Supports." In *Children's Social Networks and Social Support,* edited by Deborah Belle, 172–89. New York: John Wiley, 1989.

Blackstone, William. *Commentaries on the Laws of England,* vol. 1. Oxford: Clarendon Press, 1765–9.

Bok, Sissela. *Lying: Moral Choice in Public and Private Discourse.* New York: Vintage, 1979.

Bonsignore, John J. "Law School: Caught in the Paradigmatic Squeeze." In *Before the Law,* edited by John J. Bonsignore, Ethan Katsh, Peter d'Errico, Ronald M. Pipkin, Stephen Arons, and Janet Rifkind, 257–62. Boston: Houghton Mifflin, 1984.

Boyle, Christine L. M., Marie-Andree Betrand, Celine Lacerte-Lamontagne, and

Rebecca Shamai. *A Feminist Review of Criminal Law*. Ottawa, Canada: Minister of Supply and Services, 1985.

Broughton, John M. "Women's Rationality and Men's Virtues: A Critique of Gender Dualism in Gilligan's Theory of Moral Development." *Social Research* 50 (Autumn 1983): 597–642.

Brown, Lyn M., Mark B. Tappan, Carol Gilligan, Barbara A. Miller, and Dianne E. Argyris. "Reading for Self and Moral Voice: A Method for Interpreting Narratives of Real-Life Moral Conflict and Choice." In *Interpretive Investigations: Contributions to Psychological Research*, edited by M. Packer and R. Addison. Albany: SUNY Press, in press.

Chesterton, G. K. "The Twelve Men." In *Tremendous Trifles*. New York: Sheed & Ward, 1955.

Chodorow, Nancy. *The Reproduction of Mothering: Psychoanalysis and the Sociology of Gender*. Berkeley: University of California Press, 1978.

Code, Lorraine B. "Responsibility and the Epistemic Community: Woman's Place." *Social Research* 50 (Autumn 1983): 537–55.

"Coding Manual: A Guide to Reading for Self and Moral Orientation in Real-Life Moral Conflicts." Gender, Education, and Human Development Study Center, Harvard Graduate School of Education. Working Draft, February 1986.

Curtis, Charles. "The Ethics of Advocacy." *Stanford Law Review* 4 (1951): 3–23.

Deloria, Vine. *American Indians, American Justice*. Austin: University of Texas Press, 1983.

Dickens, Wenda, and Daniel Perlman. "Friendship over the Life Cycle." In *Personal Relationships*, edited by Steve Duck and Robin Gilmour, 91–133. London: Academic Press, 1981.

Dinnerstein, Dorothy. *The Mermaid and the Minotaur*. New York: Harper & Row, 1976.

DuBois, Ellen C., Mary Dunlap, Carol Gilligan, Catherine MacKinnon, and Carrie Menkel-Meadow. "Feminist Discourse, Moral Values and the Law – A Conversation." *Buffalo Law Review* 34 (1985): 11–87.

Epstein, Cynthia F. *Women in Law*. New York: Ballantine, 1981.

"The First Year Report of the New Jersey Supreme Court Task Force on Women in the Courts." *Women's Rights Law Reporter* 9 (1986): 129–77.

Flanagan, Owen J., Jr. "A Reply to Lawrence Kohlberg." *Ethics* 92 (1982): 529–32.
——— "Virtue, Sex and Gender: Some Philosophical Reflections on the Moral Psychology Debate." *Ethics* 92 (1982): 499–512.

Flanagan, Owen J., Jr., and Jonathan E. Adler. "Impartiality and Particularity." *Social Research* 50 (Autumn 1983): 576–96.

Fletcher, Joseph F. *Situation Ethics*. Philadelphia: Westminister Press, 1966.

Fox, Priscilla. "Good-bye to Gameplaying." *Juris Doctor* (January 1978): 37–42.

Frank, Jerome. *Courts on Trial: Myth and Reality in American Justice*. Princeton, N.J.: Princeton University Press, 1949.

Frankel, Marvin E. "The Search for Truth: An Umpireal View." *University of Pennsylvania Law Review* 123 (1975): 1031–59.

Frankfurter, Felix, to Rosenwald, May 13, 1927, Felix Frankfurter Papers, Harvard Law School Library.

Freedman, Monroe H. "Judge Frankel's Search for Truth." *University of Pennsylvania Law Review* 123 (1975): 1060–6.

   Lawyer's Ethics in the Adversary System. New York: Bobbs Merrill, 1975.

   "Personal Responsibility in a Professional System." *Catholic University Law Review* 27 (1978): 191–205.

   "Professional Responsibility of the Criminal Defense Lawyer: The Three Hardest Questions." *Michigan Law Review* 64 (1966): 1469–84.

Freud, Sigmund. "Some Psychical Consequences of the Anatomical Distinction Between the Sexes." In *The Standard Edition of the Complete Psychological Works of Sigmund Freud,* edited by James Strachey, 19: 248–58. London: Hogarth Press, 1961. (Originally published 1925.)

Fried, Charles. "The Lawyer as Friend: The Moral Foundation of the Lawyer–Client Relation." *Yale Law Journal* 85 (1976): 1060–89.

Gibbs, J. C., K. D. Arnold, and J. E. Burkhart. "Sex Differences in the Expression of Moral Judgment." *Child Development* 55 (1984): 1040–3.

Gilligan, Carol. *In a Different Voice: Psychological Theory and Women's Development*. Cambridge, Mass.: Harvard University Press, 1982.

   "Woman's Place in Man's Life Cycle." *Harvard Educational Review* 49 (1979): 431–47.

Gilligan, Carol, and Jane Attanucci. "Two Moral Orientations: Gender Differences and Similarities." *Merrill-Palmer Quarterly* 34 (1988): 223–37.

Gilligan, Carol, Lyn Mikel Brown, Annie G. Rogers. "Psyche Embedded: A Place for Body, Relationships, and Culture in Personality Theory." In *Studying Persons and Lives,* edited by A. Rabin et al. New York: Springer, in press.

Gilligan, Michele, and M. Lou Luchsinger. "Intimidated? Or Intimidator?" *Women Lawyers Journal* 72 (Winter 1986): 1–2 and 22.

Gluckman, Max. *The Judicial Process among the Barotse of Northern Rhodesia,* 2nd ed. Manchester: Manchester University Press, 1955.

Goodpaster, Kenneth E. "Kohlbergian Theory: A Philosophical Counterinvitation." *Ethics* 92 (1982): 491–8.

Hardin, Garrett. "The Tragedy of the Commons." *Science* 162 (1968): 1243–8.

Hazard, Geoffrey C., Jr. *Ethics in the Practice of Law*. New Haven, Conn.: Yale University Press, 1978.

Henley, Nancy M. "Psychology and Gender." *Signs: Journal of Women in Culture and Society* 11 (1985): 101–19.

Hess, Beth. "Friendship and Gender Roles over the Life Course." In *Single Life,* edited by Peter Stein, 104–15. New York: St. Martin's Press, 1981.

Heymann, Philip B., and Lance Liebman. *The Social Responsibility of Lawyers*. Westbury, N.Y.: Foundation Press, 1988.

Hilary, Rose. "Hand, Brain and Heart: A Feminist Epistemology for the Natural Sciences." *Signs: Journal of Women in Culture and Society* 9 (1983): 73–90.

Hoebel, E. Adamson. "Three Studies in African Law." *Stanford Law Review* 13 (1961): 418–42.

Iannone, Carol. "The Barbarism of Feminist Scholarship." *The Intercollegiate Review* (Fall 1987): 35–41.

Karst, Kenneth L. "Women's Constitution." *Duke Law Journal* (1984): 447–508.

Kegan, Robert. *The Evolving Self.* Cambridge, Mass.: Harvard University Press, 1982.

The Sweeter Welcome: Martin Buber, Bernard Malamud and Saul Bellow. Needham Heights, Mass.: Wexford, 1977.

Kerber, Linda K., Catherine G. Greeno and Eleanor E. Maccoby, Zella Luria, Carol B. Stack, and Carol Gilligan. "On *In a Different Voice:* An Interdisciplinary Forum." *Signs: Journal of Women in Culture and Society* 11 (1986): 304–33.

Kohlberg, Lawrence. "The Claim to Moral Adequacy of a Highest Stage of Moral Judgment." *The Journal of Philosophy* 70 (1973): 630–46.

The Philosophy of Moral Development: Moral Stages and the Idea of Justice. New York: Harper & Row, 1981.

"A Reply to Owen Flanagan and Some Comments on the Puza-Goodpaster Exchange." *Ethics* 92 (1982): 513–28.

"Stage and Sequence: The Cognitive Developmental Approach to Socialization." In *Handbook of Socialization: Theory and Research,* edited by D. Goslin, 347–480. New York: Rand McNally, 1969.

Kohlberg, Lawrence, and R. Kramer. "Continuities and Discontinuities in Childhood and Adult Moral Development." *Human Development* 12 (1969): 93–120.

Langdale, Sharry, and Carol Gilligan. "The Contribution of Women's Thought to Developmental Theory: The Elimination of Sex Bias in Moral Development, Work and Education." Interim Report Submitted to National Institute of Education.

Law, Sylvia. "Rethinking Sex and the Constitution." *University of Pennsylvania Law Review* 132 (1984): 955–1040.

Lever, Janet. "Games Children Play." *Social Problems* 23 (1976): 478–87.

Llewellyn, Karl N. *Bramble Bush: On Our Law and Its Study.* Dobbs Ferry, N.Y.: Oceana, 1981.

Lloyd, Genevieve. "Reason, Gender, and Morality in the History of Philosophy." *Social Research* 50 (Autumn 1983): 490–513.

Lubin, David. *The Good Lawyer: Lawyers' Role and Lawyers' Ethics.* Totowa, N.J.: Rowman & Allanheld, 1984.

Lyons, Nona. "Two Perspectives: On Self, Relationships and Morality." *Harvard Educational Review* 53 (1983): 125–46.

McBroom, Patricia. *The Third Sex.* New York: William Morrow, 1986.

Maccoby, Eleanor. "Social Groupings in Childhood: Their Relationship to Prosocial and Antisocial Behavior in Boys and Girls." In *Development of Antisocial and Prosocial Behavior: Themes, Research and Issues,* edited by Dan Olwens, Jack Block, and Marian Radke-Yarrow. San Diego: Academic Press, 1985.

MacKinnon, Catharine A. "Femininism, Marxism, Method, and the State: An Agenda for Theory." *Signs: Journal of Women in Culture and Society* 7 (1982): 515–44.

"Feminism, Marxism, Method, and the State: Toward Feminist Jurisprudence." *Signs: Journal of Women in Culture and Society* 8 (1983): 635–58.

Mellinkoff, David. *The Conscience of a Lawyer.* St. Paul, Minn.: West Publishing, 1973.

Melville, Herman. *Billy Budd.* New York: Penguin, 1979.

Menkel-Meadow, Carrie. "Women as Law Teachers: Toward the 'Feminization' of Legal Education." In *Humanistic Education in Law.* Monograph 3, Essays on the Application of a Humanistic Perspective to Law Teaching, 16–32. Columbia University School of Law, 1981.

Miller, Jean Baker. "The Development of the Feminine Sense of Self." Work in Progress, Paper #12, Available from the Stone Center for Developmental Services and Studies, Wellesley College, Wellesley, Massachusetts.

Toward a New Psychology of Women. Boston: Beacon Press, 1976.

Mindes, Marvin W. "Trickster, Hero, Helper: A Report on the Lawyer Image." *American Bar Foundation Research Journal* (1982): 177–233.

Nader, Laura. "Forums for Justice." *Journal of Social Issues* 31 (1975): 151–70.

"Styles of Court Procedure: To Make the Balance." In *Law in Culture and Society,* edited by Laura Nader, 69–91. Chicago: Aldine, 1969.

Nader, Laura, and Harry F. Todd, Jr., eds. *The Disputing Process – Law in Ten Societies.* New York: Columbia University Press, 1978.

Nicholson, Linda J. "Women, Morality, and History." *Social Research* 50 (Autumn 1983): 514–36.

Noddings, Nell. *Caring: A Feminine Approach to Ethics and Moral Education.* Berkeley: University of California Press, 1984.

Noonan, John. "The Purposes of Advocacy and the Limits of Confidentiality." *Michigan Law Review* 64 (1966): 1485–92.

"Open Letter to the Law School Community." Minorities and Women at Yale Law School. Unpublished document, 1984.

Piaget, Jean. *The Rules of the Game.* London: Routledge & Kegan Paul, 1932.

Plato. *Republic.* Translated by Paul Shorey. In *The Collected Dialogues of Plato,* edited by Edith Hamilton and Huntington Cairns, 575–844. New York: Bollingen Foundation, 1961.

Statesman. Translated by J. B. Skemp. In *The Collected Dialogues of Plato,* edited by Edith Hamilton and Huntington Cairns, 1018–85. New York: Bollingen Foundation, 1961.

Postema, Gerald J. "Moral Responsibility in Professional Ethics." *New York University Law Review* 55 (1980): 63–91.

Pound, Roscoe. *Introduction to the Philosophy of Law.* New Haven, Conn.: Yale University Press, 1922.

Puza, Bill. "An Interdisciplinary Treatment of Kohlberg." *Ethics* 92 (1982): 468–90.

Rawls, John. *Theory of Justice.* Cambridge, Mass.: Harvard University Press, 1971.

"Report of the New York Task Force on Women in the Courts." *Fordham Urban Law Journal* 15 (1986–7): 11–198.

Rhode, Deborah L. "Ethical Perspectives on Legal Practice." *Stanford Law Review* 37 (1985): 589–652.

"The 'Woman's Point of View'." *Journal of Legal Education* 38 (1988): 39–46.

Richards, David A. J. "Moral Theory: The Developmental Psychology of Ethical Autonomy and Professionalism." *Journal of Legal Education* 31 (1981): 359–74.

Ruddick, Sarah. "Maternal Thinking." *Feminist Studies* 6 (1980): 342–67.

Sartre, Jean-Paul. *Existentialism and Humanism.* Brooklyn: Haskell Booksellers, 1977.

Sassen, Georgia. "Success Anxiety in Women: A Constructivist Interpretation of Its Source and Its Significance." *Harvard Educational Review* 50 (1980): 13–24.

Scales, Ann C. "The Emergence of Feminist Jurisprudence: An Essay." *Yale Law Journal* 95 (1986): 1373–1403.

Scarr, Sandra. "Race and Gender as Psychological Variables." *American Psychologist* 43 (1988): 56–9.

Schneider, Elizabeth M. "The Dialectic of Rights and Politics: Perspectives from the Women's Movement." *New York University Law Review* 61 (1986): 589–652.

Sharwood, George. *Essay on Professional Ethics.* 1854. Reprinted in *Reports of the American Bar Association* 32 (1907).

Sherry, Suzanna. "Civic Virtue and the Feminine Voice in Constitutional Adjudication." *Virginia Law Review* 72 (1986): 543–616.

Simon, William. "Ideology of Advocacy: Procedural Justice and Professional Ethics." *Wisconsin Law Review* 29 (1978): 30–144.

Sophocles. *Antigone.* Translated by Dudley Fitts and Robert Fitzgerald. In *The Great Books Foundation* no. 1, set 1. Chicago: The Great Books Foundation, 1966.

Strachan, Nell. "A Map for Women on the Road to Success." *American Bar Association Journal* 70 (May 1984): 94–6.

Surrey, Janet. "The 'Self-in-Relation': A Theory of Women's Development." Work in Progress, Paper #13, Available from the Stone Center for Developmental Services and Studies, Wellesley College, Massachusetts.

Tronto, Joan C. "Beyond Gender Difference to a Theory of Care." *Signs: Journal of Women in Culture and Society* 12 (1987): 644–63.

Turiel, Elliot. *The Development of Social Knowledge: Morality and Convention.* Cambridge: Cambridge University Press, 1983.

Turow, Scott. *One L.* New York: G. P. Putnam's Sons, 1977.

Uviller, Richard H. "The Advocate, The Truth, and Judicial Hackles: A Reaction to Judge Frankel's Idea." *University of Pennsylvania Law Review* 123 (1975): 1067–81.

Vasudev, J., and R. C. Hummel. "Moral Stage and Sequence and Principled Reasoning in an Indian Sample." *Human Development* 30 (1987): 105–18.

Wald, Patricia M. "Yale Was There." *Yale Law Report* 34 (Fall 1987): 77–9.

Walker, James C. "In a Diffident Voice: Cryptoseparatist Analysis of Female Moral Development." *Social Research* 50 (1983): 665–95.

Walker, Lawrence. "Sex Differences in the Development of Moral Reasoning: A Critical Review." *Child Development* 55 (June 1984): 667–91.

Wasserstrom, R. "Lawyers as Professionals: Some Moral Issues." *Human Rights* 5 (1975): 1–24.

Westkott, Marcia. *The Feminist Legacy of Karen Horney.* New Haven, Conn.: Yale University Press, 1986.

Winter, Bill. "Survey: Women Lawyers Work Harder, Are Paid Less but They're Happy." *American Bar Association Journal* 69 (1983): 1384–8.

Court cases

Bradwell v. Illinois, 83 U.S. (16 Wall) 130, 21 L. Ed. 442 (1893).

Byrn v. New York City Health and Hospitals Corporation, 31 N.Y. 2d 194, 335 N.Y.S. 390, 286 N.E. 2d 887 (1972).

De Shaney v. Winnebago County Department of Social Services, 55 L. W. 4218 (1989).

Gideon v. Wainwright, 372 U.S. 335, 9 L. Ed. 2d 799, 83 S. Ct. 792 (1963).

Lyng v. Northwest Indian Cemetery Protective Association, 485 U.S. __, 99 L. Ed. 2d 534, 108 S. Ct. 1319, 56 L. W. 4992 (1988).

Miranda v. Arizona, 384 U.S. 436, 16 L. Ed. 2d 694, 86 S. Ct. 1602 (1966).

Nix v. Whiteside, 475 U.S. 157, 89 L. Ed. 2d 123, 106 S. Ct. 988 (1986).

People v. Belge, 372 N.Y.S. 2d 798, Aff'd mem., 376 N.Y.S. 2d 771 (1975), Aff'd per curiam, 41 N.Y. 2d. 60, 390 N.Y.S. 2d 867, 359 NE 2d 377 (1976).

Shapero v. Kentucky Bar Association, 486 U.S. __, 100 L. Ed. 2d 475, 108 S. Ct. __ (1988).

United States v. Dougherty, 473 F.2d 1113 (1972).

United States v. Wade, 388 U.S. 218, 18 L. Ed. 2d. 1149, 875 Ct. 1926 (1967).

Index

Abrams, Ed, 88–9
achievement, standards of, 141, 143
American Bar Association Commission on Women in the Profession, 132–5
Andrews, Darcy, 86–7
Andrews, Frances, 23–5
Antigone, 2–5, 13, 15, 22, 41, 50, 62, 64, 138, 158, 169
Aristotle, 16, 17, 64, 83, 113, 168
autonomy, 1, 7–8, 19, 31, 56, 170

best interests of child standard, 80–2; *see also* hypothetical dilemma of child custody
Billy Budd (Melville), 13–14
Blackmun, Supreme Court Justice Harry, 206n16
Blackstone, Sir William, 47–8
Bok, Sissela, 65
Bonsignore, John, 44–5
Bradwell, Myra, 21
Bramwell, Baron, 33
Brennan, Supreme Court Justice William, 206n16
Brougham, Lord, 32
Burger, Chief Justice Warren, 70, 81

Camus, Albert, 160
care orientation
  childhood precursors of, 85
  defined, 6–11
  developmental psychology and, 5–12
  examples of, 23–5, 56–9, 66–8, 71–2, 114–16, 118

and legal system, 93–4, 154–5, 167–8
  see also women in law
Cartwright, Diana, 112
Chesterton, G. K., 168
child custody hypothetical dilemma, *see* hypothetical dilemma of child custody
Chodorow, Nancy, 6–7
code of ethics, 100, 102, 123
  origins of, 162–5
Colby, Kathryn, 46, 117–18, 124, 137–44
confessed murderer hypothetical dilemma, *see* hypothetical dilemma of confessed murderer
confidentiality, 31, 38–9, 79, 86–8, 92, 116, 124
Constans, Susan, 46, 87–8, 98, 150
Constitution, U.S., 8, 20, 27, 73, 74
courts of equity, English, 47–8
Creon, 2–5, 15, 22, 41, 50, 62, 66, 158, 168, 169
Crowell, John, 47, 76–8, 118, 161, 162
Curtis, Charles, 33, 39, 40

De Shaney v. Winnebago County Department of Social Services, 206n16
detachment, 148, 150, 151, 160
  stoic, 40–1, 104–5, 119, 120, 131
Dickens, Charles, 28
dispute resolution
  Aristotelian model of, 16
  commercial arbitration and, 18–19